W9-BIL-655

# Routledge Research in Education

# Language Teaching Through the Ages

Konrad Koerner, a leading historian of linguistics, has long said that an academic field cannot be considered to have matured until it has history as one of its subfields. The history of linguistics is a growing area, having come into its own in the 1960s, especially after Noam Chomsky looked for historical roots for his work. In contrast, the history of language teaching has been neglected, reflecting the insecurity and youth of the field. Most works on the subject have been written by linguists for other linguists, and typically focus on a specific period or aspect of history. This volume concentrates on the basic issues, events, and threads of the history of the field—from Mesopotamia to the present—showing how a knowledge of this history can inform the practice of language teaching in the present.

**Garon Wheeler** is Campus Dean at the New York Institute of Technology, Abu Dhabi, UAE.

# Language Teaching Through the Ages

**Garon Wheeler**

Routledge
Taylor & Francis Group
NEW YORK   LONDON

First published 2013
by Routledge
711 Third Avenue, New York, NY 10017

Simultaneously published in the UK
by Routledge
2 Park Square, Milton Park, Abingdon, Oxon OX14 4RN

*Routledge is an imprint of the Taylor & Francis Group,
an informa business*

*Library of Congress Cataloging-in-Publication Data*
Wheeler, Garon.
  Language teaching through the ages / Garon Wheeler.
    cm. — (Routledge research in education ; 93)
  Includes bibliographical references and index.
  1. Language and languages—Study and teaching—History.  I. Title.
  P61.W44 2012
  418.0071—dc23
  2012038144

ISBN13: 978-0-415-65789-1 (hbk)
ISBN13: 978-0-203-07645-3 (ebk)

Typeset in Sabon
by IBT Global.

Printed and bound in the United States of America on sustainably sourced
paper by IBT Global.

# Contents

## PART III
## Modern Times

# Figures

# Preface

My original plan was, simply, to write a history of foreign-language teaching. It soon became apparent, though, that there was nothing simple about it. Foreign-language teaching has rarely conformed to what we have in mind when we think of history. There is no long chain of events that has steadily and gently led us to where we are today. Trying to link all the significant events of the last five thousand years in the field would drive all but the most determined author and researcher over the edge. It would also turn the work into one more suited for the reference shelf. That was not my intention. I've found through the years that foreign-language teachers rarely have a knowledge of the history of the field from before the last half-century or so. I'll leave it to my Introduction to make the case for studying language-teaching history, but in brief, what I have done is create an "anecdotal" history: it covers the main points of the last five thousand years by focusing on people and events that I find both relevant and interesting. Purists of history will object to omissions, simplifications, the promotion of minor figures to prominence, and no doubt other faults; nevertheless, my goal has been to cover the story in a less academic style than many readers would expect. I have written a book that I hope will appeal to an international audience of teachers and others interested in the topic.

The book is of historical necessity focused primarily on the West and drawn from Western sources, mostly English, Latin, and French. Although other civilizations such as India, China, and the Arab world have distinguished histories in the field of language study, there are few records in a Western language that describe how languages were taught outside the West through the centuries. That's unfortunate, and I hope that more resources will become available in the future.

Readers who are interested in a more detailed study of the field are encouraged to read the excellent *A History of English Language Teaching* by Anthony P. R. Howatt and to explore the astoundingly detailed *25 Centuries of Language Teaching* by Louis G. Kelly. I also recommend *Évolution de l'enseignement des langues: 5000 ans d'histoire* (Evolution of the Teaching of Languages: Five Thousand Years of History) by Claude Germain.

I'd like to thank a few people for helping me with and tolerating this long project. My wife, Gehan, comes first of course for reading the work and putting up with hundreds of lost weekends. I am also grateful to James Lewelling for his continuous support and encouragement, Mark Vevers for reading early chapters, Shobha Rebello for technical assistance, Barry Velleman for reviewing a chapter that relies on his work, Maria Tsiapera for getting me started in the history of linguistics, and Konrad Koerner for giving me breaks along the way and assistance whenever asked. I am also very grateful to Cynthia Walker, Christine Coombe, and Wes Weaver for reviewing the draft. Finally, I thank the staff of the University of Amsterdam libraries for their unwavering help and countless favors during my research visits.

# Introduction
## Why Study the History of Language Teaching?

"Indifference to history isn't just ignorant; it's a form of ingratitude."[1]

Back in the 1970s, I was chosen to be a Peace Corps Volunteer in Morocco.[2] I had no technical skills—I couldn't teach rural Moroccans how to dig a well or increase their crop production like some of my fellow volunteers, but my French was fair, so it was decided that I'd become an English teacher in a public secondary school. This was good, because I'd always loved languages. I'd started with Spanish in kindergarten and had studied several languages to varying degrees of fluency all the way through my university days. As a result, I thought that I knew a thing or two about learning a foreign language. I was sure I could become an ace English teacher in no time.

A large part of our training during the first months consisted of learning some Moroccan Arabic. Each day for up to six hours we were face-to-face with our teacher. Not one word of English was ever used by the teacher during the lessons. No matter how stumped we were by a grammar or vocabulary point, everything was communicated through actions, gestures, and the knowledge that we'd managed to accumulate up to that time. "What a brilliant idea!" I thought. "This is just like learning a language in the real world—why hasn't anyone ever thought of this before?" Well, someone *had* thought of this before. The "direct method" that we were using in 1976 was popular in the late eighteen hundreds; it was employed most usefully for immigrants. But I didn't know that for a long time, even after I did become an ace English teacher.

During my studies for a master's degree, I became a big fan of Stephen Krashen and his "natural approach." Ah, modern language teaching at its best—state of the art, so to speak—cutting edge and all that. I was again unaware that similar ideas about comprehensible input and the importance of psychological factors can be found in works from centuries ago, and that the umbrella term "natural methods" is more than a hundred years old.

In my later graduate studies I became interested in the history of linguistics and was occasionally surprised that a supposedly recent idea had actually been around for hundreds of years, or even longer. I also found some interesting stories and characters along the way. As a language teacher, my interest naturally drifted back to the history of our field. To make a long story shorter, that's how I happen to have written this book.

Why should a language teacher be well versed in the history of the field? It's a simple question, but to answer it we need to start big. Because we're talking about a form of history, the starting point becomes why study any history? Already you might see that we're in trouble, because who can give a convincing answer to that? The study of history is something that almost anyone would agree is important, but just try to give a few reasons and you'll see that it's not easy. As one scholar says, historians don't carry out heart transplants, improve our roads, catch crooks, or do any other tangible, headline-grabbing activities.[3] For most of us, it probably comes down to a meek assertion that it's just "good for you." End of discussion. Or maybe we'll recite that nugget of wisdom from George Santayana that those who cannot remember the past are condemned to repeat it. But this is language teaching we're talking about, and neither is a very satisfactory answer in our case. So instead, let's look at some arguments given by historians themselves.[4]

History can help to explain the current state of affairs, they say. It's been said that a person who knows no history is like an amnesiac, because he or she is missing a sense of earlier events and is therefore unable to distinguish between cause and effect. Everything happening now in our profession has some cause, some root in the past, something that has led to that action, belief, or technique. Adapting a metaphor of one historian, history must serve as our laboratory, and experiences of the past must serve as evidence in our efforts to figure out why our profession has arrived where it is today.[5]

Another reason for studying history is that it's a tool for thinking. One writer makes an interesting argument:

> As a high school football player, I spent quite a bit of time in the weight room. [But] never on the field did I ever grab an opponent and bench press him ten times. . . . There was however a transfer of the strength I derived from bench pressing to my performance on the field. As a stronger athlete I was able to perform better.[6]

What this means for us is that our knowledge of teaching practices in the eighteenth century, for example, may never come up in our classroom, but in the end it might well make us better teachers.

More convincing, perhaps, is the argument of what history can do for the intellect. The study of history develops our judgment, which can be defined as the synthesis of memory and situation. Our memory of what has happened before in the same circumstances dictates how we act. A reasonable conclusion is that the more memories we have, the more likely it is that our decisions will be the correct ones. History is, in a way, a collection of memories. The more we know about the past of language teaching, the more memories we have upon which to base our actions. As a result, we're wiser in our choices and can better assess evidence and conflicting interpretations.

There is one other reason to study history that's particularly relevant to our discussion. A leading historian of linguistics stresses that an academic field cannot be considered to have matured, to have come of age, until it has history as one of its subfields.[7] Historians say that it gives us a collective memory. Usually that means that it helps to forge a national or cultural identity. It helps us to know who we are. But this can be applied to language teaching, too. Although ours is an ancient profession, it has developed into a modern skill only in the last century. It's young, it's still very much in its adolescence,[8] and it's international, including as many varieties of teachers as there are human beings. The history of language teaching can serve as a unifying force in our profession, something to give us a professional identity.

Consider this: the social sciences, which we can consider language teaching and linguistics to be part of, have been battling an inferiority complex for a long, long time. The problem goes back to the early nineteenth century, when the new industries and technology that arose during the Industrial Revolution created a tremendous respect for the hard sciences. Ever since then, the road to respectability has had to be via science and the harder the science the better. It doesn't help that *everyone* is an expert on language or that foreign-language teaching is sometimes seen as a transient, stopgap job until something better comes along, or as a way to travel around the world. The result is that language teaching is always trying to appear as scientific as possible in order to gain respect. Our field therefore tends to look to the future and dismiss the past, viewing it as full of misguided ideas and techniques. It's hard to build a history with discredited ideas. The result is professional amnesia on a grand scale.

Ours is a profession in which we are often unable to analyze and classify our accumulated knowledge, but we know more than we realize. Adding some history to that accumulated knowledge can only be of benefit— maybe to make one a better teacher, perhaps to increase one's confidence, or maybe to improve the reputation of the profession. I just hope that I can convince a few teachers along the way that it's an interesting and useful topic, and give it a gentle nudge toward acceptance.

# Part I

# In the Beginning

# 1 An Introduction
## In the Beginning

"In the beginning . . . " It would be very satisfying if we could start an account of foreign-language teaching with these words. But that, of course, is impossible. Who knows how long people have been learning a second language? As long as humans have possessed the faculty of speech (which is at least forty thousand years), groups speaking different languages have come into contact with one another. Surely some distant ancestors made a determined effort to learn the speech of their neighbors instead of just assimilating it by trial and error through frequent contacts. Did they ever hire some sort of teacher? Did teacher and student meet regularly? Was there any kind of plan, or was it just pointing and repeating? Silly questions, maybe, but it's always interesting to ponder who the first person to do something was, even if it's merely a pointless diversion, as it is in this instance. A similar case arose in the seventeen hundreds, when philosophers, linguists, and other deep thinkers confronted the age-old question of how language began. Eventually, it became clear that the answer was nowhere in sight in spite of the theories and speculations of some of the leading scholars of the day.[1] In fact, linguistic societies in Paris and London banned further discussion of the matter in the mid-eighteen hundreds— enough was enough. The same applies to our question. We'll never know how language teaching started, whether it's of a first or a second language. All we can do is go as far back as history allows us and follow the thread from that point.

At least two historians have written histories that speak of five thousand years of language teaching.[2] And indeed, that seems to be as early as we'll ever have any information about it because that's as far back as any historical records go. To start, let's have a quick look at a timeline of the ancient world, since it can be difficult to grasp the huge expanses of time that we're talking about.

The Romans are the most recent of the ancient civilizations we'll examine. When Rome was sacked in AD 476 and the last emperor was deposed, it had been almost exactly one thousand years since the founding of the Roman Republic. The influence of Rome and the Latin language persisted for another millennium, into the Renaissance, but when we think of the glory days of Rome, we're talking a period of roughly five hundred years, from the third century BC until the third century AD, when barbarian tribes began a series of invasions that would eventually cause the fall of the empire.

Before that, though their dates overlap somewhat with the Romans, there were the Greeks, whose civilization was much admired and emulated by the Romans. Their civilization stretched back to before 1000 BC, but the Greece of Aristotle and the Acropolis was from approximately 600 BC to 300 BC. We're barely halfway through the five thousand years.

The Egyptian civilization lasted longer than any other, its power enduring from about 3000 BC until approximately 300 BC. At the time the Greeks were just beginning their remarkable achievements in everything from science to literature, the Great Pyramids of Giza had been standing for well over a thousand years.

We'll look at these three civilizations, but first, if we want to go back as far as possible, we can't ignore another civilization as old as that of the ancient Egyptians: Mesopotamia.

# 2 Mesopotamia
## The First Records

Six thousand years ago there were already villages in lower Mesopotamia, what is now modern-day Iraq. Over the next thousand years, this prehistoric agricultural society gave rise to what became known as Sumer, which was actually a group of city-states, much like what the Greeks had centuries later. And it was around this time—the best guess is about 3300 BC-that the Sumerians devised the first writing system, marking the beginning of history. So what do you suppose that they wrote about, given the very first opportunity *ever* to write and to preserve their thoughts for posterity? The heroic and glowing adventures of their ancestors? Religious texts to appease the gods? No, writing was first used for bureaucratic purposes—for recordkeeping, as a tool to keep the administration of government activities running smoothly. Adventure and religion came later.

Now that the Sumerians had a writing system to record transactions, it was necessary for people to learn it. Sumerian schools came into existence in order to create scribes to serve the state. These were no servants, however. Learning to read and write was reserved for the sons of the wealthy and powerful. We know because so many records were left behind that one scholar was able to match the students' fathers with a sort of Who's-Who of the day.[1]

The writing system that the Sumerians created for their language was originally pictographic; that is, it was similar to the hieroglyphics of Egypt in that words were represented by drawings. Through the following centuries, the symbols were gradually simplified and stylized until they became what is known as cuneiform (from Latin, meaning "in the shape of wedges"). We've all seen it somewhere in our schooldays; it was writing that consisted of wedge-shaped symbols made with the tip of a stylus, a pointed writing tool. These characters were pressed into clay that was then left in the sun to dry, making an impressively permanent record. Thousands of these tablets have been found, telling us about all sorts of matters from dull government records of food inventories to news about a spectacular murder case.[2] There are even countless practice tablets of young students who were learning to write.

Being a first effort, the Sumerian writing system was understandably not the easiest the world has ever seen. It consisted of six hundred or so symbols that represented syllables of the language instead of individual sounds (it was therefore called a syllabary rather than an alphabet). Mastering the system was not easy. Students started by learning the symbols and the sounds they represented as well as some phonetically simple words. The next step was to memorize some common words. These were presented in lists of logically related words such as the names of animals, trees, rocks, and minerals.[3] Practice consisted of a lot of copying onto tablets—that's why there are so many of them. Students in the next stage learned the more difficult words—for example, compound words whose meanings weren't clear from their individual components. In short, learning to read and write Sumerian was above all a matter of learning thousands of words of vocabulary. It was a long, arduous process that took at least ten years.[4]

By 2350 BC, Sumer had been taken over by the Akkadians, a civilization they had been in close contact with for centuries. The Akkadians were stronger militarily but they certainly were not a more developed society. In fact, the Akkadians held the Sumerians and their culture in the highest regard—so much so that something happened that was contrary to the usual pattern of conqueror and conquered: the Akkadians learned Sumerian, the language of the defeated population. This doesn't mean that they gave up their own language (which, not coincidentally, was written in cuneiform borrowed from the Sumerians), but Sumerian was seen as the language of education and social achievement.[5] Still, it was not the language of the ruling Akkadians, so within a few centuries Sumerian did indeed die out as a spoken language. But it certainly didn't disappear; it remained very much alive as a language for education and religion. And as the Akkadians studied Sumerian, at last we can talk about the first genuine second-language learning and teaching scenario that we know about.

After such a long wait, though, it might be a bit disappointing to hear that we've already read how foreign languages were first taught and learned: in just the same way Sumerian was taught to its native speakers. That is, Akkadian students started out by mastering the cuneiform writing system and simple words, then memorizing lists of thousands of words of increasing difficulty. The only innovation was that this created the need for the first bilingual dictionaries of sorts. A Sumerian child would already have known most of the words on his lists. An Akkadian speaker, on the other hand, needed translations of these words (which, of course, tells us that he was already literate in Akkadian), so the lists included the Akkadian word next to it. These sometimes even had illustrations, so if we want, we can consider these to be bilingual illustrated dictionaries—very avant-garde.[6]

So the first evidence we have of the study of a language is from about five thousand years ago as Sumer developed a writing system and had need of people to learn it for governmental purposes. To most people a language is seen as simply a collection of words, so their way of teaching it was what probably most people would do without the benefit of experience: they just learned vocabulary. There was no literature to study and there were no essays to write. When the Akkadians studied Sumerian a thousand years later, they made no distinction between learning a first language and learning a foreign language. It would have been naïve to expect anything more, and in fact this is how it went for a long, long time.

# 3 Egypt
## The Effect of Language Change

As brief as our stop was in Sumer, here it will be even shorter. In fact, when it comes to second-language teaching there isn't much point in talking about Egypt for the first two thousand years. Or maybe not at all, you may think, because the situation turns out not to be what you'd expect. Nonetheless, it *is* Egypt and it *is* three thousand years of history, and that makes it rather hard to ignore. The ancient Egyptians, who spoke what is simply called ancient Egyptian, certainly had good reasons to learn a few foreign languages during all those years. As a major power there obviously was contact with other nations, whether from trade or through diplomacy or conquest. Knowing the other person's language is clearly a benefit in business. It also is useful in administering an empire, and it's believed that some Egyptian diplomats learned the language of their host countries.[1] When conquering, though, unlike the Akkadians in Sumer, the Egyptians were perfectly content to follow the natural course of things and have the conquered learn the language of the victors.

Overall, there is sufficient evidence that knowing a second language was not unheard of in ancient Egypt. The title of "chief interpreter" existed in the Old Kingdom, meaning sometime in the mid-third millennium BC.[2] In addition, there are multilingual documents from as early as roughly 2000 BC, as well as numerous instances of foreign words used in the writings of scribes.[3] There are other documents showing communication with outsiders.

The problem is that we have no idea how foreign languages were generally learned in ancient Egypt. There weren't even schools until 2000 BC, give or take a few hundred years, and it's thought that foreign languages were not part of the curriculum when there were. The logical possibilities are private lessons from a native speaker or spending time abroad. Either way it indicates that knowing another language was likely to be an achievement of those from well-to-do families, not of typical students.

The first instance of second-language learning in ancient Egyptian schools that we can verify isn't even really that of a second language. Let's look first at a situation in English from hundreds of years ago. At some point you may have studied something in Old English (that is, written about a thousand years ago), and you'll remember how difficult it is to decipher passages like this, the first words of the Bible:

> On angynne gescēop God heofonan and eorðan. Sēo eorðe sōðlīce wæs īdel and æmtig, and þēostra wǣron over ðǣre nywelnysse brādnysse; and Godes gāst wæs geferod ofer wæteru.[4]

> In the beginning God created the heavens and the earth. Now the earth was formless and empty. Darkness was over the surface of the deep, and the Spirit of God was hovering over the waters.[5]

Now just imagine how much more difficult it would be if this had been written in a completely different alphabet than the one we use today. No thanks, most of us would probably say. But what if, as this passage hints at, it contained the wisdom of the ages and its memorization was absolutely necessary to be a good citizen? Wouldn't it be like learning a foreign language? That's the situation that Egyptian students faced later in their history, long after the pyramids had been built.

The original Egyptian writing system was the hieroglyphics that we're all so familiar with. This pictographic method, whose name means "sacred carving," was developed about 3100 BC, soon after the Sumerians came up with cuneiform. It was used for nearly three thousand years (the last known usage was 394 BC)[6] and was always the script of choice for writing on the stone of monuments and temples. As beautiful as it was, the flaw is obvious: it was difficult and time-consuming to produce on any surface. This led to the creation of a simplified version of hieroglyphics, one that was much faster to use and became the preferred form for writing on papyrus. It existed side by side with the original, more ornate hieroglyphics. This newer style was called "hieratic," or "priestly" style, though it was used for much more than religious texts.

It was in this hieratic script that certain treatises of great significance were written. An important part of Egyptian life was a quality called *maat*, embodying truth, justice, and virtue.[7] It was believed to have been instilled by the gods at the creation of the world, and its pursuit served as a religious and moral guide to proper conduct for both the individual and the state. The principles of *maat* were contained in what were commonly known as the Books of Instruction, written in hieratic script. As often happens—it seems to be human nature—the language of these texts was regarded as special and untouchable, so they had to be studied in their original form. These books served as textbooks, in a way, for Egyptian schoolchildren in scribal schools. However, along the way the Egyptians had developed a third form of writing that was even faster and easier to use than hieratic. This final form, a cursive version of previous scripts, was called *demotic*, which means "popular" in the sense "of the people." Language change is inevitable and the Egyptian in which the Books of Instruction had been composed was considerably different from the language that students spoke many years later. Eventually the Books were as unintelligible to a scribal student as Old English written in a foreign alphabet would be to us.

What to do? These texts had to be learned in order to spread the message of *maat*, but they had to be learned in their original version. The goal was not to master archaic Egyptian, but to learn enough to comprehend the texts, which for the most part were maxims, or sentences that conveyed general truths. Here are some examples:

Do not be proud of your knowledge,

Consult the ignorant and the wise.

He who steps gently, his path is paved.

He who frets all day has no happy moment.[8]

What the teachers did was simply have the students memorize the entire sentences. There was no individual vocabulary analysis; the maxims were learned as units along with their meanings. Students were able to read and recite the maxims as well as write them from the teacher's dictation.[9] There also was some grammar work, such as a few verb conjugations, but it played a minor part.

That's it. All this work to find out that second-language knowledge was not unusual in ancient Egypt but that we don't know how these languages were learned; we do know that later students had to memorize quasi-religious proverbs for correct living that were recorded in an unintelligible form of their own language. We're starting to see why some histories of language teaching don't start until after the Egyptians.

# 4   The Greeks
## The Foundations of Western Education

In Greece, we find another example of second-language learning that wasn't really second-language learning, but was instead a case of studying an outdated form of the native language. The ancient Greeks were never particularly interested in communicating with outsiders. The main reason was that the Greeks understandably had a very high opinion of their own civilization, accomplishments, and language, regarding non-Greeks with disdain. There was no reason they could think of to learn the way of speaking of their uncouth neighbors. The best evidence of this is that the word "barbarian" and its cognates in many languages come from the Greeks' comical, dismissive imitation of the gibberish that emerged from a foreigner's mouth: "bar-bar-bar." A "barbarian," then, was a person who didn't speak Greek.

So why study the Greeks here, if they never turned their attention to the study of foreign languages? It's simple, really. The Greeks developed a complete system of education, the best the world had seen to that point. The Romans, as they were accustomed to doing, later borrowed heavily from the Greeks' ideas. The Romans then studied Greek and Latin, but in the same way that the Greeks had learned their first language. The Roman system of education, which was really much like the Greek, then spread throughout Europe, North Africa, and the Middle East, so when we later examine the study of Latin in, say, the fifteen hundreds, we're still seeing methods that were deeply influenced by the Greeks. In other words, in language teaching as in nearly everything else in Western civilization, the influence of the ancient Greeks lived on for an amazingly long time. Let's look, then, at how reading and writing were taught to young Greeks.[1] Children began school at the age of six or seven. Although girls sometimes received at least primary education, it was the boys who went off to school. A school was typically located right in the middle of town, perhaps in an unused shop or in a park. Students sat on stools arranged around the teacher, while their pedagogues (slaves who accompanied them to and from school) sat nearby. These servants, responsible for the boys' conduct and protection, played an important part in the boys' education.[2]

## LEARNING TO READ AND WRITE

The method of teaching reading couldn't have been more straightforward. The students first learned the twenty-four letters of the Greek alphabet. Once they had been mastered, it was time to start reading two-letter syllables. Every possible combination was brought out and practiced again and again. From there the students went on to three-letter syllables. At last it was time to read some words, and the process followed a similar build-up. Students started with those of just one syllable and slowly worked their way up to longer ones, one additional syllable added at each stage. Some of the practice words were chosen specifically for their difficulty. The Greeks believed that it was a matter of toughening the student: if they could master the pronunciation of even difficult words at an early age, it would make later studies easier. From there it was a big jump to reading selected passages from famous authors. Early on, the words were divided into syllables to help the students. Later, though, they had to face the real thing, and it wasn't easy. Greek in those days was written in *scriptio continua*: thismeansthatthewordsallrantogetheranddidnotevenhavepunctuation Perhaps the idea of toughening the students with obscure and difficult words in the practice lists made more sense than it seems to us at first. These passages were learned by heart and recited before the class. Incidentally, all reading then was done out loud, presumably because the aim was to be able to recite literature. Silent reading, as hard as it is to believe, was virtually unknown in Greek and Roman times. In fact, it was rarely mentioned until the twentieth century, which suggests that it's a relatively recent practice.[3]

Writing was taught in the same way as reading and accompanied it step by step.[4] There was no need for desks in the class because the students' wooden writing boards allowed them to use their knees for support. This board was something like an empty picture frame with a wooden backing. It was filled with wax, which served as the writing surface (papyrus existed but was too expensive for everyday use, especially for children just learning to write). The writing instrument was a sort of stylus—a tool with a point on one end for writing and a rounded opposite end for smoothing out mistakes. The teacher would draw the letters faintly on the children's tablets so that they could trace the form and then copy it. From there it was syllables of increasing length and then words, and at last the literary passages for reading, recitation, and writing. These passages for primary school were short not just for the sake of young learners: the students had no books. In a time when a book meant a hand-copied scroll of parchment or papyrus perhaps ten feet long, it's easy to understand why they weren't standard classroom materials.[5] Instead, these passages were written on whatever was handy, even pottery fragments. It's hard not to wonder what the students would have thought if they'd known that their primary school classwork might survive for two thousand years.

It's not a good idea to look at long-ago events through modern eyes, but I think we would agree that this educational routine sounds quite boring. Students plugged away at each level until it was mastered. What this means is that the entire process took several years, because they generally didn't start higher education till the age of eleven or twelve. It was year after year of copying and memorization. The Greeks just expected education to be a dull duty. According to a Greek saying, "The roots of education are bitter, but the fruits are sweet."[6] Even the great Aristotle had this to say about learning: "It is not difficult to see that one must not make amusement the object of the education of the young, for amusement does not go with learning—learning is a painful process."[7] This highlights a characteristic of education that persisted until quite recently, historically: there was a complete lack of consideration for the needs of children as learners, who from the beginning were treated as small adults. This was certainly not unique to the Greeks and their successors and imitators; it was the way things typically were in Western education until the eighteen hundreds (which, not coincidentally, is when psychology came into existence). We know from many comments that ancient Greek children behaved just as we'd expect them to. Discipline was a constant problem and corporal punishment was the rule. On top of that, primary school teachers were an unfortunate lot, underpaid and looked down upon by society.[8] They often were men down on their luck—exiles, outsiders, or even drifters just working their way through town. All together, an ancient Greek primary school classroom doesn't sound like an appealing place for learning.

## SECONDARY EDUCATION

Matters seem to have improved when the students started secondary school.[9] At last, after the years of primary school drudgery we find a more thoughtful approach to learning language. Anyone who was willing and literate was able to carry on higher studies. Language study at this level meant a close examination of Greek literature—poets, epic poets, and historians, mostly. The objective wasn't just a thorough understanding of these works; a mastery of all the minor details—the names, places, and so on—was the mark of an educated person.

The first step was to compare everyone's copy of the work under study. After all, each was written by hand, so it was necessary to check that each copy was complete and free from mistakes. A detailed study of the text followed; remember that it was written in *scriptio continua*, so students worked diligently to separate the words and study the tone and inflections required for a dramatic recitation. This close study undoubtedly paid off when the students then committed the work to memory.

For writing at this level, there was a series of exercises called *progymnasmata*,[10] again proceeding from the simple to the complex. There was a unity to their logic: the goal was to improve one's oratorical abilities, so the emphasis was on argumentation and style.[11] The first exercise, for example, was for the student to retell a short and simple story that he had read or had read to him. Another exercise would impose a limit on the number of lines that the student could write in a summary. Henri I. Marrou, in his book *A History of Education in Antiquity*, describes one of the more advanced exercises, usually based on a saying or an action of a famous person. Let's return to a saying we encountered a short while ago:[12]

> Suppose [a student] was given the following: "Isocrates says, 'The roots of education are bitter but the fruits thereof are sweet.'" This had to be treated in its proper order in eight paragraphs:

> 1. Introduction to Isocrates and a eulogy on him.
> 2. A paraphrase of his aphorism in three lines.
> 3. A brief defence of his opinion.
> 4. Proof by contrast, refuting the contrary opinion.
> 5. Illustration by analogy.
> 6. Illustration by anecdote—borrowed from Demosthenes, for example.
> 7. Quotations from old authorities in support—Hesiod, etc.
> 8. Conclusion: "Such is Isocrates' excellent saying about education."

Over our heads today, probably, but it serves to show the sophistication achieved in Greek secondary education.


## HOMER

Now that we've considered the basics of Greek literary studies, we can turn to the star of this section, the most famous Greek writer of all time, the epic poet Homer. But first we require some very basic Greek history. The "Golden Age" of ancient Greece was during the fifth century BC, give or take a century. But a full millennium before then there was a flourishing, highly developed Greek civilization named for the city of Mycenae.[13] In about 1200 BC, this civilization was destroyed by invaders who pushed Greece into a dark age that lasted several centuries. By the eighth century BC, recovery was well on its way, and it was in this period of renewed culture that the poet Homer probably lived. It would be very difficult to overestimate his significance to Greek history. His two epic poems, the *Iliad* and the *Odyssey*, recount the story of the Trojan War and the adventures of Odysseus during his long journey home from the fighting. The Greeks believed the war had taken place back in the earlier Mycenaean age. Whether there is any historical basis for the war is debatable, but the ancient Greeks regarded it as a fact and a glorious tale from their history. Those were the days—and they were celebrated in epic poetry, an elemental part of Greek life. Whereas the primary school teacher had the clear task of instructing students in reading, writing, and counting, the secondary schoolmaster's responsibility was above all moral. An essential aspect of the study of literature was finding and assimilating the moral lessons provided by the great authors—especially the epic poems.[14] These works were much more than lengthy, entertaining adventures in verse. Based on the doings of both humans and gods, they served to instruct and inspire as well. They represented what it meant to be Greek. They demonstrated virtues such as courage, loyalty, and achievement; in short, they exemplified the characteristics of an ideal Greek. (They served, we can say, a purpose very similar to that of the Egyptian *maat*.)

Homer's *Iliad* and *Odyssey* became cultural staples. Although the city-states such as Athens and Sparta spoke different dialects of Greek and frequently quarreled with each other, there was never a time when they didn't feel a sense of family, no matter the politics of the day. In the end, a Greek was a Greek, and the *Iliad* and the *Odyssey* belonged to all of them.

But as we've noted, language change is inevitable. In English we can see this easily by reading Shakespeare's writings of four hundred years ago and then comparing the language to that of Chaucer in the thirteen hundreds or that of the Bible in Old English from a thousand years ago. This happens in all languages—no exceptions. It's also usual to hold earlier forms of the language in higher regard than today's. When it comes to culturally important literature, this regard for the old forms is especially strong. We'd never dream of studying Shakespeare in modern English, and some people are still convinced that the King James Version of the Bible from the seventeenth century is more appropriate than recent translations.[15]

By the fifth century BC, the *Iliad* and the *Odyssey* were no longer intelligible to Homer's descendants. Retelling it in contemporary Greek was no more an option than rewriting *Hamlet* today in twenty-first-century English. Predictably, the language of Homer was considered to be purer and nobler than that spoken by the Greeks of later days. Homer's works were a major part of a student's education, so the solution was obvious: learn the archaic Greek of the eighth century to be able to study the greatest literary works of the greatest civilization (and not just the works of Homer).

Here is how it was typically done.[16] The story and its plot were introduced to the students in their own form of Greek. There likely would have been dramatic readings of the original text. The students then studied "bilingual" versions of the text, with the original text alongside a current translation. A word-by-word understanding was needed, so a bilingual vocabulary list could be referred to. In other words, it was studied just as the Sumerians and Egyptians had done, a common sense approach of translating word by word. Ultimately, the goals were the same as for any poem: a thorough understanding of the vocabulary and the use of the language, a mastery of the content and smallest of details, and above all, taking to heart the many lessons about life as a Greek.

## DIONYSIUS THRAX AND THE STUDY OF GRAMMAR

It wouldn't be right to move on without a mention of a very important grammar book. Unfortunately for the author, a man named Dionysius Thrax, the printing press and author's royalties didn't exist then, or he and his heirs would have been extremely wealthy. Nowadays an author is lucky if a textbook goes through more than one printing and is used for more than a decade. Imagine this, then: Dionysius wrote a short description (it's only fifteen pages) of the Greek language in the first century BC that was still in widespread use more than a thousand years later![17] That's truly astounding. But it isn't just for its longevity that it needs to be mentioned: it provided the model for language description that was adopted by the Romans and then passed on through the ages, all the way down to us today. Dionysius was hardly the first Greek to speculate about the nature of language. Quite a few scholars had done so, including Plato and Aristotle. But Dionysius's work was the first complete description of the language and certainly the most influential. We'll see more of its influence later.

The point of his little book was not to aid in teaching languages but to help students attain a deeper understanding of their own first language so that they could better appreciate literature. Dionysius himself said that "the appreciation of literary compositions . . . is the noblest part of grammar."[18]

Dionysius starts with a description of the Greek letters and their sounds before moving on to the word and the sentence. He discusses grammatical concepts like gender, number, case, mood, voice, and tense. Most of this is of note more to historians of linguistics than to language teachers, but in fact, the best-known section of his work is of interest to all of us. Dionysius Thrax provided the first modern list of the parts of speech, as they are commonly called; this list is the one that has been around with slight modifications ever since. The list may seem obvious to us today but it was anything but that in ancient times. Plato divided words into just two categories, what can be thought of as the noun and the verb components of a sentence. Dionysius came up with eight categories: noun, verb, participle, article, pronoun, preposition, adverb, and conjunction. Notice what's missing? As odd as it sounds, the adjective was not considered a separate category for a long time. One reason is that in Greek and Latin, adjectives agree with nouns in gender, number, and case, so they look similar. But let's also consider two structurally similar sentences: *John is a man* and *John is old*. In both sentences the words following the verb are what is asserted of the subject. Because both a noun and an adjective can therefore serve to describe the subject, they were put into the same category of noun.

And that's it for the ancient Greeks. Even though they never ventured into the study of foreign languages, the methods they created to study their own language exerted a strong influence on foreign-language teaching that has lasted to this day.

The Romans, in contrast, were much more open-minded when it came to the study of languages, as we'll now see.

# 5   The Romans
## Refining the System

There was an extraordinary difference between the Greeks and the Romans when it came to learning foreign languages. The Greeks were content with their monolingualism and had no pressing need to learn another language. The Romans could easily have assumed the same attitude; after all, they were the creators of the greatest empire the world had ever seen and were certainly in a position to dictate who would learn whose language. Yet they showed a much greater willingness to borrow from other cultures. Throughout their history, the Romans showed themselves to be an extremely practical people who were willing to learn from outsiders. And they certainly knew that they had a lot to learn from the Greeks, whose culture they had the utmost respect for. They particularly recognized the superiority of the Greeks in fields such as art, architecture, and literature. They even ended up borrowing much of their religion from the Greeks (which is why the ancient gods have two names: Zeus in Greek and Jupiter in Latin, for example). The Roman poet Horace, referring to Greek influence on Roman civilization, said, "Captive Greece took her savage conqueror captive."[1]

### THE STATUS OF GREEK

The Romans weren't interested in all foreign languages; they understandably were never concerned with learning the languages of their barbaric neighbors and conquered peoples such as the Goths or the Celts. (In fact, the Romans borrowed the Greek word *barbaroi* and referred to an uncivilized person as *barbarus*, which is ironic, since the Romans themselves would have been classified as such by the Greeks.) But when it came to the Greeks it was an entirely different matter. The Romans, in their efforts to copy the Greeks in so many things, readily and enthusiastically studied the Greek language, to the point that for several centuries it was a second language of the empire.

By the second century BC, in fact, it was a matter of pride for a Roman to be able to speak Greek.[2] It was a prestige language, and its mastery was a sign of education and refinement, even among those who weren't really so educated or refined. There is ample evidence of the widespread usage of Greek. If the situation was one of business or other serious matters Latin was used. Greek, on the other hand, was the language of fun, of diversion.[3] Even in conversation, native Latin was heavily sprinkled with Greek words. The playwright Plautus, known for lowbrow humor that appealed to the uneducated, could safely assume that his audience nevertheless had an understanding of the many Greek terms he used. The poet Juvenal made fun of women who annoyed their husbands with their constant speaking of Greek. And the famous public speaker Quintilian tells us that the emphasis on early learning of Greek was so great that some Roman children spoke Latin with a Greek accent.[4] It's not surprising, really, because originally Latin and Greek were taught together. A family often had a Greek-speaking slave who ensured that the children learned to speak Greek as well as Latin before they started school.

## ROMAN EDUCATION

On the whole, there is little to add about Roman education, for it was essentially a matter of refining the Greek system.[5] Children started school at six or seven and learned to read and write in much the same way as their Greek counterparts.[6] There was the progression from letters to syllables to words to sentences to short passages and moral sayings. The classroom was similar as well; it was typically a room just off the main market square. Teaching was still a lowly profession, and primary school teachers were the lowest of all, badly paid and again often of dubious background.[7] Unfortunately, there remained the same disregard for the psychological needs of children as learners. Motivation was provided mainly by the threat of physical punishment. It must have been as grim as it sounds. Saint Augustine, who was educated in the mid-fourth century in Roman schools, talks about his wretched days as a young student in his *Confessions*. We see in this short passage the unfortunate weight of tradition in education—this was toward the end of the Roman Empire, after centuries of the same old system:

> I now went through a period of suffering and humiliation. I was told that it was right and proper for me as a boy to pay attention to my teachers, so that I would do well at my study of grammar and get on in the world. . . . I was too small to understand what purpose it might serve and yet, if I was idle at my studies, I was beaten for it, because beating was favoured by tradition. Countless boys long since forgotten had built up this stony path for us to tread and we were made to pass along it. . . . My elders and even my parents, who certainly wished me no harm, would laugh at the beating I got.[8]

At the age of eleven or twelve, the children could then go on to secondary education to focus on literature and the art of speaking. The status of the teacher was appropriately higher: though still hardly a respected position, it paid four times as much as that of the elementary teacher.[9] The methods again were the same as those used in Greece. The goal was to improve public speaking, so reading with expression was of paramount importance. This presented the same difficulties as in Greece, because Latin was also written in *scriptio continua*. No mistakes were tolerated. The students attentively studied the rhythm of the verses and the vocabulary. They lingered on the historical, geographical, and mythological references, for they copied the Greeks in this love of details. Written translations were common, especially at the higher levels. The focus was not comprehension, as we might think, but style. A good translation was rendered in the style of the famous authors, thereby improving the rhetorical (i.e., speaking and argumentative) skills of the student as well. Quintilian summed up the pre-reading activities:

> At the stage of *praelectio* [pre-reading] the teacher will have to analyze even the most minor details of the passage in order to arrive at the parts of speech and the properties of the metrical verse feet. In verse these must be so analyzed that the knowledge will also be applicable to prose. In addition, the teacher must censure writing that is barbarous, unfitting, and ungrammatical.[10]

This close attention to the correctness and style of writing brings up the matter of grammar. We've already noted that Dionysius Thrax's grammar book set the standard for grammatical analysis of a language. So great was the respect of the Romans for Greek culture that they always had a bit of an inferiority complex when it came to their own language.[11] Considering the high regard that future generations had for Latin, this seems hard to believe, but at the time many felt that Greek was a richer, nobler, more capable language than Latin. A Roman writer named Varro made a grammar book that was an adaptation of Dionysius's. His was one of several grammar books by Roman scholars, but it was the most influential. Varro did his best to match the structure of Latin to that of Greek, which wasn't always easy even though the two languages are quite closely related. What this did, though, was strengthen the idea of how languages should be described grammatically. Because this was how the mighty Greek and Roman civilizations did it made it sure that this was how Western languages would be written about and analyzed all the way until today.

## HERMENEUMATA AND OTHER TECHNIQUES

Eventually, however, Greek started to lose ground as a prestige language when Latin slowly asserted itself, especially in the fields of literature and public speaking. The illustrious statesman, writer, and orator Cicero[12] had much to do with this shift in thinking, as did the epic poet Virgil. The mark of an educated person from then on was one who knew his Cicero and Virgil. The result was that even though Greek remained an important language in Rome, it was not always understood by the educated population and often had to be learned at school after Latin was mastered.

In the later years of the empire we find the first manuals intended specifically for foreign-language teaching, the magnificently named *Hermeneumata Pseudodositheana*, pronounced

hair-may-nay-oo-ma-ta psay-oo-doh-doh-see-thay-ah-na.

That's fourteen syllables. Let's just call them the *hermeneumata* for short, though that's a questionable improvement. The first word means something that explains (there is, in fact, an English word, "hermeneutics," meaning "the art or science of interpretation"); the second word tells us that they were written by someone in the style of Dositheus, a fourth-century grammarian (and were once thought to have been his work). There were several of them, very similar in content and format, but they were not what we'd call a series. They were truly bilingual; though they may well have been intended to teach Latin to Greek speakers, they were arranged so that they could be used in the instruction of Greek to Latin students, which is how they were apparently most often employed.[13] These manuals featured at least one old tried-and-true method we've already seen, namely, bilingual word lists. Another section featured words grouped according to subject matter such as gods and goddesses, animals, vegetables, and so on. Following this, the students encountered several short, elementary readings. Here is an example, one that refers to an everyday incident involving the emperor Hadrian. The original text would have had the Greek and Latin in parallel:

> A man asked [the emperor] Hadrian to take him into his army. Hadrian said, "Where do you want to serve?" The man replied "In the Praetorian Guards." Hadrian asked him, "What is your height?" "Five and a half feet." Hadrian said, "For now you must enter the Urban Guards, and if you are a good soldier, after three years of service you may transfer to the Praetorians."[14]

There could also be paternal advice, for example, or a simple history lesson on the Trojan War, depending on the version of the *hermeneumata*.

There was also typically a section of daily conversations. Here is an example. Two friends are talking:

> "If you wish, come with me."
> "To where?"
> "To see our friend Lucius. Let's visit him."

"What's wrong with him?"

"He's ill."

"Since when?"

"A few days."

"Where does he live?"

"It's not far. If you want, let's go."

"That's his house, I believe. Here is his porter. Ask him if we can enter and see his master."[15]

One modern writer gleefully points out that *nihil sub sole novi*—"there is nothing new under the sun" (not even that old adage, apparently)—and calls this section of the *hermeneumata* a precursor to functional or communicative methods of our day.[16] Recall that until then, early language learning had been essentially a matter of memorization of vocabulary and working up to short, authentic literary passages. Here, instead, were dialogues purposefully written for students to reflect the right level of vocabulary and in familiar situations to make the language lessons more meaningful. That's quite a leap!

The most common reading in the various *hermeneumata* describes the typical day of a schoolboy of the third century. It's a foreshadowing of an activity known as a cycle, in which an activity is presented by breaking it down into its components. This allows a strict control of the vocabulary and grammar of the lesson. Here is an excerpt from one of several versions:

> I woke up before daylight, got out of bed, sat down, and put on my socks and shoes. I asked for water for my face. I washed first my hands and then my face. I took off my nightshirt and put on a tunic and a belt. I perfumed my head and combed my hair. I wrapped my cloak around my neck. . . . I left the room with my pedagogue and nanny to go greet my father and mother. I greeted and kissed both of them. Then I left home to go to school. When I entered, I greeted the teacher and he kissed me. [The passage then describes the work done by the class] . . . When we had finished our work, he sent us home for lunch. I had bread, olives, cheese, dried figs, and nuts. I drank some cool water. After lunch, I returned to school. The teacher was reading when I arrived, and he told us to start working.[17]

There are some other techniques that show us the beginnings of modern teaching. Sometime in our own foreign-language study or teaching, we all have experienced that classic technique known as the substitution drill, a written or oral exercise in which the student substitutes one word for another, making any additional changes that might result:

TEACHER.     I speak Spanish. (She)

STUDENT.     *She* speaks Spanish.

Many people assume that such drills began with post-war methods in the 1950s. And yet a fourth-century grammarian named Diomedes[18] recommended the use of something similar to help students master the case endings of Latin or Greek.[19] Here's one of his own examples:

> Nominative (subject):
> *Marcus Porcius Cato* dixit litterarum radices amaras esse, fructus iocundiores.
> Marcus Porcius Cato said the roots of literature are bitter but the fruit is quite enjoyable.
>
> Genitive (possessive):
> *Marci Porcii Catonis* dictum fertur litterarum radices amaras esse, fructus iocundiores.
> Of Marcus Porcius Cato it is reported that he said the roots of literature are bitter but the fruit is quite enjoyable.[20]

Finally, we note that the idea of abridging a literary work goes back to ancient Greece, and by the time of the Romans, students sometimes made use of shortened versions of famous works.[21] Later, around the sixth century, anthologies of extracts ranging from the Bible to classical authors appeared. In both cases, abridgement made it easier for students to have access to the works of the greatest authors and speakers, and helped them to improve their style of writing and speaking.

Nevertheless, we should remember that we're simply noting the existence of these materials. It's difficult to know the extent of their usage, but it's clear that they didn't have any revolutionary effect. It's important to be reminded again that this has hardly been an overview of a typical lesson from Roman days. There's just too much time, too many places, and not enough information to be able to draw such a picture. What matters, though, is that we see how language teaching is starting to develop after so many centuries of stagnation. Learning a second language and learning a first language are still seen as essentially the same thing, yet at least we begin to see a bit of imagination at work, an attempt to present the task in a more palatable way. And in doing so, we also have already found some ancestors of modern, supposedly new techniques.

# 6  The Middle Ages
## A Few Bright Spots

By the third century AD the Roman Empire was in decline. Corruption and misrule were on the rise and barbarian tribes were making persistent attempts to gain Roman territory. In 395 the empire split in two and Constantinople became the capital of the eastern part. Rome was sacked in 410 and 455 by Goths, and the end finally came in 476 when the city was overrun and the last emperor deposed. The long period between the fall of the Western Roman Empire and the beginning of the Renaissance about a thousand years later is referred to as the Middle Ages. Of course, the people who lived through it didn't see it as the middle of anything; the name was applied by Renaissance scholars who saw their era as reconnecting with the culture and knowledge of Rome and Greece. The Middle Ages are commonly thought of as a time of widespread ignorance, especially during the first six hundred years, which are often referred to as the Dark Ages. Actually, the Eastern Roman Empire lived on for many centuries, doing quite well in most ways, and certainly didn't fit the image of a collapsed empire. Nevertheless, scholarship in general suffered a severe setback with the collapse of the Roman Empire. Overall, it wasn't as dark as the name and legend imply, but compared to the glories of ancient Rome and Greece, "dark" is a suitable word to describe the times, especially in western Europe.

With the collapse of local government in much of the continent, it was the Church that kept education alive throughout the Middle Ages. Since Latin was the common language of the fallen empire as well as the language of the Church, it naturally remained the means for a person to become educated and cultured. School subjects were taught in it, yet the Latin that was familiar to most of its speakers was slowly diverging from the language of Cicero and developing into other languages. Eventually, students had to learn "proper" Latin before they could begin their true studies, which in the Middle Ages typically meant a syllabus of grammar, rhetoric (public speaking and effective use of language), logic, arithmetic, music, geometry, and astronomy.

As usual, it's not realistic to give a simple answer to the question of how languages were taught in a particular period. Moreover, we're talking about a thousand years and much of Europe. Nevertheless, we can try.

Because most education took place in church schools, much of the emphasis was on religious education. This was seen not just as a means to learn about Christianity but as a way to acquire Latin, the language that students needed for studying. A child usually began his studies between the ages of five and seven. After learning the letters and putting them together into syllables, it was time to get to work. The first task was to learn the Lord's Prayer, the Credo (the statement of Christian beliefs), and other important parts of the church service.[1] Most of this would have been in a classical Latin that was unintelligible to the children, so the teacher relied above all on the most basic of teaching methods: translation, repetition, and memorization. Just as in earlier times, the students didn't have books to refer to, since copying by hand didn't lend itself to mass distribution of texts. Instead, the teacher would say the words and the students would repeat them over and over. The lack of books also meant that dictations were common. Another likely activity was to have the students practice their writing on those erasable wax tablets that had been in use since at least Greek times.[2] Either way, it strikes us as the same stiflingly tedious way to learn a language.

It was only after the students had a foundation in the language from their religious studies that they began to tackle Latin as an object of study in itself. Usually this meant studying Latin grammar from one source: Donatus.

## DONATUS

It's unlikely that you've ever heard of Donatus,[3] a Roman grammarian from the fourth century, but for the educated classes he was a proverbial household name in the Middle Ages. Like Dionysius Thrax several centuries earlier, he wrote a book that was still considered the final word on the subject more than a thousand years later. Donatus's book was a Latin teaching grammar for beginning students—that is, it was written specifically for use in the classroom, unlike Dionysius's work, which was a description of the language for anyone who was interested.

We know very little of the life of Donatus, which isn't surprising since he was a teacher, not some political or philosophical figure. He seems to have been good at his job: one of his pupils became Saint Jerome, who achieved fame by producing the definitive translation of the Bible into Latin; it is in fact still the standard Bible of the Roman Catholic Church.

Donatus's little masterpiece—it was only about forty pages long and covered just the parts of speech—was commonly known as the *Ars minor*, which was a shortened form of the complete Latin name, translated as "The Lesser Study of Donatus of the Parts of Speech."[4] There is evidence from all over Europe of its extensive use for many centuries. So great was its influence that the term *donat* or a variation of it entered several European languages to mean the first principle of any field of study.[5] The book was widely used into the fifteen hundreds. One historian gives evidence that it was used in some Italian schools as late as the early twentieth century![6]

Surely, you might think, this must be an amazing book of remarkable originality to have had such phenomenal success and longevity. Let's have a look, then. Here's how the book begins, though of course it would have been only in Latin. Keep in mind that it most likely would have been taught in the same way as the children's earlier religious studies: translation, repetition, and memorization.

### Concerning the Noun

What is a noun? A part of speech that signifies with the case a person or a thing specifically or generally. How many attributes does a noun have? Six. What are they? Quality, comparison, gender, number, form, case. In what does the quality of nouns consist? It is two-fold, for either it is the name of one alone and is called proper, or it is the name of many and is called common.[7]

That's not really what we would expect from one of the all-time classics. It gets even denser later as Donatus gives a complete listing of the declensions, or forms, of nouns. Here is just one example using the Latin word for teacher:

*Magister* is a common noun of masculine gender, singular number, simple form, nominative and vocative case, which will be declined thus: in the nominative, *hic magister*; in the genitive, *huius magistri*; in the dative, *huic magistro*; in the accusative, *hunc magistrum.*[8]

And so on. It really doesn't grip one's attention at any point. Moreover, it's clear from all this that psychological factors, rarely considered in ancient times, continued to be ignored throughout the Middle Ages. Although the *Ars minor* was intended for young students (below the age of ten, most probably), its style was what we would expect for adults.

Why, then, was it so successful? Perhaps Thierry de Chartres, the head of a well-known French school and a leading thinker of the twelfth century, explained it best:

Donatus has taught the grammar with an admirable brevity, condensing it skillfully, and explaining it subtly. To start the children in this subject he made [the *Ars minor*] in which he has taught what is necessary to ask and to answer. He has done this so well that he has condensed all the grammar into several chapters, and with numerous illuminating examples, while the others have made it tedious, by introducing an almost infinite number of questions, and hindering it with many errors and difficulties.[9]

This would do very well today as the blurb on the back cover of any grammar book, especially coming from such an eminent scholar. The *Ars minor* was short, complete, well organized, and full of useful examples—at least by the standards of those times. The question-and-answer format made it easy to use for the teacher and helped the students in their memorization of the information. We have to remember that teachers just didn't have much to work with—a classroom, one copy of a text, and a few wax tablets. Seen from this perspective, at least, Donatus's book was appropriate and skillfully written.

But in truth it wasn't anything innovative. The question-and-answer style was not original. It had long before been noted, especially because students rarely had their own books, that it was easier to memorize material when presented this way.[10] The grammatical information was certainly not new, either. It's not hard to trace it directly to other Roman writers, and much of it ultimately to the Greeks. Nevertheless, it was thanks largely to Donatus that their grammatical ideas managed to live on long after the end of their respective civilizations and to work their way into every aspect of language study. Even today most of the grammatical terms we use for any language—for example, "gender," "conjugation," "possessive," "imperative," or "gerund"—are those that the Romans used to describe their own Latin language. It was because of Donatus's little book that these terms lived on until they became part of our own terminology. This was also a result of the influence that Donatus had on other grammar writers of the Middle Ages. Donatus himself had merely gathered and summarized the work of earlier generations; grammarians of the Middle Ages tended to find their inspiration and sources in Donatus as well as in the work of another grammarian, Priscian.

## PRISCIAN

Donatus was not the only famous grammarian of the Middle Ages. His name is inextricably linked with that of Priscian,[11] a sixth-century grammarian from Constantinople. While Donatus's *Ars minor* was intended for beginners, Priscian's works were meant for a more advanced audience. Together, Donatus and Priscian cornered the market on medieval grammatical studies.

Donatus had indeed tried to be the complete grammarian by writing the *Ars maior* (the "greater" work compared to his "lesser" *Ars minor*), which was five times the length of his shorter work and tackled issues such as punctuation, division of syllables, poetic license, common errors of usage, and so on. It was successful, but gradually faded into disuse over the centuries in favor of a similar work by Priscian.

Priscian's *Institutiones grammaticae* (usually translated as "Grammatical Foundations") was a massive eighteen volumes and covered every aspect of Latin grammar and usage. Like Donatus, Priscian drew most of his ideas from earlier sources. Some of his work, in fact, shows the influence of Donatus himself, who had preceded him by about two hundred years and was well known to him.

It would be misleading and simplistic to imply that Donatus and Priscian were the only grammarians in vogue for a thousand years—though not by much. There were other writers, of course, but they tended to draw from Donatus and Priscian, and their influence was much less felt. Priscian and Donatus were unquestionably the premier grammarians of the Middle Ages.[12] Still, we can note a few interesting points from other writers of this long period.

There was an English monk named Aelfric from around the year 1000 who also wrote grammar works for the classroom. Their popularity never approached that of the works of Donatus and Priscian, but they were by comparison surprisingly modern. His book of conversations (*Colloquy*) went beyond the sterile question-and-answer format of most teaching texts and harked back to the dialogues from the *hermeneumata*. They used carefully chosen vocabulary related to themes of everyday life of the time. The most notable feature, though, was Aelfric's use of the students' native language, Old English (Anglo-Saxon), to translate the conversations. They were written in an interlinear format, meaning the Latin and Old English were written in alternating lines.

An obvious question arises: why was using the students' own language noteworthy? Answer: Simply because it hadn't been done. Learning Latin or Greek had always meant studying a book written entirely in Latin or Greek. If your native language was anything other than either of those, your task was significantly more daunting than that of a Roman or Athenian child. We're probably all familiar with the notion of a direct or immersion method of learning a language; it's considered to be one way to achieve communicative ability relatively quickly. But in olden days this method was not used with any educational philosophy to back it up. Texts were written only in Greek or Latin because they were thought to be the only languages worthy of being written. We've talked about how languages change; it wouldn't have made sense to most scholars of the Middle Ages in France or Italy, for example, to translate "perfect" Latin into the students' Old French or Old Italian. These were seen as not real languages but just bad and corrupted forms of Latin—the very language that the students were trying to learn. Surely it's not a coincidence that Aelfric used Old English, simply because it was considered a completely different language from Latin, not a corrupted version of it like French or Italian.

## THE LATER MIDDLE AGES

A curious thing happened about 1100, a good six hundred years after the fall of the Western Roman Empire. After such a long period of relatively little intellectual activity in Europe, there was an awakening of sorts. This "renaissance" occurred a full two to three hundred years before the more famous one—the one with a capital R—and marked the end of the so-called Dark Ages. Europe gained access to forgotten knowledge of the Greeks and Romans, as well as contemporary scientific works from the Arabs and Jews. Some of these were brought back by Crusaders who had visited what had been the Eastern Roman Empire; others appeared through contact with the highly developed Moorish (i.e., Arab) civilization in Spain. Most important of all was the recovery of the works of Aristotle. Together, these had a tremendous effect on scholarship in the coming centuries.

A few thinkers began to ask big questions about the nature of language, of the type that hadn't been asked in many hundreds of years. The Modistae,[13] as they were called, tried to prove that deep down, there was one universal grammar for all languages—that the thought processes of any speakers start out the same—and that it was only quirks of fate (that is, the vocabulary and grammatical rules of each language) that made the output different among speakers of different languages. Regrettably, they wrote some of the most high-mindedly unintelligible prose you'll ever encounter and no summary of their ideas will be found here.[14] They're of interest mainly as a historical curiosity for their foreshadowing of modern ideas of deep and surface structure. Their fully developed theory of how language works was a remarkable but underappreciated achievement. Although it had no effect on language teaching, it was an indication that philosophers were no longer content just to describe language.[15]

Priscian's venerable grammar began to be supplanted at about this time by the *Doctrinale* of Alexander of Villedieu.[16] Interestingly, Alexander's grammar, written about 1200, taught a Latin that was no longer purely classical but reflected a more contemporary version of "correct" Latin. Another departure from centuries of tradition, though it didn't originate with Alexander, was his use of verse to explain the grammar, as an aid in memorization.[17]

Another good idea appears to have originated toward the end of the Middle Ages. We saw earlier that abridged readings could be found in Roman and Greek schools. It wasn't until the fourteen hundreds, though, that anyone thought of creating what today we'd call a simplified reader. Guarino Veronese's version of Julius Caesar's autobiography, itself a perennial favorite for Latin students, marked the debut of this teaching technique.[18]

Before we move on, here's a quote that neatly summarizes the role and enduring importance of grammar in the Middle Ages. It was written in the twelfth century by a bishop and author named John of Salisbury but refers approvingly to the words of a sixth-century writer, Martianus Capella. Grammar is personified as a no-nonsense wielder of weaponry in the battle for correct speech:

> Martianus . . . depicted Grammar carrying a scalpel, a cane, and a jar of ointment. Let her cut away the vices of the mouth with her scalpel, and she will trim down the tongues of children. . . . At the same time she will be teaching them not to blurt out grammar mistakes and unfitting turns of phrase.[19]

The scalpel was for cutting the children's tongues into shape for proper speech; the ointment would have been to soothe the wounds, and the cane to administer punishment to those who offended the sensibilities of this tyrannical muse. It's grimly amusing today but it's unlikely that medieval students saw any light side of it. It's more evidence of the unpleasant reality of education in times past.

## THE TOWER OF KNOWLEDGE

When I was a graduate student doing research in the history of linguistics, I stumbled across a fascinating drawing. It interested me so much that I photocopied and framed it, and the picture has never been off my desk or office wall ever since. It's from a sort of early encyclopedia, called the *Margarita Philosophica*. Have a look at the drawing.

*Figure 6.1* The Tower of Knowledge, showing the steps in education in the Middle Ages. The first stop is Donatus's classroom.

Our eyes are drawn first to the lower left of the picture, where a woman is leading a young boy into a curious building. It's a tower built in layers, rather like a wedding cake. The boy, who's carrying a bag over his shoulder, is probably a typical lad of his day. The woman, smiling faintly, is much larger than the other figures. She's holding a board in her right hand and grasping the handle of the tower door with her left. On the two bottom floors we see both adults and children. It's hard to tell what they're engaged in, but judging by their faces it's a rather serious business. In the windows of the upper floors we see an intriguing series of important-looking men gazing out in all directions. Their expressions give few clues to what's on their minds. Near each head is some Latin writing. Alone at the top of this remarkable pyramid sits a most serene figure, lost in thought as he looks up from reading a book.

The building in this drawing from the year 1504[20] is none other than "The Tower of Knowledge"—or at least one anonymous artist's rendering of what such a lofty structure could look like. It's interesting just by itself, but it also shows us the different stages in medieval education.

What we have then is a young fellow—let's call him the son of a middle-class merchant to give him a bit more life—who is about to embark on the great adventure of education. And what better guide to see him off safely on his long trip than the Muse of Wisdom herself? Her hand on the door, she's moments away from leading her young charge into the first level of the Tower of Knowledge. The object she's holding in her other hand is the board that the child will write on in chalk as he learns his ABCs.

When the boy enters the tower, his first stop will be the ground floor. That first room he's going to enter is a classroom. Look at the label just to the left of the window. All the inscriptions on the tower are written in a nearly illegible form of Latin, but the label says "Donatus." On the floor above we see a similar scene and again there is a label to the left of the window. This time it says "Priscian." We'll come back to this in a moment.

As for the gentlemen peering out of the tower from above, we find that there are some famous names and some that are not so famous anymore. The man on the bottom left is Aristotle. He represents the art of logic, the sign tells us. Next to him is Tullius, better known to us as Cicero, the most famous Roman master of rhetoric and poetry. And so on. Next to Tullius/Cicero is the philosopher Boethius,[21] who teaches arithmetic. Directly above Tullius is Euclid, whom we still associate with geometry. To his left and right we spot the teachers of astronomy and music, respectively, Ptolemy and Pythagoras.[22] In the next-to-last layer we have Pliny,[23] the master of physics (natural science), and Seneca, who represents the subject of morals. Finally, in the top position, the man with the best view of all is the teacher of theology and metaphysics, a twelfth-century bishop named Petrus Lombardus, who wrote the standard theology textbook of his day and long afterward.

You may notice that the subjects are arranged in a roughly logical order. At the top are the ultimate objects of study: God, religion, and the meaning of life. Below those are the subjects of what is right and wrong and the science of the natural world. Beneath these we find music, geometry, astronomy, logic, rhetoric and poetry, and arithmetic, which are six of the seven elements in a typical medieval curriculum. What the tower is telling us is that in order to reach the summits of knowledge—physics, morals, and especially theology—our schoolboy will have to pass through the other subjects in the tower. But what is the first subject that he's going to study? What subject is the foundation of all the others? It's grammar. In order to study anything from arithmetic to theology, first you have to master grammar—or to put it in more modern terms, you have to be literate.

What this means is that our young hero is going to begin his education by studying the work of Donatus—that would be the man himself who's leading the class. Once our boy has mastered the basics of grammar, he'll move on up to the works of Priscian to become a more accomplished reader and writer. You can even see one schoolboy on his way upstairs at this moment to Priscian, and another who appears to be leaving Priscian to begin the study of the subjects he'll need to be a well-educated young man.

This drawing tells us about the medieval system of education, which was based on the study of a set of topics that had been fixed for centuries. The entire system in fact went back to the days of the Romans, whose own educational system was taken largely from the ancient Greeks. In other words we have before us a good, simple summary of the way education was conducted for many students in the Western world for a couple of thousand years.

# Part II
# The Early Modern World

# 7   William Lily's Famous Grammar

## THE SIXTEENTH CENTURY

Milestones on the timeline of language teaching in the Middle Ages are not a common sight. Although any period can be of interest, it's not until we reach the Renaissance and the sixteenth century that our timeline becomes dotted with personalities more worthy of note. Not only was there a real increase in intellectual activity, something approaching what we'd call modern thinking, but it was a time of great movement in Europe as a result of wars and religious strife. Combine Renaissance thinking with a growing need for second-language learning and disillusionment with traditional teaching results, and we see the first real changes in the way language learning is viewed since the Greeks. Nevertheless, we find that Greek and especially Latin still hold sway as *the* languages of education in Europe, so we find ourselves in another foreign-language teaching and learning situation.

Learning grammar had usually been seen as the key to acquiring a language, and the traditional way to do this, of course, was through the study of grammatical rules, probably from Donatus and Priscian. The sixteenth century saw some scholars rebel against this philosophy of deductive learning.[1] They viewed memorization of rules as an obstacle to fluency. A few even went so far as to call for the abolition of grammar teaching. Georgius Cominius (early sixteenth century, not to be confused with the more famous Jan Comenius of the next century) claimed that readers were either bored by detailed grammars or confused by the shorter ones; the dismal result for the student was the same.[2] Scholars like Cominius believed that an inductive approach was superior (though not all were as fanatical as he was); that is, language success was more likely to result from using the language than from studying the rules. Grammar follows usage, that is. What these thinkers were advocating is what we would label today with a term such as "direct" or "natural method," "communicative skills," or any number of related concepts. Inductive learning was not new (it was known to the Greeks), and according to one historian, both inductive and deductive teaching had always been done in the language classroom. However, it was during the fifteen hundreds that an inductive approach began to gain more favor than in the past and continued its ascent into the sixteen hundreds before deductive methods won out for a time.[3] We'll see varying degrees of acceptance of induction—that is, not teaching grammar explicitly—during the sixteenth century.

We'll examine the views and works of a few representative scholars. The personalities we'll look at during the sixteenth century are of two types. The first are those who encountered success in the classroom, usually because of the teaching materials they created. They were, in other words, our ancestral colleagues, but few are well known to us today.

On the other hand, we have some celebrities. In ancient times it had been perfectly normal for a scholar to be interested in many things. Aristotle, certainly one of the greatest minds of all time, wrote about everything from ethics to the weather, from politics to dreams. This idea of the polymath, or person of great and varied learning, never really disappeared, of course, but it flourished during the Renaissance. In fact, the term "Renaissance man" has long been applied to someone whose interests and accomplishments span a wide range of experience. Some, like Leonardo da Vinci, whose interests ranged from painting to anatomy to science and inventing, preferred the more concrete, practical challenges. Others stuck to matters of the mind. Who knows what Leonardo would have had to say about language learning, but fortunately we have no shortage of other Renaissance polymaths who've left behind their opinions on the best ways to teach and learn another language. The good news is that we're sifting through the thoughts of some of the great thinkers of their day. The bad news is that none of them ever set foot in a classroom as a teacher.

## WILLIAM LILY

Let's start with a success story of sorts. But in fact, it's more of an enigma. William Lily (1468?–1522) illustrates the traditional view of grammar in language teaching—the one that some other scholars would rebel against as time went on in the fifteen hundreds. Lily was an outstanding scholar of the Greek language and eventually was appointed as the first headmaster of the famous St. Paul's School in London. After his death, his grammatical works were used as the basis of a textbook for young students called *A Short Introduction of Grammar,* or as it's more commonly known, "Lily's Grammar." It's unfair, really, to consider it simply "Lily's" book, because Lily was dead when it appeared and he had nothing to do with the actual production of the work. Moreover, several other scholars contributed to the book, but since it was mostly his work and because of his fame, that's how it has always been known. It's arguably the most successful textbook of all time (and certainly a worthy competitor to Donatus) and was in common usage in schools in England and even the United States well into the eighteen hundreds.[4] Success at the outset was guaranteed, actually, because King Henry VIII authorized it as the official Latin textbook throughout the kingdom from 1540—that's ten years before there was even an official

Bible, oddly enough.[5] This meant that generations of English students (including Shakespeare, who refers to it in several of his plays) became intimately familiar with Lily.

With that kind of background, you'd think Lily would be a towering figure in the history of language teaching. Yet there is little mention of him in language-teaching histories.[6] This lack of enduring fame is puzzling. Where did it all go wrong?

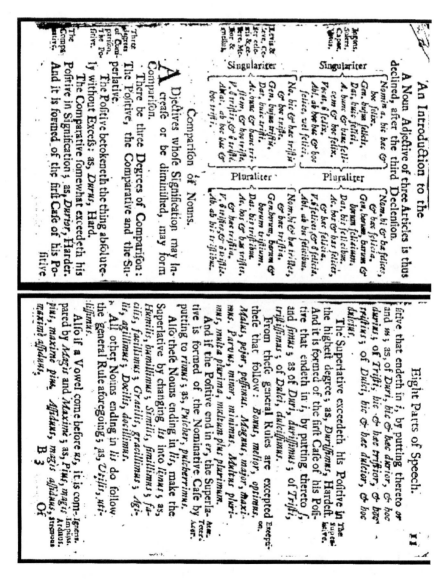

*Figure 7.1*   A page from what is commonly called "Lily's Grammar." Note: the letter s is sometimes written as ſ or ∫.

The popular notion of the book has long been that it was an ordeal suffered by generations of students. You can almost imagine the rolling of eyes and contorted faces of survivors at the mention of Lily's Grammar. The introduction to the book ("To the Reader"), nonetheless, certainly offers a promising start. It says many things that strike us as quite modern, even enlightened compared to previous works.[7] Refreshingly, it considers the feelings of the young pupils. For example, it notes that students require a great number of examples, which should be graded from easy to more difficult. This would lead not to a simple memorization of the subject matter but to an all-important understanding of the "reason of the rules." But the most important principle is not to push the children too fast—they need to "rehearse" till they get it right.[8] No moving ahead, then, until most of the students have mastered the material under discussion. This makes them happier and unafraid to proceed—a thoroughly modern outlook on the psyche of the learner, it seems. It will also encourage teachers when they see better results. One thing is clear, then—whoever wrote the introduction (it's unsigned and Lily was already dead) had no intention of making children suffer; in fact he must have thought he was being considerate.

It's surprising, then, that the book itself is very unlikely to strike any youngster as friendly. As historians, however briefly, our rule is not to evaluate a work through modern eyes, but in this case we should surely be granted an exemption. The text is in two main parts. The first, approximately seventy pages, is "An Introduction of the Eight Parts of Latin Speech." Considering Lily's traditional bent, it's no surprise at all to find that the section is essentially Donatus's *Ars minor* revisited. For example, after listing the parts of speech, it begins thus: "A noun is the name of a thing that may be seen, felt, heard, or understood: as the name of my hand in Latin, is *manus*; the name of an house, is *domus*; the name of goodness is *bonitas*."[9] The grammar is extensive, covering all the points related to each part of speech, such as cases and declensions and moods, and so on. In spite of calling for wise principles of plentiful examples and sufficient time for mastering each step, the introduction also calls for daily drilling of verb forms until students can recall any form of it and can even recite its conjugation both backward and forward. This activity "shall make the great and heavy labour so easy and so pleasant for the framing of sentences, that it will be rather a delight unto [the students], that they be able to do well, than pain in searching of an unusual and unacquainted thing."[10] In other words, the success encountered from this extensive daily drilling will be a great encouragement. It's hard to reconcile this with the earlier emphasis on learning "the reason of the rules" rather than memorizing without comprehending. Curiously, the introduction claims that three months is sufficient for students of average abilities to reach an acceptable level of Latin. Centuries of experience tells us that this is not so, despite the book's enduring success.

At least it's in English, the students' native language. Or at least it is until about a quarter of the way through the book. Immediately following this first section, we find a sort of intermission between the two main parts, a poem in Latin called "Carmen de Moribus," meaning a poem on morals or good behavior.[11] It's two pages of couplets advising the young scholar on proper conduct, mostly in the classroom: "A penknife, quills, ink, paper, and books—may your tools for studying always be ready." "While engaged in your studies, you shall speak in a soft voice; when you reply to me, your voice shall be harmonious."[12] (These are translations, of course; the poem was in Latin.) All in all, it includes examples of most of the Latin grammar to be studied. After that comes the third and longest part of the book: the "Brevissima Institutio" or "Very Brief Foundation" of Latin grammar. These remaining two hundred or so pages are again a Latin grammar, but this time in Latin, just as Latin grammars had always been. The information contained in the already detailed English portion is now repeated and expanded upon, but new topics are added: pronunciation and punctuation, figurative language, and poetic meters, for example.

Why the book was so successful is not clear, especially if we keep in mind that the typical user of Lily's Grammar was no more than ten years old. The introduction's words of concern for pupils seem oddly inappropriate. Although the book was standard for English classrooms and despite recommendations for usage, it's a safe bet that most often the book was used for simple rote learning, given that the typical Latin teacher of the day was no scholar of Lily's level. In other words, the age-old habit of children's reading and memorizing without genuine understanding continued.

Most likely the book's success can be explained in the same way as that of Donatus's grammar. Both seem deadly dull and uninspired to us, but both were phenomena of their genres for centuries. As the respected scholar said about Donatus's *Ars Minor*, it's complete, well organized, and full of useful examples (though he also said Donatus's was short, which does not really fit Lily's Grammar, in spite of the title of the Latin section). In those times it was enough. Perhaps Donatus, seen as a medieval figure, is judged more kindly, whereas Lily, a Renaissance figure, suffers today from unrealistic expectations in hindsight. As one twentieth-century scholar sums it up, "Few will maintain that Lily's Grammar is one of the world's 'Great Books,' but fewer still will minimize the influence of the basic schoolbook in England for three hundred years."[13]

# 8  Erasmus's Ideas on Education

The next of our sixteenth-century personalities is Desiderius Erasmus (1466?–1536) of Holland. Rather hard to categorize like many other "Renaissance men," he's known mainly for religious writings and his involvement with the Reformation.[1] He provides a neat introduction to how ideas on education, including language, were maturing into what we would consider modern. His thoughts on what constituted good educational practices were laid out in 1511 in a treatise entitled *De ratione studii* (On the Method of Study).[2] They were firmly rooted in the past, but at the same time he showed insights that would have caused a few murmurs among the ancients.

Erasmus starts with a clear assertion: the basis of all education rests upon a mastery of language, because the truths of this world, without the words to express them, are unintelligible and of no use to us. Therefore, the first steps in educating children are teaching them to speak and understand speech. Obviously, children possess both these skills in their native language when they begin school, but this is the early fifteen hundreds, so Erasmus is not referring to the students' mastery of their native French, Dutch, Italian, or whatever other language. The great civilizations of Greece and Rome had not been rivaled in more than a thousand years, and thinkers such as Erasmus still looked up to them as the ideal. Anything serious was most likely written in Latin; scholars wrote even their personal correspondence in the language of Cicero. Thus, after his declaration of the essential importance of mastering language, he makes it clear that he is talking about mastering Latin and, if possible, Greek.

Erasmus's respect for the languages and the ways of the Greeks and Romans was boundless. Their languages, he claimed, contained all the useful knowledge that had ever been acquired, and he probably wasn't far off the mark, speaking as a European of five hundred years ago. He also assumed that the Romans had gotten it basically right in their system of education. He was a great admirer of Quintilian, the famous first-century Roman orator and writer. "Quintilian has left a very thorough treatment of these matters, so that it would seem the height of impertinence to write about a subject he has already dealt with."[3] In fact, Erasmus expressed no criticism of traditional methods, and many of his suggestions were taken straight from the earlier days.

*Figure 8.1*   Erasmus.

Nevertheless, we find some interesting new ideas. Throughout his writings, we find a concern for the students' motivation. Good results, for example, can be achieved if the teacher encourages student efforts and displays patience in correcting errors. Like the Greeks and Romans, he promoted the use of games and prizes to encourage students, as well as having the top students involved in the supervision of activities. Unlike the ancients, however, he urged that students of lesser abilities also be chosen sometimes for prizes when they do well in order to maintain their interest and morale.

This concern surfaces in other ways. He mentions several times that the materials under study, whether a reading text, discussion point, or writing topic, must be of interest to the students. He also understood that studying grammar was not a favorite activity of children. Knowledge of the rules was needed, of course, but in the early stages of language education, there should be as few rules as possible:

> Nor have I ever agreed with the common run of teachers who, in incul-cating these authors [i.e., of grammar books], hold boys back for sev-eral years. For a true ability to speak correctly is best fostered both by conversing and consorting with those who speak correctly and by the habitual reading of the best stylists.[4]

In other words, grammar should be taught inductively to begin with; a more formal approach can be used at later stages.

His disdain for studying rules applied as well to the teaching of writing. Style is acquired not by studying the rules of rhetoric but by writing and writing and more writing. But beyond this, truly good writing also requires general knowledge, which as we noted was in Latin and Greek, the target languages for learning. It's a bit circular, but we can say that learning in general and proficiency in language go hand in hand, because the better your language skills, the more you can understand and learn from the two languages. The more you understand, the more you can know, and the more you know the more you can write. The more you write, the better your style becomes. In brief, though, once again we are avoiding the dry memorization of rules.

The acquisition of knowledge is based on memory. Three factors are required for remembering: (1) you have to understand what you are try-ing to learn, (2) it must be in its correct order (that is, memory depends on logical ordering of the subject matter—you need a proper informational background), and (3) it requires lots of repetition and review.[5]

Another refreshingly different viewpoint of Erasmus is his high regard for teachers—or at least, his ideal teachers—since the success of education lies more with them than with their pupils:

> A teacher can expect success in the classroom if he displays the quali-ties of gentleness and kindness and also possesses the skill and ingenu-ity to devise various means of making the studies pleasant and keeping the child from feeling any strain. Nothing is more harmful than an instructor whose conduct causes his students to take an intense dislike to their studies before they are sufficiently mature to appreciate them for their own sake.[6]

Erasmus's language teacher is extremely well read and informed, and able to discuss a tremendous variety of subjects. He's patient, kind, and a com-plete master of the language or languages he teaches, with excellent pro-nunciation that provides the perfect model for his students, whom he cares about sincerely. No doubt he was good-looking as well![7] Erasmus realized that such a person was necessary to put his ideas into practice. Only a well-educated man could choose the best materials to study and topics for discussion; only he could help the students achieve the goal of a thorough understanding of a text.

Erasmus marks a transition between the Middle Ages and modern times, between Latin and the vernacular languages.[8] Erasmus's scheme is essentially a refinement of the Roman system, though it probably was more of a break with tradition than even he realized (for example, he didn't seem to think that paying attention to psychological factors was groundbreaking). And he wasn't much of a realist—he describes an ideal home and classroom environment. If possible, children were to learn Latin and perhaps Greek at home from their parents before even starting their formal education. The local language could be learned easily through contact with others outside the home. Obviously, his plans referred to an elite class, not the typical students of his day.

Still, we should give credit for forward thinking where it is due. We're not trying to pass Erasmus off as a pioneer in applied linguistics. Instead, we should think of him as one of numerous examples we could examine in a search for enlightened thinking in the classroom. Some of his ideas were quite interesting and indeed a welcome change.

# 9 Roger Ascham and His Double-Translation Technique

Our next scholar is the Englishman Roger Ascham,[1] who lived from 1515 to 1568. Unlike Erasmus, his reputation today rests mainly upon his work as an educator. Like Erasmus, he looked to the Romans for right and wrong in education, but instead of following Quintilian's musings on the subject, he focused on mastering literature; therefore, he took advice from Cicero and even Caesar. He came from a prominent family and received his early education in the care of a renowned tutor. He entered Cambridge University at the age of fifteen (quite normal in the fifteen hundreds) where he made a name for himself as a student of Greek. His academic reputation eventually earned him the prestigious post of tutor to the king's sixteen-year-old daughter, Princess Elizabeth, who later would become Queen Elizabeth I.

## A FATEFUL DINNER

Ascham was a noted scholar in his day. His legacy derives from a book called *The Schoolmaster*, or *The Scholemaster* to give it its contemporary title, which was written in the 1560s and published in 1570, shortly after his death. In "The Praeface to the Reader" he tells the interesting story of how he came to write the book. On December 10, 1563, he was dining at the queen's residence with a few government officials and other notables. One of them made a comment that created a lively discussion:

> I had strange news brought me this morning, said Mr. Secretary, that several scholars of Eton[2] have run away from the school for fear of being beaten. Mr. Secretary then wished that many schoolmasters used more discretion in their methods of correcting students. Many times, he said, they punish a weakness of nature rather than a fault of the scholar. As a result, many students who might otherwise do well are driven to hate learning before they know what learning truly is, and are then eager to give up their books for any other kind of living.[3]

Another guest disagreed. The rod was the sword that "keeps the school in obedience and the scholar in good order"[4]—a philosophy as old as philosophy itself. Both flogging and anti-flogging had their supporters at the dining table. One participant asserted that the best schoolmaster of the day was also "the greatest beater"; Ascham diplomatically declines to furnish the name of this shaper of young men.

After dinner, a gentleman who had remained silent throughout the debate sought out Ascham for a private conversation. All the talk of classroom punishment had affected him deeply, he confided. He agreed wholeheartedly with the secretary's aversion to severe physical punishment:

> I can be good witness to this myself. For a foolish schoolmaster, before I was fully fourteen years old, drove me with a fear of beating from all love of learning. But now that I know what a difference there is to have learning and to have little or none at all, I feel it is my greatest grief, and find it to be the greatest hurt that has ever happened to me, that I had the misfortune to encounter such a vulgar schoolmaster.[5]

The man was Sir Richard Sackville, under-treasurer of the exchequer. He hoped to benefit from this unfortunate event of his own past to ensure that it couldn't happen to his two-year-old grandson. What, he wanted to know, were the best methods of educating a young gentleman? After all, here in front of Sir Richard was a prominent scholar who had educated the queen. Their discussion so impressed Sackville that he beseeched Ascham to put down his thoughts on paper. A little flattery served its purpose. Sackville continued:

> Seeing that God did so bless you as to make you the pupil of the best tutor and then the teacher of the best pupil [Queen Elizabeth I] that ever was in our time, surely you would please God, benefit your country and honour your own name if you would take the pains to impart to others what you learned from such a master and how you taught such a scholar.[6]

Who could resist such an invitation? The result was *The Schoolmaster,* a two-hundred-page discourse on the upbringing of a young person that covered religion, morality, and the correct methods (the "right order") in learning.

## THE SCHOOLMASTER

The methods section is of most interest to us here, but Ascham's concern for the total education of the child underscores the awakening to the needs of the young as a distinct group of learners. He criticized the foreign-language teaching methods commonly used in the schools of his day. Students were cheated both by the vocabulary chosen without thought and by their lack of understanding of what to do with the words. The results were poor habits and errors that became set for a student's lifetime. Ascham advocated a technique that solved these problems. What better way to learn the best vocabulary and grammar than to study the works of the most eloquent writers in history? This wasn't innovative, obviously, but he favored an activity called "double translation" that seemed new to his contemporaries. It wasn't actually an original method either (Ascham clearly said that it wasn't), yet his name became the one most closely associated with it.

Double translation was introduced to the pupils after they'd learned the parts of speech and some basic grammar and vocabulary. It could first be applied to maxims that promoted virtuous principles for everyday life, but the true aim of the method was a detailed study of the best writing. The activity commenced with the teacher "cheerfully and plainly" explaining in English the context and background of a text[7]—a letter by Cicero was the premier teaching tool, Ascham urged. It was then translated orally by the teacher into English as much as necessary for the child to have a clear understanding of it. Then came identification of the parts of speech. Until this point, it had all been reading and oral work, but next the learner advanced into the heart of the method. The child sat alone and, with no help, translated the passage from Latin into English, relying only on the text itself and the knowledge gained through the earlier exercises. He then showed it to the master, who took the Latin text away. After a pause of least one hour, the student translated his own English text back into Latin as accurately as he could. The teacher would then go through the text with the student, gently pointing out errors and praising good work. Demonstrating kindness was essential, "For I assure you, there is no such whetstone to sharpen a good wit [i.e., mind] and encourage a will to learning as is praise."[8] Likewise, "For I know by good experience that a child shall take more profit of two faults, gently warned of, than of four things, rightly hit [i.e., done correctly]."[9]

Having children speak before they were ready was discouraged. The common practice in even many of the best schools in England, Ascham said, was to have students talk just for the sake of talking. But talk about what? "The Master careth not, the scholar knoweth not, what."[10] Ascham warned of the consequences of having youngsters apply their limited knowledge at too early a stage: "Confusion is brought in, barbarousness is bred in young wits"[11] to the point that their speaking abilities and judgment may never be put right again. In contrast, Ascham wished them to "speak so . . . it may well appear that the brain doth govern the tongue, and that reason leadeth forth the talk."[12] The double-translation method provided the foundation for proper speaking by ensuring that students were exposed only to a thorough study of the best authors.

Grammar, then, was taught inductively, for the most part—that is, the rudiments were studied traditionally—but once the students reached a level that allowed double translation, grammar was learned by doing, not by memorization, and by asking questions, not by doing exercises. Ascham swore by this method. The best evidence was furnished by his prize pupil, the future Queen Elizabeth I, who

> never took yet Greek nor Latin Grammar in her hand, after the first declining of a noun and a verb, but only by this double translating . . . daily . . . for the space of a year or two, hath attained to such a perfect understanding in both the tongues . . . as they be few in number in both the universities, or elsewhere in England, that be, in both tongues, comparable with her Majesty.[13]

Ascham's methods went beyond double translation, as we'd expect from a renowned language scholar. Nevertheless, the basis of his teaching even at higher levels was translation, a lot of writing, and eventual imitation of classical writers.

Perhaps double translation could be a useful activity in a classroom. However, in spite of Ascham's claims, drawbacks to relying so heavily on double translation are not hard to find. It focuses so heavily on style and imitation that it's hard to imagine that a practical knowledge of the language could be achieved. Moreover, his chipper assertion that the princess did nothing but double translations day after day after day for up to two years makes us wonder whether it was more a case of royal self-control and determination that led to success. Ascham was well known and respected, so his interest in the method meant that it received a great deal of attention and imitation. It shows us as well the continuing respect given the ancient Romans and Greeks even during the Renaissance, with its "rebirth" of intellectual activity.

# 10 Claudius Holyband
## "A Frenchman Which Doth His Dutie"

We'll turn now to a Frenchman who had quite a successful career as a language teacher and school owner in sixteenth-century London. He's known by several names, but we'll use Claudius Holyband, an anglicization of his birth name, Claude de Sainliens. It's not known when he was born, but he was one of thousands who fled France in the mid-fifteen hundreds to escape religious unrest. He came to England in about 1565. Holyband had been a teacher in France,[1] so he continued his profession in England and achieved a very comfortable living. He owned a succession of schools and wrote a few very successful textbooks.

Holyband was a contemporary of Roger Ascham, whose *Schoolmaster* was published five years after Holyband's arrival. Holyband even lived for a while in the distinguished household of the Sackville family; it was Sir Richard Sackville who had been Ascham's benefactor and patron for *The Schoolmaster*. It's certainly no coincidence that one of Holyband's best-known works is called *The French Schoolmaster*.

Holyband had a different perspective from the language teachers we've seen until now: his primary goal was not to teach Latin (though that was part of the curriculum of his schools), but to teach practical language skills in French to the children of well-to-do merchants—the language was more a future business tool than a symbol of prestige. Although Holyband wrote a number of books, including texts for Latin and Italian, he's known chiefly for two: *The French Schoolmaster* and *The French Littelton* (also spelled *Littleton*). They were both intended for French instruction,[2] but as we'll see, they were suitable for teaching English to French speakers as well. They were actually very similar in content and style.[3] Though Holyband was Ascham's contemporary, we encounter a completely different style of language teaching and learning from what we've just seen in Ascham, who was concerned with language learning based on the works of the best ancient authors.

Holyband's students learned French through a well-thought-out program that had reading and a strong emphasis on correct pronunciation as the foundations.[4] Grammar was a part of it, but not mindless memorization of rules. Holyband preferred to emphasize work on verb forms. It was only then that the focus shifted to acquiring a large vocabulary, with an understanding of the proper usage of the words. The heart of Holyband's method was teaching through dialogues. Dialogue work was not original, as we've seen, and was fairly common at the time, though written conversations were more typically intended as survival guides for adults. Holyband's students still memorized and recited a lot, but the materials were strikingly different. The dialogues, written by Holyband himself, cleverly and skillfully taught essential vocabulary and grammar, and were written with a keen eye for the students' levels, interests, and experiences. They're quite lively and often humorous, and were surely successful in holding the attention of a classroom of children. The dialogues and their translations were laid out side by side, so even though they were actually French books, they could in fact be used for either French or English instruction. They served, then, to teach French to English children in a familiar context and to teach cultural information to French newcomers who were studying English. The dialogues are fascinating, not just because they're something new, but because they also tell us about the most mundane details of daily life in sixteenth-century London.

*The French Schoolmaster* and *The Littelton* consist principally of dialogues, vocabulary lists, and proverbs.[5] The dialogues were the heart of both books, so let's see some examples. The first dialogue of *The Littelton* is "Of Scholars and School." It deals with the pupils and happenings in Holyband's own school. The students most likely were no older than ten. As it had for centuries, a typical schoolday began early in the morning, seven o'clock usually, and continued until probably five o'clock, with a one-hour break for lunch. The dialogues contain a varied cast of characters, both at home and at the school. We see parents, servants, an assortment of pupils, class clowns (one is named John Nothingworth), and the strict but caring teacher (Holyband). There are many instances of humor, something we're not accustomed to seeing. The teacher is constantly threatening to beat the children, but it's clear that he rarely does so and is far from being one of those feared teachers discussed at dinner by Ascham and company.

Early in the dialogue, we find a gentleman accompanying his son to school on his first day. They run into a woman they know:[6]

WOMAN: Whither go you so early? Whither lead you your son?
MAN: I bring him to schoole, to learn to speake Latine and French: for he hath lost his time till now: and you know well that it were better to be unborne than untaught: which is most true.
WOMAN: You say true: it is true certainly; but whither goeth he to schoole?
MAN: In Paules Church yard, at the signe of the golden ball: there is a Frenchman, which teacheth both the tongues . . . and which doth his dutie [that is, he does his job conscientiously].
WOMAN: It is the chiefest point [the most important thing]: for there be some which be verie negligent and sluggish . . . they care not very much, if their scholers profit or no.
MAN: They be folke of an evill conscience: the same is a kind of theft.
WOMAN: Who doubteth of it? What is his name?

MAN:     I cannot tell truly: I have forgotten it. John, how is thy master called?

JOHN:    He is called Monsieur Claudius Holyband.

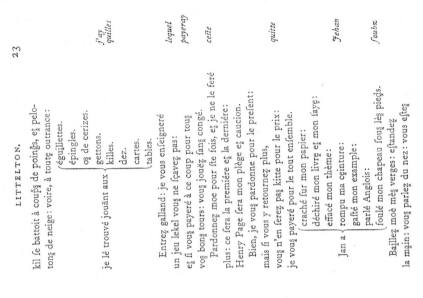

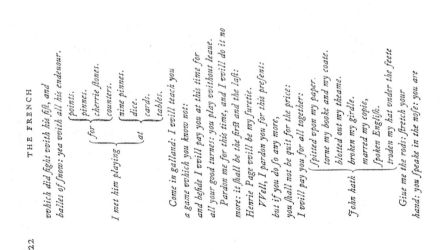

*Figure 10.1*   A page from Claudius Holyband's French Littelton. Silent letters in French have a small x under or above them. Remember that the letter s is sometimes written as ſ or ʃ.

Holyband has slyly combined a lesson in morality and an advertisement for his own services. Later on the father is dismayed to learn how much Monsieur Holyband charges for his services, but the teacher tells him that if his son learns, it is money well spent.

Holyband made use of a practice that was becoming popular in the sixteenth century—a sort of substitution table. To give one example, when a student is tattling on John Nothingworth, Holyband gives a list of possible transgressions that one might commit in the classroom. The villain, reports the student (take your pick), "hath: spitted upon my paper, torne my booke and my coate, blotted out my theame, broken my girdle [i.e., belt or sash], marred my copie, spoken English, troden my hat under the feete."[7] All these offenses are duly translated into French. Similarly, this technique could be used to show the lack of a one-to-one translation of a word. In the sentence "My father . . . sendeth you his ring for a token," we see in French that "his ring" can be translated as *son anneau, sa bague, son cachet,* or *son signet.*

A useful practice of Holyband's was the marking of the many silent letters in French, an obstacle for any student of the language. He placed a small *x* under or above any letter that should be passed over. It's a very handy device even today as we try to read his dialogues.

The use of dialogues meant that grammar was taught inductively. This was a deliberate choice; Holyband tells us in his introduction that learners should not get bogged down in the rules of the language at the beginning, but should involve themselves directly with the language through the dialogues. He wasn't dismissing the importance of grammar, though: a rudimentary grammar could be found in both books. Repetition was a key feature of the dialogues, though it's not always obvious, thanks to Holyband's genius for writing realistic conversations. Grammatical structures and vocabulary are repeated in slightly different contexts, permitting the student to see more than one solitary usage as would normally happen if they were studying an authentic text of a classical author.

It feels like we're moving toward modern times. There's not the emphasis on Latin. The language learned will serve practical purposes, not just as a badge of class and education. We also see, in this case at least, the teacher as a respected figure instead of the shady character of questionable morals and cloudy past. In Holyband's case, and undoubtedly that of other higher-class teachers, the pay was good. Though that was certainly not the rule, it shows at least that teaching could be a respectable and profitable business.

# 11 Michel de Montaigne
## The Last Native Speaker Of Latin?

Sometimes it's enjoyable to stop at a story not for its great importance but just because it's a good tale. The ancient Greek historian Herodotus tells us that the Egyptians had always believed themselves to be the oldest race on earth, but the pharaoh Psammetichus (seventh century BC) wanted to prove it.[1] His clever but heartless experiment was to take two newborn children and entrust them to a shepherd's family in the countryside. They were to be kept apart from any other human contact as much as possible and never spoken to. Why? It was thought that language would appear spontaneously in a child, even without hearing any other speech. Whatever language was the first to be uttered by these children, Psammetichus believed, would be the original language, that of the first civilization. The story goes that at the age of two, both children one day rushed up to the shepherd on one of his visits to check on their needs and both exclaimed their first word: *bekos*! The shepherd was unsure what to make of this at first and waited, but when the children repeated this word several times on later visits, he took them to the pharaoh. What was this word, *bekos*? Inquiries were made and it was discovered, undoubtedly to the enormous dismay of Psammetichus, that *bekos* was the word for bread in Phrygia, a kingdom in what is now Turkey. From then onward, Herodotus says, the Egyptians had to accept that they were the second oldest people in the world.

That may or may not have really happened (Herodotus himself advised caution when reporting matters of which he didn't have personal knowledge), but we do know of another youthful language learning experiment, also of questionable morality, that really did happen. Michel de Montaigne[2] (1533–1592) was a sixteenth-century French author best known for his *Essais*, or essays. In fact, he's usually credited with the creation of the essay as a literary form. His personal reflections filled dozens of essays on a tremendous range of topics. His interest in language learning was no more than typical for a person of his standing, and in fact he talked about it only briefly. But what little he wrote about it is remarkable, for Montaigne tells us how he grew up as a native speaker of Latin, almost certainly the first and only one in many centuries.

Montaigne's family was rather wealthy, and his father, a highly educated man, took an exceptionally close interest in the education of his son. From his discussions with the wisest men he could find, he was convinced that the years spent learning Latin and Greek created a delay in a child's education that could never be overcome. This time and effort wasted in mastering a language that had come naturally to the ancients "is the only reason that we are unable to attain the same greatness of soul and knowledge as the ancient Greeks and Romans"[3]—or so thought Montaigne's father. He came up with a fascinating and bizarre experiment to test this belief. As an infant, Montaigne was entrusted to a German doctor who spoke no French but was fluent

*Figure 11.1*  Michel de Montaigne: a giant of French literature and a native speaker of Latin.

in Latin. The doctor and a few servants who assisted him were instructed never to speak anything but Latin to young Michel. His parents, of course, followed the same rule. We can only assume that he had no contact with any other children or adults. Montaigne doesn't go into details of how he was taught, but the philosophy of it is clearly stated: his father had been advised "to educate my soul in complete gentleness and liberty, without compulsion or force."[4] The atmosphere was to be playful whenever possible.

Montaigne says nothing about the social consequences of his upbringing, but informs us (not surprisingly, from a modern perspective) that he spoke Latin with the same ease as any other child would speak his first language. "Without trickery, without a book, without grammar or rules, without whipping and without tears, I had learned Latin as pure as that of my master."[5] The experiment was such a success that several of his tutors, extremely learned men and scholastic authors, confessed later that they were intimidated by his fluent Latin as a child of no more than six years of age. At that time, he claims, he knew no more French than he knew Arabic (i.e., none at all), a remarkable statement from one of the giants of French literature.

So what advantage did he gain from this unique upbringing? None. The most significant reason was his father's failure to follow through with the experiment. In spite of his ardent desire to provide Michel with the best education, he at last gave in to common opinion and sent the boy off to a top private school when he was six. School rules were broken to provide him with special attention, but nevertheless,

> My Latin immediately deteriorated, and since then, through lack of practice, I have lost all usage of it. And this novel method of education of mine served only to allow me to skip some of the early classes; I finished my courses at thirteen, and in truth, without any benefit from it that I can tell even today.[6]

As drastic and even cruel as this experiment seems, Montaigne expresses no regrets. On the contrary, he even criticizes his father for giving up on it, comparing him to a bird in flight who must follow the leader. Yet he reminds us of "the care and affection of such a good father, to whom no blame should be attached if he did not gather any fruit from such an exquisite cultivation."[7]

At the beginning of the story Montaigne says the method guarantees much greater success than one will obtain by traditional scholastic means. Montaigne offers evidence of the benefits of a stress-free learning environment at a very early age—but then, it's really just a case of a child's acquisition of his first language, even though for him it happened to be a dead one. The rapidity with which he lost his native fluency at a young age was obviously a surprise to him in hindsight and just as newsworthy to his readers as the experiment. In the end, it's of interest simply as a historical curiosity. "Make use of it as you wish," he says dryly.[8] Fortunately no one else has, as far as anyone knows.

# 12  John Brinsley's Advice to Teachers

## THE SEVENTEENTH CENTURY

The seventeenth century can be considered the beginning of modern history in many ways, especially in the sciences and arts. Descartes, Newton, Locke, Galileo, Peter the Great, Francis Bacon, Shakespeare, Rembrandt, Molière, Louis XIV, and Bach, to name a few, have more in common with us today than with their predecessors of just a few generations earlier. As one scholar said, "In 1600 the educated Englishman's mind and world were more than half medieval; by 1660 they were more than half modern."[1] Much of this credit belonged to the French philosopher René Descartes, whose rationalist outlook popularized experimentation and reason in the search for truth, rather than relying on the speculation and persuasive arguing that had always been the norm. This would show up in language studies as a concern for the nature of language and the mind. Religion still played a major role in everyday life, of course, and on a geographically and politically larger scale than in the past. It also continued to play a major role in the work of our language scholars in this section.

The sixteen hundreds were a time of grand ideas in education. In a way, we'll take a break from the past centuries and talk about some ideas that aren't really related directly to language teaching—certainly not in a practical sense—but they're just too interesting to pass by without notice. The word "universal" keeps popping up, and we can't dream any bigger than that. We'll encounter an ambitious goal to institute universal education. We'll then consider the efforts of one group to create a description of the grammar that underlies all languages, and how it influenced language teaching for many years afterward. This notion of universal grammar caught the attention of Noam Chomsky in the 1960s and helped establish the history of linguistics as a respected subfield. After that, we'll examine one man's dream of creating a universal language. Linguistically, the universal language movement represented by these episodes defined the century: "No other linguistic project engaged and influenced more scholars from as many countries for as many years as the seventeenth-century universal language movement. No other movement was as characteristic of its age."[2]

This seems to suggest that the seventeenth-century classroom was much more modern as well. It's fortunate, then, that we can start by examining a book that gives us a sense of how languages were actually often taught in the early sixteen hundreds. Let's see how big the ideas were.

## JOHN BRINSLEY

Two old friends, both teachers, see each other for the first time since their university days twenty years earlier. But it's not a coincidence; Spoudeus has sought out his old friend Philoponus for advice to help him get through a crisis in his professional life. He's had enough of the teaching life: he's worn out, both mentally and physically. Their conversation runs like this:[3]

SPOUDEUS: Thank God I have my health, at least. But for the last twenty years I've been teaching in a poor school out in the countryside— I'm trapped in a fruitless, tiresome, and thankless job. But I hear you've been doing the same type of work so I imagine you understand my troubles.

PHILOPONUS: Indeed I do understand. But what brings you here? It's been so long that I hardly recognize you. You've aged so much, to be honest. Only your voice hasn't changed.

SPOUDEUS: Well, I've heard that you've always been a conscientious teacher, and that in recent years you've devoted yourself to finding the best ways of teaching. And I hear you've had considerable success. I've come all this way for your help: I'll always be grateful if you can tell me some of the results that you've managed to achieve. I've worked so hard and so long without any real success, and I'm so tired of my job that I've begun to question whether this is what God really wants me to do.

PHILOPONUS: For most of my career I knew just how you feel. But ever since I decided to investigate the best teaching practices and carry them out, I've managed to put the bad old days behind me. Not only do I have fewer problems at work, but now I enjoy the activities and progress of my children so much that I dare say it gives me more satisfaction than anyone can get from his favorite pastimes. The best part is after the work is done, when I can reflect on the success I've had. I also know that I've made a real contribution to society— even though most people still don't realize that. If I'd known from the beginning what I know now, I could have accomplished ten times as much and my life would've been much more pleasant. Oh, it's true that even in the darker days my efforts were never entirely wasted—I've managed to send some students off to university each year—but it's nothing compared to what I might have done.

SPOUDEUS: Just the fact that you've experienced both the bad and the good gives me some hope that you can help me.

PHILOPONUS: It'll be my pleasure and my duty. It's only right that we share what we've learned with others.

SPOUDEUS: I'm ready to do whatever you recommend. I just hope my last years of teaching can be enjoyable and make up for the past, which I'd really rather just forget.

PHILOPONUS: There've been so many learned men in recent times that if we're willing to learn from them and put into practice their advice, our teaching can give us greater rewards than we've ever experienced. It's a pity, but until now some of the most useful knowledge has been ignored.

## *Ludus Literarius:*
### OR,
# The Grammar Schoole.

### CHAP. I.

*A Discourse betweene two Schoolemasters, concerning
their function. In the end determining a conference
about the best way of teaching, and the manner
of their proceeding in the same.*

---

SPOUDEUS.          PHILOPONUS.

---

*Spoud.*
GOD save you, good Sir: I am glad to see you in health.
*Phil.* What, mine old acquaintance, M. *Spoudeus?*
*Spoud.* The very same, Sir.
*Phil.* Now, I am as right glad to see you well; you are heartily welcome to this my poore house.
*Spoud.* Sir, I give you many thankes.
*Phil.* But how have yo done these many yeeres?
*Spoud.* I thanke God I have had good health, ever since we lived in the Colledge together: but for my time, I have spent it in a fruitlesse, wearisom, and an unthankfull office; in teaching a poore countrey schoole, as I have heard, that your

*The Schoole-master's place oi dinarily weari-some, thankless*

*Figure 12.1* The first page of John Brinsley's *Ludus Literarius*.

Expand this conversation and put it into the English of 1612 and we have the opening lines of a remarkable book by an English schoolteacher, John Brinsley (born 1564 or 1565), called *Ludus Literarius, or the Grammar Schoole*. *Ludus* means "game" in Latin. *Literarius* doesn't have to refer to literature; it can also mean learning in general, so the best translation is "The Game of Learning." Poor Spoudeus saw nothing playful in his chosen profession, and Brinsley recognized that England, especially in the smaller and poorer schools in the countryside, was full of long-suffering teachers like Spoudeus, who had the will but not the knowledge to improve their teaching and their lives.

Brinsley was not an innovator. As he says through Philoponus, he looked into the opinions and practices of leading scholars and teachers from both his time and the past. His idea of the best teaching practices simply meant the proper application of the same methods that had been used since ancient times, with a few refinements thrown in. In most chapters he begins by having Spoudeus explain how the teaching point under discussion was done in the real world of the early sixteen hundreds. What this accomplished, no doubt, was to establish a bond with the reader: to the Spoudeuses of the world, he seems to say, "You're not the only one who does it this way. I understand and will help you change."

What we have, then, is a true picture of how classrooms in 1612 functioned (in England and presumably much of Europe), as well as a blueprint for the ideal classical education. Brinsley is talking about education in general, but in fact in the classroom of a 1612 grammar school, it was still all about learning classical languages (hence, we're reminded of the origins of the name "grammar school"). The times were beginning to change, but we can say that Brinsley tells us how it *should* have been done for hundreds of years.

## TWO TEACHERS, TWO WORLDS

It's no wonder that Spoudeus is depressed. He used to possess enthusiasm for his job and a sense that he was being called by God to do it. Yet years of rote teaching and learning and unappreciative students and parents have sent him to Philoponus in a glum final attempt to revive his career. Brinsley doesn't dwell on the methods used by teachers like Spoudeus, but we can piece together a few scenes of what the classroom was like. Today we think of the four skills of reading, writing, listening, and speaking, but in the classrooms of Spoudeus and Philoponus the big skills were grammar, reading, translation, writing, and speaking.

### Grammar

As would be expected in a "grammar" school, the study of grammar was the foundation of all learning, just as it had been for centuries with Donatus and Priscian, for example. Lily by this time had replaced Donatus, at least in England. Spoudeus gives few details about how he teaches grammar other than to have the students memorize rules, translate them "a little," and then apply them to their readings. The parts of speech receive a great deal of attention.[4]

Philoponus would have agreed completely with the artist of the Tower of Knowledge: mastery of grammar was the key to everything, the foundation of all learning. The job of the teacher is to turn his pupils into "absolute Grammarians"[5] who know Lily's rules by heart and actually understand them. Students are drilled daily on the rules, typically by the type of short questions and answers used in Donatus's textbook. For example, with their books in front of them, the teacher can ask, "What gender are proper names of Females? How many kinds of them are there? What is the rule for them?"[6] The teacher may ask and receive answers in either English or Latin, depending on the level and ability of the class.

## Reading

For reading, the main technique employed by Spoudeus is again old-fashioned memorization and recitation. The alphabet is memorized as a whole—students can recite it forward and backward. They spend little if any time working with individual letters. The teacher reads and translates the lesson (often on topics that are alien to the students) and parses it.[7] The pupils repeat the passage after the teacher. They then read, recite, and parse on their own. Spoudeus laments that some of his students can't read well even after six or seven years of school.

Philoponus begins by teaching the names of the letters, one at a time; the children then practice letter recognition by finding examples of the letter in text. Then, just as in ancient times, they move on to working with syllables, which teaches both reading and spelling, and so on, to longer words. He makes sure that they understand what they are reading. In fact, the more familiar the subject matter, the better. Thorough memorization is still required, though, to ensure mastery of vocabulary. The teacher reads the material, translates it, and explains everything. He asks many short questions in Latin, but in the same order as the reading. At first he even answers them himself; only then does he repeat for the students to answer.

## Translation

In Spoudeus's classroom, learning to translate is much like learning to read. Typically, the teacher gives the students a text and, as with reading, goes through it word by word. The students, with a little help from the teacher, then write out translations in English. At a later stage, students are expected to translate a passage within a time limit and with no help. Errors must be dealt with strictly. Translations are normally done only from Latin into English. Spoudeus admits that it's not a very useful way to do things: "Translations in Schools have not been found to bring any such benefit, but rather much hurt."[8]

Philoponus observes once again that the foundation of this skill is a thorough knowledge of grammar. The typical method used by Spoudeus focuses just on the meanings of the words, but without explanation of how things fit together. This confuses the students and leads to a dislike of translation. Philoponus, on the other hand, advocates the "golden rule of construing" as stated in various forms by previous grammarians, based on a point-by-point analysis of each sentence.[9] After the students have carried out this careful translation, they can put it back into its original Latin—a double translation as recommended by Ascham. In another activity, the students make three columns on a page. In the first, they copy the teacher's English translation of a Latin text. In the second column they turn this into a literal Latin translation, and in the third the students attempt to put it into their best literary Latin. The student who comes closest to the author's original words and order is the winner.

## Writing

For both Spoudeus and Philoponus, writing means composing themes and poetry in the style of the classical authors. In Spoudeus's classroom, the simplest exercise is the daily copying of a text given by the teacher. It is just expected that the students will pay attention to the style. He then assigns a theme, asking the class to expand the topic. They might use Cicero or another author for inspiration.

Learning to write themes was neither a popular nor successful activity for students. Says Spoudeus:

> But yet (alas!) that which my children have done hereby for a long time, they have done with exceeding pains and fear, and yet too-too weakly, in harsh phrase, without any invention, or judgement; and ordinarily so rudely [primitively], as I have been ashamed that anyone should see their exercises.[10]

The result? The teacher gets angrier than he would like with the beleaguered students ("the poor boys," Spoudeus calls them), discouraged students quit school if their parents will let them, and some decide that any rotten job at all is better than the beatings and embarrassments suffered in school. And in the end it must be admitted, says a despondent Spoudeus, that many of his graduating students are incapable of writing even an acceptable letter to a friend in any language. Learning to write poetry goes no better, though at least a lack of skill in this art carries no such disastrous consequences.

For Philoponus, endless practice in double translation and parsing should have taken care of the technical foundation for composition. What

Spoudeus and others don't realize, he claims, is that in composition by children, content comes before form. That is, it's wrong to expect young students to write intelligent themes if they've had no worldly experience. Before beginning a plan of composition, the teacher should establish a different kind of framework that will give them something to write about. Start with sentences from authors that contain useful moral teachings and good virtuous advice; study exemplary poems and themes to serve as models. There should be daily writing homework, even for the youngest, that the teacher checks the next day. Students can then begin writing, but short themes of just twelve to sixteen lines. You can also have students read letters of ancient authors (Cicero, especially) and have them copy the style, perhaps to write a letter to a friend. Only then will students achieve the complete foundation to write themes.

## Speaking

Since ancient times, scholars and teachers had decried "barbarisms" in both writing and speaking. Because correctness and style are the prized goals of a grammar school education, and speaking is the least controllable skill, speaking is discouraged in Spoudeus's lower forms because of the risk of mangling the language. Hence, there is little practice for the youngest children.[11] The natural result is that students never develop the habit of speaking Latin, and in higher levels, when it is time to do so, students insist on speaking English when the teacher wants Latin.[12] Teachers often resort to snitches who report students who have been speaking English. These assistants might even be given a paddle to enforce the rule, but this leads to resentment in and out of class.

In contrast to the common practice, Philoponus urges that even the youngest pupils be encouraged to speak the foreign language in class.[13] Pronunciation is of the highest importance. Philoponus actually calls on the teacher to mimic the students' bad pronunciation to show the difference between the correct and the incorrect.[14] It's more than pronunciation of individual sounds, though. To develop pleasing and acceptable intonation and expression, the children should think of it as acting. Urge them to imagine saying it first. If that doesn't work, they can practice it in English and then try to capture that style in Latin.[15]

An essential part of Philoponus's classroom is a friendly atmosphere. Brinsley was a great admirer of Ascham, the writer who talked of the horrors of physical punishment for students. Philoponus refers approvingly to Ascham's belief that students learn better in caring, encouraging surroundings, free from fear. This results in fewer disciplinary problems, but justice must nevertheless be carried out strictly when required. Spare the rod whenever possible but use it when necessary.[16]

This has been merely a summary of the advice that Philoponus gives Spoudeus for more than three hundred pages. There are plenty of other interesting incidental bits: for example, the best time to practice handwriting is at one o'clock, when the students' hands are "warmest and nimblest."[17] He calls on teachers to enforce an attendance policy, saying parents should be told either to send their children regularly or keep them away. He even recommends a maximum of thirteen unexcused absences in a quarter, after which the student should be booted out.[18]

Brinsley's book was quite well known in its day. It provides us with an unusually realistic look at the language-teaching classroom as it was for centuries, both in its weakest and its strongest versions. It's also of particular interest because for our purposes, it marks the last time we'll see such praise for the classical method.

# 13  Eilhard Lubinus
## A Call For Change

From Brinsley we move on to a scholar who is more representative of the changes of the seventeenth century. If you look up Eilhard Lubinus[1] (1565–1621), you won't find much—and most of it will be in German or Polish. What you'll discover is a typical "Renaissance man": he was a German professor of philosophy, mathematics, literature, and theology, as well as a mapmaker of the late sixteenth and early seventeenth century. Like many others of his time, he dabbled in other areas, including language learning. In the early sixteen hundreds he published a trilingual New Testament. Of interest to us is the preface to the work, because it is there that he advocates what seem to be some novel ideas about good language teaching. This preface itself was so well received that it was translated into English and printed a number of years after his death in another book, where it gained a wide readership.[2]

Lubinus blamed the poor results of contemporary language teaching (but note that he was referring above all to Latin) on a lack of consideration of children as learners, which is becoming a familiar lament by this time. Corporal punishment should be abandoned in favor of psychological punishments, he said, such as making the student sit with the lower grades, stand in a corner, or wear a jester's clothing.[3] A better class atmosphere could be created by a spirit of friendly competition, an old idea indeed. But Lubinus claimed that it was the study of grammar that was the root of most classroom problems. In the classroom, students should love their teachers, who are like their parents. Instead, they often hate and fear them, and the cause is clear: "All this mischief is due well nigh to the inculcating of Grammatical principles."[4] A favorite complaint of his was the use of grammatical jargon in teaching a foreign language to young people. He estimated that in the commonly used materials of his time, there were about 180 words used in the description of grammar that would be unfamiliar to young children; terms such as "tense," "mood," and "aspect," even when memorized, would not have meaning for them. In syntax, there were at least seventy rules with just as many exceptions. In brief, the level of information required even to begin the study of a foreign language such as Latin was too high for the typical classroom. The rules and terminology were a hindrance, not an aid,

*Figure 13.1* Eilhard Lubinus: a great influence on Jan Comenius.

to language study. He compared it to teaching an infant to walk by starting the child on ice with slippery iron-soled shoes.[5]

In contrast, what Lubinus advocated was quite simple, really: learning should involve the senses, not just the study of rules and words on a page or their mindless repetition. Vocabulary can be learned much faster if the pupils *see* the object to be named—even better if they can touch it or draw it:

> As Naturalists know very well, there can be nothing in the understanding, which is not before in the sense. . . . That which hath been in the sense is more notable . . . and so also sticks the surer and the longer in the memories treasury.[6]

He therefore called for vocabulary to be introduced in pictures, lots of pictures: "All Things which can be perceived by the sense of the eyes, described or imagined, ought by some sure way . . . to be shewed to children and set before their eyes."[7]

It was essential that new words be introduced in sentences in conjunction with the pictures when possible, because encountering them in a context made it easier to remember them than seeing them isolated in a word list. Moreover, a word list restricted the introduction of a noun or verb to just one form: all nouns traditionally were memorized in the nominative (i.e., subject) form and in the singular, while verbs were introduced in the first person singular. Hearing and reading their usage in natural sentences exposed a learner immediately to several grammatical forms.

From this technique the grammar would follow. Young minds have the ability to acquire it through usage and practice, he argued, which is much more agreeable and profitable than spending hours on obscure and incomprehensible rules. Some formal grammar teaching was useful, however, such as listing the case endings of nouns and the conjugation endings of verbs, but only after having worked with them through natural examples.

Eventually students would be able to engage in translation, both single and double, and later venture into original composition, but the foundation of learning a foreign language was the involvement of as many senses as possible, which generally meant both seeing and touching an object in reality, or at the least by simply seeing the object in a drawing:

> [And from these] examples, by which use and exercise, if the Latine Tongue can be learned in two, or surely three years space, to what end shall we sweat and toil ten, twelve or more years? For the most certain, and most ready course of learning any Tongue is by Use, and Exercise, and by Examples.[8]

It certainly sounds enlightened. Empiricism wasn't new, but Lubinus's preface was widely read at the time and received quite a lot of scholarly attention. But what's missing here? As we mentioned earlier, many of these ideas we're talking about are being proposed as ideals and by non-practicing teachers. Lubinus was primarily a mapmaker and professor of other disciplines. He makes it clear that he himself hadn't tried to create such a wondrous book full of pictures of everything in everyday life. Nonetheless, he was certainly ready to offer moral support to anyone prepared to make this attempt. Remarkably, he thought that it would not really be such a major undertaking:

> [This project] at the first will put one to some labour and charge, yet not very much. But these Pictures once so made and procured may afterwards last alwayes. . . . And who would not redeem with a little cost so many years of mans life in many thousands of children, whose turns [needs] this one thing, when't is once provided, may serve?[9]

Lubinus's interest in the psychology of language learning in children and his push for sensual involvement in their education sets the stage for the coming years and above all, for the work of someone who actually fulfilled Lubinus's wish: Jan Comenius.

# 14 Jan Comenius
## A Full-Scale Science of Education

**INTRODUCTION**

Our next personality closely follows Brinsley chronologically and provides an intriguing contrast. Brinsley showed us the way things were in reality and how they should have been in a classical education; Comenius will show us how things should have been in an ideal school. He was truly a man of the seventeenth century.

We rarely give more than a passing thought to the people involved in historical accounts. They're just names that may or may not have to be memorized, along with dates associated with them. Unless we have a particular interest in the person, he or she is just another step to reaching the end of the story. So let's pause and get to know more about one of our language-teaching scholars.

Jan Comenius[1] was a seventeenth-century educator from Moravia, in what is today part of the Czech Republic. He's been called "a genius, possibly the only one that the history of language teaching can claim."[2] He's not well known among language teachers today, which is a pity, because he was a brilliant man whose ideas reached far beyond the classroom and education. Moreover, his life story is a fascinatingly good tale. He certainly led one of the most interesting lives of anyone in our field, but alas, "interesting" is sometimes a euphemism for "disastrous." Unfortunately for him, a good tale requires conflict, and his life had far more than its fair share. Of all the famous teachers and noted scholars in the history of language teaching, his life story is the best bet for a successful film—or in his case, a miniseries. A biographer summed it up well in his title for a book about him: *The Sorrowful and Heroic Life of John Amos Comenius.*[3]

Comenius's grand goal in this era of big ideas was to reform education by devising a framework for "teaching all things to all men" (but not excluding girls; that's merely the language of his day). Like most big dreamers, he had only mixed success in reaching his goal. Yet along the way he did manage, in the words of the prominent psychologist and educator Jean Piaget, to be "the first [person] to conceive a full-scale science of education."[4]

*Figure 14.1*   Jan Comenius: a "sorrowful and heroic life."

## IDEAS FROM THE GREAT DIDACTIC

Let's go straight to his work and ideas, because it isn't as interesting to hear the life story of someone whom one knows nothing about. In the early 1630s he laid out his ideas on education (not just language learning) in a book entitled *The Great Didactic*.[5] The goal of education, simply put, was to develop a good relationship with God, a matter that had crucial consequences for life after death. Comenius saw God as a benevolent creator who wanted to be loved and praised by those whom he created. A mastery of language was seen as the key to the education that would make this possible.

His ideas about education are highly relevant even today and his words are very quotable, as in his stated aim:

To seek and find a method of instruction by which teachers may teach less, but learners may learn more; by which schools may be the scene of less noise, aversion and useless labour, but more of leisure, enjoyment and solid progress; and through which the Christian community may have less darkness, perplexity and dissension, but on the other hand, more light, orderliness, peace and rest.[6]

Comenius noted the failures of the contemporary system of education, a familiar theme. He quoted Eilhard Lubinus, one of his heroes, who said, "I find myself always led to the conclusion, that the entire system must have been introduced by some evil and envious genius, the enemy of the human race."[7] Comenius tells us that the classroom experience was so severe, such a "terror," that the majority of students left early, preferring work to learning. As for languages, he noted that adult workers in unskilled, boring jobs learned languages two or three times faster than children in schools did: surely this was the fault of the method. Much of the trouble with schools was the lack of standardization in methodology and ignorance of the importance of organization: "The principle which really holds together the fabric of this world of ours, down to its smallest detail, is none other than order; that is to say, the proper division of what comes before and what comes after."[8]

Here are some of his recommendations and observations for improving the systems of education everywhere:

1. Comenius believed that students should be required to memorize as little as possible. Interacting with the subject matter was what created genuine knowledge; memorization just led to pseudo-knowledge. Children learn by doing, not by learning a rule first and then applying it. This means that languages are learned more easily by practice than by the study of rules.

> The pupils [should] be forced to memorize as little as possible, that is to say, only the most important things; of the rest they need only grasp the general meaning.[9]

> Now the faculties of the young are forced . . . if they are made to learn by heart or do things that have not first been thoroughly explained and demonstrated to them.[10]

> No one should be allowed to talk about anything that he does not understand, or to understand anything without at the same time being able to express his knowledge in words. For he who cannot express the thoughts of his mind resembles a statue, and he who chatters without understanding what he says, resembles a parrot.[11]

Comenius dismissed empty, memorized words as nothing more than *flatus vocis*,[12] which translates colorfully as "blowing of the voice."

Comenius suggested several playful activities that involve sensory experience and amusement, such as providing students tools to imitate handicrafts, taking them into gardens or the countryside to study plants, and giving titles such as doctor, general, chancellor, and so on to the best students during relevant discussions.[13]

2. The material to be learned should be presented in a way to make it of interest to the students.

> Every study should be commenced in such a manner as to awaken a real liking for it on the part of the scholars. . . . A general notion should be given to the pupil before the detailed consideration of the subject . . . for as the skeleton is the foundation of the whole body, so the general sketch of an art is the foundation of the whole art.[14]

He recommended, in addition, giving the students historical background on the originators of the topic under discussion and information about the times in which they lived (a good idea, because so much information was centuries old). In his classroom, there would also be summaries of the lessons posted on the wall.

3. The material should be at the right level for the students, carefully arranged in an order that allows students to master the material before moving on.

> [To teach] boys logic, poetry, rhetoric, and ethics before they are thoroughly acquainted with the objects that surround them . . . would be equally sensible to teach boys of two years old to dance, though they can scarcely walk.[15]

> All studies should be carefully graduated . . . in such a way that those that come first may prepare the way for those that come later.[16]

> The subjects learned should be arranged in such a manner that the studies that come later introduce nothing new, but only expand the elements of knowledge that the boy has already mastered.[17]

4. The number of hours in the classroom should be reduced.

> The class instruction [should] be curtailed as much as possible, namely to four hours, and the same length of time left for private study.[18]

This proposal to reduce the number of hours spent in the classroom was truly radical, but four hours well spent in meaningful study, he believed, was far superior to twice as many hours of drudgery. It also allowed more recreation time for the students, which Comenius considered to be essential for their health. There should be two hours of lessons before noon and two in the afternoon. Morning lessons were to be devoted to new material and work that requires concentration and memory. The afternoon was for review and mechanical exercises, such as copying and handwriting practice.[19]

5. The atmosphere in the classroom should be light, cheerful, and encouraging. Comenius abhorred physical punishment, no doubt as a result of his own youthful experiences.

> The very sun in the heavens gives us a lesson on this point. In early spring, when plants are young and tender, he does not scorch them, but warms and invigorates them. . . . Just such a skilful and sympathetic treatment is necessary to instill a love of learning into the minds of our pupils, and any other procedure will only convert their idleness into antipathy and their lack of interest into downright stupidity.[20]

It was up to the teacher to be a model of good conduct for the class to imitate and to set the tone of the classroom: "The keener the teacher himself, the greater the enthusiasm that his pupils will display."[21] There was to be no corporal punishment for academic shortcomings, as the fault inevitably lay with the teacher.[22] Examples of the only actions that merited real discipline were blasphemy, obscenity, premeditated misbehavior, pride, and disdain (for example, refusing to help others).[23] Beatings should be given only as a last resort. As for disciplinary problems of the everyday kind, Comenius had this to say:

> If any pupil make a mistake he should be corrected, but at the same time the cause of the error . . . should be made clear.[24]

> Discipline should be free from personal elements, such as anger or dislike.[25]

> [The teacher] should take great care to make his motive clear and to show unmistakably that his actions are based on paternal affection.[26]

> Training of the character can only be accomplished in the above-mentioned ways: by good example, by gentle words, and by continually taking a sincere and undisguised interest in the pupil.[27]

6. In keeping with his goal of teaching everything to everyone, Comenius strongly urged that education be universal—for girls as well as boys, the working class as well as the privileged, the mentally weaker as well as the brainiest. Everyone needs education, because

The mind of man cannot remain at rest, and, if not engaged with what is useful, it occupies itself with the vainest and even with harmful things.[28]

Nor can any good reason be given why the weaker sex . . . should be altogether excluded from the pursuit of knowledge. . . . They are endowed with equal sharpness of mind and capacity for knowledge (often with more than the opposite sex).[29]

The slower and the weaker the disposition of any man, the more he needs assistance. . . . Nor can any man be found whose intellect is so weak that it cannot be improved by culture.[30]

Despite lofty ideals, Comenius realized that a few children would never be fit for the classroom because of an inherently wicked nature. In that case even floggings were insufficient, and these students must be removed. He quoted Lubinus again, who warned that society in fact did not want to educate such children as "any knowledge that they may acquire will be employed for wicked purposes, and will be like a sword in the hands of a madman."[31]

8. In Comenius's time, there were two types of elementary schools. The first were the Latin Schools, similar to what had been seen for centuries, in which the curriculum was entirely in Latin. These were still considered by most families to be the best education. However, there were also the Vernacular Schools, generally for the working class to obtain a basic education, in which teaching was done in the local language. Comenius called for a standard system that began with a vernacular education; only afterward would a child switch to Latin studies at approximately twelve years of age. Lessons in a language such as Latin, which wasn't fully mastered by the students, meant that much of their learning was the *flatus vocis* that he had warned about.

What I have in view is an education in the objects that surround us, and a brief survey of this education can be best obtained from books written in the mother-tongue, which embody a list of the things that exist in the external world. This preliminary survey will render the acquisition of Latin far easier, for it will only be necessary to adapt a new nomenclature to objects that are already known.[32]

Comenius admitted that the task of a comprehensive reformation of education was not going to be easy. He listed the principal obstacles: a lack of teachers capable of carrying out reform in a methodical way, the difficulty of instituting the system in every little town and village, the struggle for poor families to send their children to school instead of putting them to work, an opposition to new ways, a lack of "comprehensive and methodical class-books," a need for qualified scholars to write the materials, and most of all, the necessity for support and money from the state.[33]

## JANUA LINGUARUM AND ORBIS PICTUS

Comenius was also the author of an intermediate Latin textbook called the *Janua linguarum reserata* (The Gate to Languages Unlocked), or just the *Janua*[34] for short. Published in 1633, it was a highly successful book that established Comenius's reputation as one of the best language-textbook authors of his day. It contains one hundred texts in Latin and the students' native language, displayed in parallel columns. What distinguishes this book is the sequencing of the readings: it was genius. The first few chapters describe the natural world, including plants and animals. Next are readings on the human body and the senses, followed by texts about daily activities and work. The next section deals with social institutions and conventions like government and law. Then we read about issues of morality and virtue: wisdom, friendship, fortitude, and so on. The book concludes with the ultimate topics of this world: death, God, and angels.

Comenius believed that language study gave students the chance not just to learn another language but to grasp important lessons in life. Thus, in a hundred readings, he leads his readers from the basic components of this world all the way to the loftiest topics any philosopher could tackle. The readings are arranged in a familiar Biblical style of verses, which also allowed frequent pauses for discussion and comprehension checks. Comenius proceeded only when he was sure that the class had understood.

This text was one of the first teaching instruments to use the principle of grouping readings by vocabulary topics. Examples of texts on everyday topics can be found from more than a century earlier, but it's doubtful that any of them could have captured the imaginations of students in the way that the *Janua* did. Comenius did an admirable job of fulfilling his own principle of making learning meaningful.

Of greater interest to us is his most famous textbook of all, published in 1658, rather late in his life. The book was called the *Orbis sensualium pictus* (The Visible World in Pictures), or the *Orbis* for short. Inspired by Lubinus, it's considered to be the first illustrated language textbook.[35] It was a logical step for Comenius's empiricist beliefs; the drawings provided a link between the words and the objects of knowledge. Title pages tended to be very "busy" artistically in those days, giving a lot more information than we'd expect to see today. From the title page of the *Orbis* we get a sense of what the book is about, especially if we keep in mind the contents and organization of his other well-known textbook, the *Janua*. The English version, under the lengthy full title in Latin, provides further description: "Johan Amos Comenius's Visible World, or a Picture and Nomenclature of all the chief Things that are in the world; and of Mens Employments therein." It then tells us that it is "A Work newly written by the Author . . . and the most suitable to Childrens capacities of any that he hath hitherto made." Underneath is a maxim attributed to Aristotle that captures the empiricist slant to the book: "Nothing is in the intellect that was not first in the senses."[36] All knowledge is derived through the senses, that is, and here was a language textbook that led to much greater sensory involvement than any that had preceded it. The *Orbis* is a higher-level textbook, so it's longer than the *Janua*: it contains

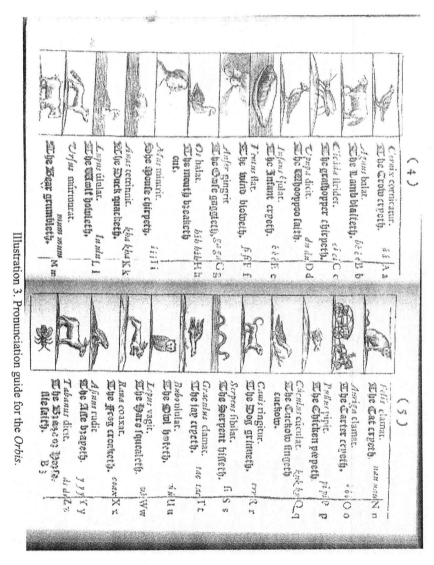

*Figure 14.2*  Part of the pronunciation chart from Comenius's *Orbis*.

150 readings in about 300 pages. Like the *Janua*, it's a summary of life itself (the final reading, fittingly, is on the Last Judgment). It also contains a clever introductory section on pronunciation. Figure 14.2 shows us a sample lesson, on the rituals involving the burial of a corpse. Like its predecessor, the texts are laid out in parallel columns, the Latin on one side of the page and the students' native language on the other.

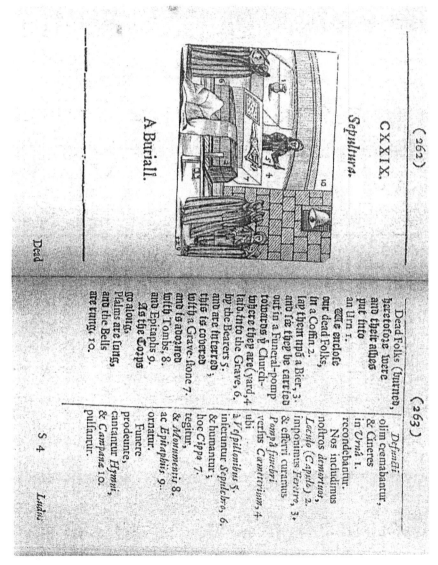

*Figure 14.3* A sample page from the *Orbis*. The numbers in the text refer to the objects in the picture.

Comenius envisaged five steps in using the book:[37]

1. Let the children look at the book and "delight themselves" as they please.
2. Examine them continually to make sure of their understanding and knowledge of all the items illustrated.
3. Whenever possible, show the students the real thing under discussion.
4. Have the pupils copy the illustrations.
5. When possible, keep in the classroom any items that are not readily available to students outside of school.

Here we can see a simple demonstration of Comenius's brilliant insights into effective language teaching. It's not just a matter of repetition and memorization; students dealt with the material through as many senses as possible.

## Comenius's Life Story

There was no reason at birth to expect Comenius to achieve greatness. He didn't come from a prominent family (in fact, not much at all is known about them), nor did he have the advantage of being born in a major cultural center. Instead, he was born in 1592 in a village in Moravia, a region that has had occasional aspirations for independence through the centuries, including during the lifetime of Comenius.

His early education was not a happy experience, because he was at the mercy of cruel schoolmasters. Comenius must have been a sensitive child because the psychological well-being of the young student, as we've seen, was later a major concern of his. The unfortunate boy was orphaned when he was twelve. It's hard to believe that a parentless, semi-literate child from a rural area in a politically insignificant country could become a famous, respected educator, but that's exactly what happened.

Rescue came from a popular regional Protestant sect called the Unity of Brethren. Thanks to them, he studied at university, where he became an educator. Besides beginning to write books on all sorts of subjects, including language, he was ordained and sent to a small Moravian city called Fulnek to be both a pastor and a teacher. There he wrote more books, and he might have remained there indefinitely, leading a nice, quiet, uneventful life if political and religious circumstances had not interfered. This was a time of religious tension all over Europe. In the first instance of bad timing that would dog him all his life, Comenius's arrival in Fulnek coincided with the outbreak in 1618 of the Thirty Years' War, a conflict between Catholic and Protestant powers that engulfed much of Europe. This had disastrous consequences for Comenius when, after five years, the town was sacked and burned: he lost his wife, his children, his house, and all his books in the attack. Protestants were forced either to flee or to hide their beliefs. Comenius chose to leave.

For the next few years Comenius led an unsettled life as a refugee, even hiding in the mountains for extended periods. He ultimately ended up in Leszno, Poland, a stronghold of the Unity of Brethren, where he did some teaching but more importantly, wrote *The Great Didactic*, which we've already seen.

Comenius's bad luck seemed to change in 1641. Though he was still in exile in Poland, he'd seen his reputation grow in recent years from his writings on a wide range of topics related to education and theology. He was invited to go to London to help found a college whose teaching would be in line with his universal education beliefs. What should have been a triumphant chapter in his life vanished when just nine months after his arrival, the English Civil War broke out, putting a premature end to his plans.

The next year he was invited to France by Cardinal Richelieu, the powerful advisor to King Louis XIII, to help reform the school system. Sadly, before Comenius could even start the project, the cardinal died.

Still, there were opportunities for him. The Swedish government was interested in his services as a textbook author, so off went Comenius and his second wife to Sweden for the next six years. Sweden, not coincidentally, was the leading power among the Protestant forces in the Thirty Years' War, so it's probable that Comenius accepted the position to use whatever influence he could with the Swedish government to secure support for the cause of Moravian independence after the war. But once again, Comenius met with bitter disappointment. At the end of the war Sweden betrayed Moravia, in his view, and independence was nowhere in sight. He returned to Leszno but he arrived alone; his second wife had died during the return journey.

So there he was, fifty-six years old, having been an exile or refugee for nearly half his life, some of that time spent hiding in the wilderness. He had lost his family and his home during these years and though he'd gained renown as a writer, his success was tainted by personal and professional setbacks. Moravian independence was a mere illusion despite his efforts. And he'd barely begun to reach his goal of a curriculum for universal education, which was far more important to him than the success of his Latin textbooks. We can only imagine the misery and suffering he experienced. But there was more to come.

Two years later, in 1650, another attractive opportunity arose. Hope springs eternal! Comenius accepted an offer to set up the curriculum for a new school in the Hungarian city of Sárospatak. He spent three years there, producing an impressive number of works and getting the school off to a good start. He returned to Leszno, seemingly after a successful interlude, but just two years later the city of Sárospatak was hit by the plague, and the school that he had spent so much effort on was forced to close. It never reopened.

The final blow, the final indignity, occurred just the following year when his town was ransacked in a Catholic raid, even though the Thirty Years'

War had ended. It was a different town but the results were the same: in the raid Comenius once again lost all his possessions, including the manuscript for a dictionary that he'd been working on for forty years.

At the age of sixty-four, Comenius and his most recent family moved in 1656 from Leszno to Amsterdam, where he spent his last thirteen years. Although he remained in exile, it was at last a period free of personal disaster. In fact, there were even some triumphs. His collected educational works since 1627, totaling two thousand pages, were published. It's also the period when the *Orbis* appeared. Comenius spent his last decade editing his previous works and focusing on religious matters in his writings. He died in Amsterdam in 1670 at the age of seventy-eight.

What should we make of Comenius? One writer cautions in the opening sentence of his glowing tribute, "Nothing is easier, or more dangerous, than to treat an author of 300 years ago as modern and claim to find in him the origins of contemporary or recent trends of thought." [38]

As language teachers today our interest in him rests in being able to draw a few parallels between his educational principles and those in modern methodology textbooks. It's a matter of both curiosity and admiration. Without much strain, we can find kinship with the notions of meaningful learning, motivational and psychological factors, schema theory, gradation of materials, and so on. He was a thinker truly ahead of his time. However, we mustn't get carried away in attributing all that we've seen to his own originality. In fact, another language-teaching historian delivers the following verdict:

> Everything that Comenius had to say had already been said by experts as diverse as Quintillian and Erasmus, but his peculiar contribution is summing up all the trends of the preceding seventeen hundred years in a clear, coherent method based on a sound theory of learning. [39]

Comenius probably thought of himself as a failure because he didn't accomplish his own goal of reforming the educational system of his day, and in fact never even succeeded in establishing a school (one that lasted, at least).

Most surprising, the success and genius of his textbooks, especially the *Orbis*, failed to shape textbook writing in succeeding generations. There is no real explanation for it. One problem may have been an increased emphasis on grammar brought about by the emergence of vernacular languages such as French and Italian, an approach not compatible with Comenius's works. Or maybe, as the English translator of the *Orbis* complained, the book was too expensive for normal classroom use because of the cost of printing the illustrations. [40] (In fact, illustrations were generally missing from language textbooks for another two hundred years, until the eighteen hundreds.) Another likely explanation is that illustrations were considered by many educators to be childish and inappropriate for a crucial undertaking such as learning a language. Education was traditionally a serious matter and language learning was no exception. Befitting the thinking of the sixteen hundreds, a few educators like Comenius or the schoolmasters at Port-Royal (treated in the next chapter) realized that psychological factors were important for success, but they remained a minority.

Comenius was rediscovered in the late eighteen hundreds when an attempt was made to reform language teaching based on modern principles of science, including psychology. The *Orbis,* for example, was reissued in both an updated version in 1883 with colored illustrations as well as in its original form in 1887. Although he was looked on with admiration and appreciation, his ideas served more as affirmation of "new" ideas of the day and he remained above all a curiosity. Nevertheless, we can say that he at last regained some of the respect that he so deeply deserved, thus giving our story at least a hint of a happy ending.

# 15 The Port-Royal Community

Since the beginning of the Middle Ages, religion and education had worked together in a mutually beneficial relationship, with the Church often providing instruction as a means to continue the Christian faith. Our next scholars continued in the same tradition, but took this principle to an extreme.

The religious community of Port-Royal started as a convent near Paris in the thirteenth century. By the mid-sixteen hundreds the community also included a group of men, who were monks in all but title. In general, they were a rather disgruntled bunch who were dissatisfied with the current state of the Roman Catholic Church. They produced a number of works proclaiming their opinions of the situation, which earned them a good deal of political trouble, but they also came out with several works on education that earned them fame, praise, and imitation. We'll look at two works related to language study they created for the school they set up on their grounds.

The Port-Royalists held a grim view of human nature, one that deeply influenced their ideas about education. The fundamental problem was Original Sin, a burden that was inherited by all children at birth, leaving them as vulnerable to temptation as lambs are to a wolf. The surest way to save them from damnation was to give them a proper education. As it had been for centuries, the key to this education was a mastery of language, specifically grammar. A true understanding of the workings of language would permit them to achieve a deeper comprehension of Church doctrine. This would be a tremendous aid in avoiding the pitfalls of this earthly life. Language study, then, was a far more serious business than learning to express oneself in smooth phrases and memorizing passages from famous authors. It was a struggle to save one's soul.[1]

## THE NEW LATIN METHOD

One Port-Royalist, Claude Lancelot,[2] was a quiet, modest man who preferred to focus on education rather than politics. In 1644 he published a Latin textbook commonly called the *Nouvelle Méthode latine* (New Latin Method). Lancelot noted that many people were dissatisfied with the traditional ways of teaching languages (meaning Latin and Greek, in most cases). Like Brinsley, he undertook a study of past opinions; Lancelot concluded that the underlying problem was the reliance on teaching the target language in the language itself. It was only common sense, he claimed, to use one's first language to acquire another. "Does it not suppose that one already knows what one wishes to learn and that one has already done what one wants to do, to propose the first elements of a language that one wants to acquire in the words of that very same language?"[3] Lancelot broke with this tradition and decided to give the rules of Latin to the students in French and only French.[4] However, children being children, who are liable to alter the wording of rules, in his biggest innovation he instead put the rules into verse. Students could no longer make changes because they were constrained by rhyme and meter. Lancelot cheerfully requested forgiveness from his readers for his weak poetic skills.[5] But there was more than Latin rules in French verse. He tells us that he did everything in his power to make the book agreeable to use. His improvements focused on the method of presentation rather than the contents of the grammar, which were really rather traditional, as in the following:[6]

1. The rules in his book generally had eight syllables per line, or about half those found in other texts, for easier memorization.
2. Each rule included many examples and comments, something he observed was not always the case.
3. Each rule was numbered and had an explanatory title.
4. All Latin words were marked for stress.
5. All the case and declension endings were written in capital letters.
6. A different style of type was used for Latin and for French.
7. Comments to the rules were in smaller print.

In the following very brief example of the results, note that the second and third lines rhyme; it's not elegant but it does read like lines of poetry:

> RÈGLE XIV: DE CEUX QUI FONT XI AU PRÉTÉRIT, SANS SUPIN
> Friger, Lucet XI recevront,
> Mais jamais de Supin n'auront.[7]
> Exemples
> FRIGEO, frixi, frigére; Avoir froid, . . .

The book was a smashing success; one of its users was little King Louis XIV.

Nevertheless, Lancelot felt the need to improve it, so he kept on with his studies. He eventually came across some works from the previous century—ponderous and profound books that had generally been forgotten by Lancelot's time—written by scholars inspired by the Modistae of long before.[8] Lancelot was fascinated by the notion of universal grammar, that is, that there is one system that underlies all languages. The real job of a grammarian, he realized, was not to prescribe rules for each language but to explore and explain this system. It's no wonder that he took this step. Port-Royalists saw language as an indispensable tool for the development of proper judgment. To ignore the inner workings of a primary component in this process would have been unthinkable. He went back to work on the *Nouvelle Méthode latine* and expanded it considerably, especially in discussing the parts of speech and by adding the observations of the rational grammarians.[9] When he finished he had, in fact, two books: a complete grammar of the Latin language beyond that of a schoolchild's textbook, as well as an abridged version similar to the first edition, which remained popular in the classroom. This shorter version was widely used in France for more than one hundred years, while the full grammar was printed in several translations in many editions as late as 1819. Lancelot also wrote popular "new method" books for Greek, Italian, and Spanish, all of which were used throughout Europe.

## THE PORT-ROYAL GRAMMAR

Another resident of Port-Royal was a member of the prominent Arnauld family, headed by one of the country's most famous lawyers. Antoine Arnauld[10] started in the legal profession but ended up heavily involved in the disputes of the day within the Catholic Church. He eventually moved to Port-Royal to lead the life of a religious philosopher and author. He and Lancelot collaborated on a book known in English as the Port-Royal Grammar,[11] published in 1660, a book that changed the course of language study in the West for 150 years—and then was more or less forgotten for another century and a half.

Inspired by Lancelot's interest in rational grammar, the Port-Royal Grammar was an attempt to find principles of language that were independent of time and place, which Arnauld and Lancelot believed could be found by examining several languages (mostly European, but also Hebrew) to see what they had in common. In line with Lancelot's earlier studies, the authors claimed that the surface forms of language are merely reflections of our thought processes (conceiving of an object and affirming something about it, for example). Because reason is universal, the rules for expressing one's thoughts must be the same for everyone. Language, then, is a manifestation of these universal rules set by reason, even though the results, whether spoken, written, or in the mind, vary from language to language. Words are the symbols that represent these thoughts, so Arnauld and Lancelot concentrated much of their book on the study of the parts of speech across languages.[12]

An understanding of these "universal" aspects of language would let students concentrate on the similarities, rather than the differences, between their own language and the target language. For students at the Port-Royal school, in addition to improving their French, this would make learning any foreign language easier. In any situation, it advanced the goal of understanding religious teachings through improved language skills.

Although the Port-Royal Grammar was essentially Lancelot's creation, Arnauld supervised the writing and his famous name guaranteed interest from the public. It was written in French, which was still something of a rarity for such a scholarly work. This had the advantage of allowing educated members of the public to share in its philosophy. As surprising as it seems, the book was widely read and discussed in the salons of Paris. What matters is that it marked a break with the prescriptivist studies of the day and the obsession with correct language and beautiful style. In the typical classroom, language teaching probably plodded along in the same way it had for centuries, but here was an indication that language could be viewed as something more than the study of literature and grammatical rules. For the next century and a half, the Port-Royal Grammar led the way for rational grammar and spawned many imitations.[13]

The Port-Royal Grammar, forgotten for many years, had a renewed fame when it was rediscovered by Noam Chomsky in the mid-1960s. He was intrigued by the Port-Royal notion of surface forms of language as mere reflections of underlying thoughts that are the same in all languages. Chomsky considered this an ancestor of deep and surface structure,[14] although he did acknowledge its sources in earlier scholars. Nevertheless, the Port-Royal Grammar's true purpose, rather than being a philosophical treatise, was above all educational and simply part of the Port-Royal plan to develop good Christians.

# 16 John Wilkins and His Rational Language

Earlier, we talked briefly about the Modistae of the twelfth and thirteenth centuries. They had the surprising idea that in spite of superficial differences, all languages operate on the same principles—universal grammar, we can call it. However, they had little influence at the time. Three hundred years later, Claude Lancelot of the Port-Royal community read earlier works that had been influenced by the Modistae; the result was a popularization of this concept of universal grammar. Another indication of this interest was a growing curiosity in the possibility of a universal language. While Latin was fading as the common language of the educated, the European vernacular languages were rising in strength and competing for leadership. Some people saw an appeal in a universal language that could avoid international politics.[1]

The implications of such a language are far-reaching. It would be tremendously useful in daily commerce all over the world, for example. It was also seen as a tool to help missionaries spread Christianity. It would even have repercussions for language teaching. In the same line of thinking as the Port-Royalists, it was hoped that creation of a universal language could reveal organizational similarities of existing languages that might benefit the teaching of languages. And it could continue the *status quo*: instead of having to teach multiple world languages, the situation of the previous centuries could continue, but with a new international language taking the place of Latin.

The newly formed Royal Society in London decided to sponsor one of its members to give it a go, to attempt to create a universal language. The man they chose was John Wilkins (1614–1672), a clergyman, scholar, and founding member and first secretary of the Society. He wasn't the first to attempt a universal language and certainly not the last, but he is probably the best known.[2]

## AN ESSAY TOWARDS A REAL CHARACTER AND A PHILOSOPHICAL LANGUAGE

When we think today of a universal language (Esperanto, for example), we see a language based on simplifying and modifying either living languages or Latin or Greek. Wilkins didn't think this way at all, though. Being a man of religion, he approached the task from a more spiritual viewpoint. There was in his day the never-ending interest in the "original" language spoken on Earth, an ancient discussion as we saw with Herodotus's tale of Psammetichus. It was widely believed that before the events of the Tower of Babel,[3] there had been one language worldwide, superior in its ability to express thoughts to any of the "corrupted" languages spoken ever since. Wilkins shared this idea that modern languages were a sad relic of the original one. He therefore didn't want to reform imperfect languages; what he wanted was much more impressive. His new language would be created from scratch and thus would not be constrained by the flaws of any existing language. In fact, it would be entirely logical. It would be, quite simply, based on a complete categorization of all knowledge. In his own words, he sought to create

> a regular *enumeration* and *description* of all those things and notions, to which marks or names ought to be assigned according to their respective natures. . . . It being the proper end and design of the several branches of philosophy to reduce all things and notions unto such a frame, as may express their natural order, dependence, and relations.[4]

Wilkins's universal language would be a great benefit and a remedy against "the Curse of the Confusion" (i.e., Babel).[5] The language would break down communication into all its semantic categories and represent them in an unambiguous form. For Wilkins, this could clear up disagreements in religion, because breaking down words into their true meanings would allow one to express ideas perfectly clearly and avoid their misinterpretation.[6] It would also promote knowledge in general: "The reducing of all things and notions . . . as here proposed . . . would prove the shortest and plainest way for the attainment of real Knowledge, that hath been yet offered to the World."[7]

In magnificent understatement, he admits, "It is no easie undertaking to Enumerate all such matters."[8] Nevertheless, what he achieved was a remarkable work of scholarship. Wilkins called his work, published in 1668, *An Essay towards a Real Character and a Philosophical Language*.[9]

So Wilkins, in the optimism of the times, thought that he could classify knowledge and summarize it in a very limited number of categories—forty, as it turned out. For example, a few of these categories (or *genuses*, as he called them) were stones, birds, measures, and personal relationships. Wilkins assigned a two-letter syllable (consonant + vowel) to each of these. The genus of "measure," for example, was represented by *po-*. Each of these large categories was subdivided numerous times into *differences*, with each difference assigned a consonant. Each difference was divided further into *species* and assigned a vowel. It sounds confusing, but the basic idea is quite easy to grasp. For example, one of the differences of the genus "measure" was time (as opposed to length, etc.). All nouns dealing with time were assigned the consonant *t*, giving us the stem *pot-* so far. But time of course is divided many ways. Add an *o* to *pot-* and we have the word for "day": *poto*. Add a *y* instead and *poty* gives us "morning."

## USING THE LANGUAGE

Wilkins's language needed a written form to have any chance of being put to real use. Interest in Chinese writing was high at the time, and it was commonly thought that the Chinese wrote with symbols that could be decoded if one knew their component parts. This is true only in some cases, but it nevertheless served as an inspiration for devising the writing system.[10] Wilkins created a completely new system whose characters were logical and contained much of the meaning within them.

It's not easy to describe a writing system, so the first step is to have a look at it.

One example of Wilkins's language in use is the Lord's Prayer.[11] Look at the second symbol. Instead of the original "father" from the English, Wilkins preferred to use "parent" to refer to God.[12] We start with the horizontal line that has what looks like a number three through its middle. That represents the genus, one of his forty categories. Here it stands for the genus "interpersonal relations." On the left end of the line is a little hook at a forty-five-degree angle. This indicates the "difference," or the next logical division of the genus. A table in the book tells us that this marks the first difference; in this case, it means a blood relationship. Therefore, any symbol with these two components will indicate a blood relative of some degree. The "species" of this blood relative is noted by the affix on the right side of the character—there is a small line that goes straight up. This indicates the second species, namely "direct ascending." A moment's thought tells us that this is the definition of a parent: a blood relative who, linearly speaking, is right above us. If Wilkins had wanted to specify the male parent, he would have added a small curved symbol above it.

The sixth symbol has a base with a vertical line through it, indicating the genus "world." The affix on the left signifies the second difference, which is "heaven." There is no affix on the right to show further division, so the word is complete as it is: heaven. And so on, at least for the content words. Grammatical variations are indicated by affixes. A hook here, a loop there, and we can change the root idea to an adjective or to the passive verb form, for example.

Other noncontent words such as pronouns and prepositions are simpler in form but still regular. The first symbol in the prayer is "our." Pronouns are represented by dots. One dot is a singular pronoun. If it is written high, it equals *I*, in the middle it stands for "you," and the lower position indicates "he" or "she." Two dots turn it into the plural, and a curved line under it makes it possessive. Thus, our two underlined dots written toward

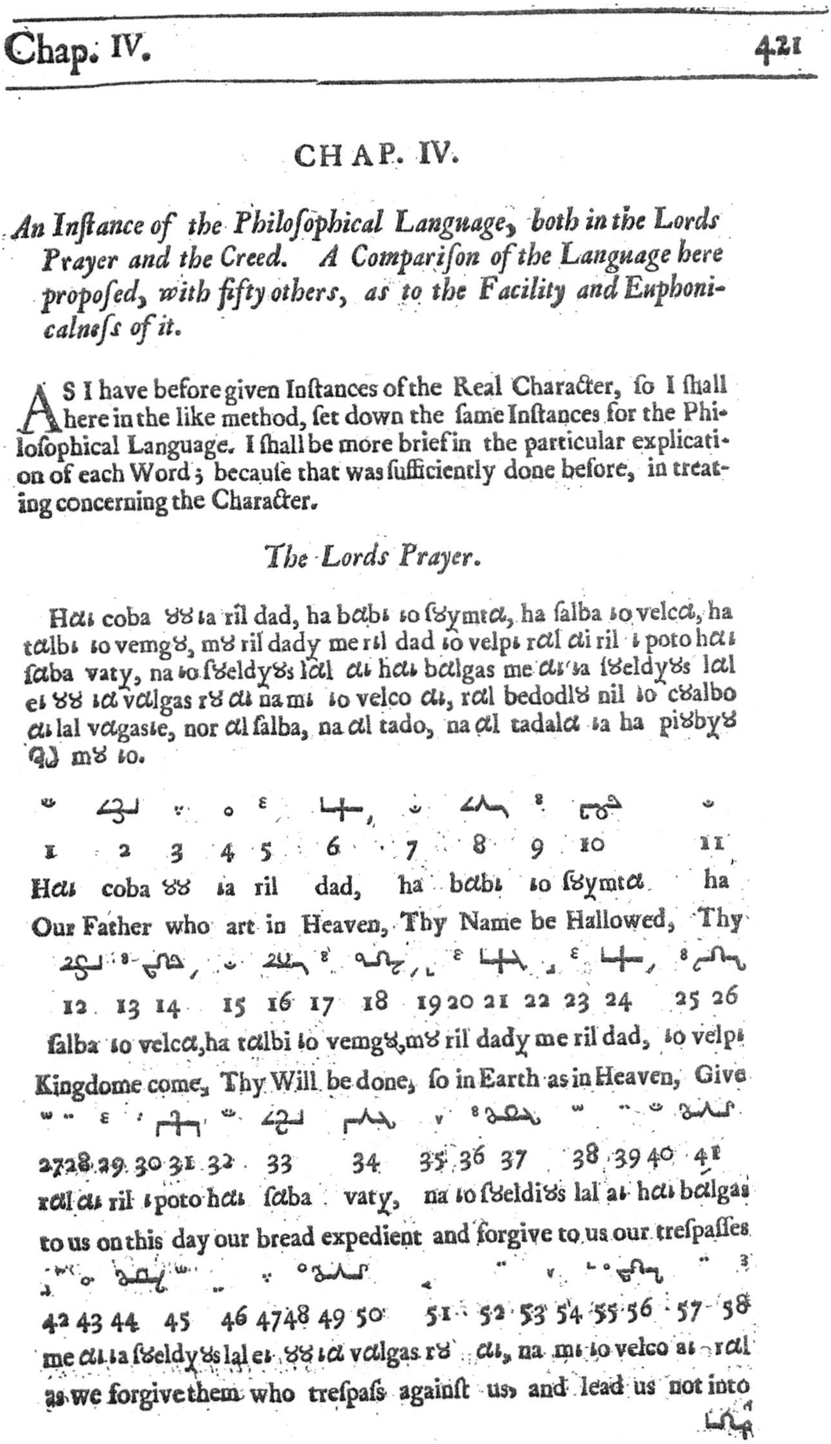

## CHAP. IV.

*An Inſtance of the Philoſophical Language, both in the Lords Prayer and the Creed. A Compariſon of the Language here propoſed, with fifty others, as to the Facility and Euphonicalneſs of it.*

AS I have before given Inſtances of the Real Character, ſo I ſhall here in the like method, ſet down the ſame Inſtances for the Philoſophical Language. I ſhall be more brief in the particular explication of each Word; becauſe that was ſufficiently done before, in treating concerning the Character.

### The Lords Prayer.

Hæı coba ꝰꝰıa ril dad, ha bæbı ıo ſꝰymtæ, ha ſalba ıovelcæ, ha tælbı ıovemgꝰ, mꝰ ril dady merıl dad ıo velpı ræl æi ril ı poto hæı ſaba vaty, na ıo ſꝰeldyꝰs læl æı hæı bælgas me æı'ıa ſꝰeldyꝰs læl eı ꝰꝰ ıæ vælgas rꝰ æl namı ıo velco æı, ræl bedodlꝰ nil ıo cꝰalbo æı lal vægasıe, nor æl ſalba, na æl tado, na æl tadalæ ıa ha pıꝰbyꝰ ꝗ mꝰ ıo.

```
 ˘   ⌐ᴶ   ˘   ˳   ε   ⌐⌐,   ˘   ⌐ᴧ   ˢ   ⌐ᵒᴧ   ˘
 1    2   3   4  5    6   7   8    9   10        11
Hæı  coba ꝰꝰ ıa ril  dad,  ha  bæbı ıo ſꝰymtæ    ha
Our Father who art in Heaven, Thy Name be Hallowed, Thy
```

```
 2ᵍᴶ  ˢ ⌐ᴧ,    ˘  2ᴧ,   ˢ  ᵒᴧ,  ε  ⌐⌐,   ε  ⌐⌐,   ˢ ᴧ
 12 13 14   15 16 17  18  19 20 21 22 23 24    25 26
ſalba ıo velcæ,ha tælbı ıo vemgꝰ,mꝰ ril dady me ril dad, ıo velpı
Kingdome come, Thy Will be done, ſo in Earth as in Heaven, Give
```

```
 ˘   ˘  ε   ˈ  ⌐⌐  ˘  ⌐ᴶ  ᴧᴧ  v  ˢ ᴧᴧᴧ  ˘   ˘ ˘ ᴧᴧ
27 28 29 30 31 32  33   34  35 36 37  38 39 40 41
ræl æı ril ı poto hæı ſaba vaty, na ıo ſꝰeldıꝰs lal aı hæı bælgas
to us on this day our bread expedient and forgive to us our treſpaſſes
```

```
  ˈ ˘ᵒ ᴧᴧᴧ ˘    ˘  ᵒᴧᴧᴧ     ˘    v  ˹˘ ᴧ   ˘ ˘ 3
42 43 44  45  46 47 48 49 50   51  52 53 54 55 56  57 58
me æı ıa ſꝰeldyꝰs lal eı ꝰꝰ ıæ vælgas rꝰ   æı, na mı ıo velco aı ræl
as we forgive them who treſpaſs againſt us, and lead us not into
```

```
                                                       ᴧᴧᴧ
```

---

*Figure 16.1* John Wilkins's universal and rational language in use.

the top give us "our." The fifth symbol is a final example: all prepositions are curved figures; in this case we have the word "in."

A few paragraphs can give only an inkling of his scheme. Wilkins himself needed about five hundred pages to explain it. He had hopes for this undertaking but he suspected it wouldn't be an immediate success, and certainly not in his lifetime. He compared it to the slow acceptance of two inventions from earlier in the century, shorthand and logarithms.[13] Alas, his mammoth work of scholarship never achieved even a modest usage; however, Wilkins is commonly cited as a key inspiration for Peter Roget in the creation of his *Thesaurus of English Words and Phrases* in the nineteenth century.

# 17 John Locke
## Who Needs Latin?

John Locke (1632–1704) was an English philosopher and leading proponent of empiricism, the belief that learning occurs primarily through the senses and actual experience. Although most famous for *An Essay Concerning Human Understanding*, from 1690, another well-known work of his, *Some Thoughts Concerning Education* (1693), is of greater interest to us. It had similar roots to Ascham's *Scholemaster*. A prominent gentleman and parliamentarian named Edward Clarke inquired about the best way to educate his son. Locke sent him a series of letters with advice, and these were gathered a decade later and published. The book was quite a success. Locke was already a famous and respected personality, so his opinion counted. The book was widely read for a century, and in fact some have argued that it was Locke's most influential work. Actually, second-language learning was only a small part of the essay. Most of it stressed how to impart virtue and critical thinking to the child, for these were considered the roots of the love of knowledge.

Locke hated grammar rules, as would any good empiricist. Or maybe it's better to say that he hated how they were considered the foundation of typical language teaching, no matter what the situation. We've already seen that putting grammar in the background (inductive grammar learning), was popular in theory, if not in widespread practice, in the sixteen hundreds. Locke is yet another voice, and a very distinguished one, in support of this. "And I would fain have any one name to me that tongue, that any one can learn, or speak as he should do, by the rules of grammar. Languages were made not by rules or art, but by accident, and the common use of the people."[1]

Detailed study of the grammar of languages was fine later on for those few who chose to make them their study—language teachers, presumably.[2] In general, however, he argued that grammar is more usefully studied in your *native* language, which you use all the time in both speaking and writing, and by whose accuracy you will be judged throughout your life. The simple fact that the Greeks and Romans studied the grammar of their own language first was, he believed, a strong argument for his position. And yet very few ever engaged in this study in his day—and in fact most didn't even

*Figure 17.1*   John Locke.

think it possible; it was something you did when learning a foreign language. On the other hand, he believed that studying the grammar of Latin or Greek or any other foreign language, which you will probably rarely use, is a waste of time because the mistakes you make will be excused—precisely because it is a foreign language! What a revolutionary idea and how far we have come from the standard teaching since ancient times.

In the late sixteen hundreds the national languages were taking over as Latin faded from daily educated life. It was nevertheless the language of the highest discourse and still used in some publications, but few students of the day would be writing international letters or publishing scientific treatises like Isaac Newton. Children didn't like studying Latin, either, Locke noted. He called it "nothing but the learning of words, a very unpleasant business both to young and old."[3] Most children would be better off focusing on handwriting and arithmetic, skills useful for all professions. Yet even farmers sent their children to grammar schools where they studied Latin.

Why? Tradition and nothing else, Locke claimed. Most students, though, were more likely to need a living foreign language for commerce.

Locke insisted that the best way to learn a language was through use, not through the study of grammar. Talk to the child and the grammar will follow.[4] This is how it happened with him in English as a child, so this seemed to be the most natural way to learn a living language. But what about learning Latin, which was still a fact of academic life? It was not a living language; nevertheless, the principle was the same. Locke undoubtedly knew the work of Montaigne. Continuing the child analogy, he asserted Latin was no more strange to a student than English was to an infant and could still be learned in the same way.[5]

An obvious objection can be raised—how does one propose to implement this plan in the classroom, a plan that requires a fluent Latin speaker? After all, the letters that constituted the book were written for a young nobleman with a tutor, and were not a proposal for some kind of national reform of education in the public schools. In fact, Locke addressed the question of what to do if no satisfactory teacher was available.[6] In that case, he realized that practicality won out over ideals. He called for the use of a lot of translations and readings. Have students translate simple readings literally into English and then use those texts to translate back into Latin—a form of double translation, clearly. Despite his anti-grammar claims, he admitted that basic grammar is useful here, such as memorization of the conjugation and declension endings. That's all that's needed till later, he said. Asking detailed grammar questions early on spoils the fun and wastes time.

Locke's other suggestions were also quite radical. All the age-old practices for teaching Latin were virtually useless, for none of them improved the students' performance in English, which was what was needed in real life. Write poetry in Latin? Not unless the children are going to be Latin poets: "If any one will think poetry a desirable quality in his son . . . he must need yet confess, that, to that end, reading the excellent Greek and Roman poets, is of more use than making bad verses of his own, in a language that is not his own."[7] The same applied to making speeches in Latin,

> a language which your son, it is a thousand to one, shall never have an occasion once to make a speech in as long as he lives. . . . If the Latin tongue [is] to be learned, let it be done in the easiest way, without toiling and disgusting the mind by so uneasy an employment as that of making speeches.[8]

It was far preferable to practice unrehearsed speeches in one's own language on topics suited to the students' ages and interests.[9]

Theme writing was even worse, for as it was typically done in the schools, it required the children to sound off about topics like love ("Love conquers all," for example) and war ("You cannot make a mistake twice in war"), areas that students know nothing about.[10]

Nevertheless, Locke was short on concrete ideas about what to do in their place. After all, he was a philosopher, not a classroom teacher, so he can't really be blamed for the lack of details and apparent lack of interest in this situation. The ideal way to learn a language is the same way that infants learn. That's philosophical. Giving specifics for a real classroom is not.

But speaking of how to treat learners in general—that's philosophical, and Locke had plenty to say about that. By this time it's not a surprise to hear a scholar speak of the child's mind, but Locke is more explicit. He emphasizes the short attention span of children, their love of novelty, and the need to make the material meaningful and to create a relaxed atmosphere.

> The natural temper of children disposes their minds to wander. . . . It is a contradiction to the natural state of childhood, for them to fix their fleeting thoughts.

> Novelty alone takes them. . . . They quickly grow weary of the same thing, and so have almost their whole delight in change and variety.

> [The teacher] should make the child comprehend (as much as may be) the usefulness of what he teaches him; and let him see, by what he has learned, that he can do something which he could not do before; something which gives him some power and real advantage above others, who are ignorant of it.

> Passionate words or blows from the tutor fill the child's mind with terrour and affrightment, which immediately takes it wholly up, and leaves no room for other impressions. . . . It is impossible children should learn any thing, whilst their thoughts are possessed and disturbed with any passion, especially fear. . . . Keep the mind in an easy calm temper, when you would have it receive your instructions, or any increase of knowledge.[11]

In summary, Locke thought that the traditional emphasis on Latin was no longer relevant to the youth of the late seventeenth century. He made it clear that a modern foreign language was of greater benefit. In fact, his disdain for simple language learning was deep. The right teacher for one's child was someone "who thinks Latin and language the least part of education." The moral aspect of education was what really counted. Without a virtuous soul, "languages and sciences, and all the other accomplishments of education, will be to no purpose, but to make the worse or more dangerous man."[12]

# 18 César Chesneau du Marsais, Philosophy, and Grammar

## THE EIGHTEENTH CENTURY

Let's start with a little review after the previous busy century. What have we seen in the last century or so? Latin was still taught as a usable language well into the seventeenth century. We saw John Brinsley advocate the classical tradition and show us how it should be done instead of the way it was actually carried out in many classrooms. By the mid-sixteen hundreds we find unmistakable signs of a shift to more modern educational thinking, well exemplified by Comenius and his student-centered, empirical approach that demonstrated a deep concern for the well-being of the students. Language learning was not just for communication but for teaching about all aspects of life.

At the same time, we find the Port-Royal community and their introduction of rational grammar into language teaching, which linked philosophy to language for many years to come. In addition, Port-Royal's religious goals depended on the students' genuine comprehension of their language studies, so pupils were taught through French rather than directly in Latin and Greek. Though there had been earlier attempts to teach the target language in the students' native language (most notably Aelfric's grammar of the early eleventh century), it wasn't until the success of Port-Royal that it started to gain acceptability. By the seventeen hundreds it was not an unusual practice, and later on in the eighteen hundreds it became the norm.

Although important scholarly works continued to be published in Latin in the first half of the sixteen hundreds, by the end of the century it was much more common to use the vernacular languages for international communication. The philosopher John Locke even declared that the study of Latin was a largely irrelevant activity, one that should be subordinated to the study of a child's native language.

In contrast to all this activity, the eighteenth century was a surprisingly quiet time in language teaching. Unlike the sixteen hundreds, there are few outstanding works. What we find are representatives of a gradually evolving field. As always, we risk oversimplifying the many threads and stories of a historical period, but we can feel confident that we are following the main developments. The biggest story continues to be the decline and changing role of Latin studies. At the beginning of the century it is still the first language of prestige, but its status has gradually shifted from that of a *lingua franca*[1] to a badge of education and an intellectual exercise. On the other hand, Latin's decline means the emergence at last of the vernaculars.

The developments we'll see are thus the results of the changing needs of learners. It was becoming less necessary to develop smooth and persuasive writing and speaking in Latin. This does not at all mean that grammatical studies were outmoded, though. The interest in the national languages created a desire for their standardization, which could be achieved only through the traditional interest in detailed grammar. Talk of "correct" spelling and grammar was not a new concern (national language academies had already been set up in France and Italy, and the author Jonathan Swift proposed one for English in 1712), but it could now take center stage. While few new Latin and Greek grammars were produced, there was a flood of native language grammars to assist speakers in their own languages, as well as grammars for teaching foreign languages. In either case, the emphasis had shifted from teaching literary aspirations to a concern with rules and accuracy. In a way, this marks a return to the normal state of affairs throughout most of history, but it ultimately leads to the grammar-translation method, which was very different from applying rules in order to imitate the writing and speaking style of Cicero, for example.

We'll start in 1722 by looking at a French scholar's book on the best way to learn Latin. César Chesneau du Marsais's book is one of many that followed in the Port-Royal tradition of general grammar. His is an excellent example of the high point of a philosophical approach applied to foreign-language teaching, using the students' own language, just as in the Port-Royal community. We'll then turn to later in the century and see how much the underlying principles had changed among the field's top scholars, when we encounter two more of those hugely successful school grammars known to generations, as were those of Donatus and Lily. This time, though, they're grammars not of a foreign language, but of English students' native language. By the time Robert Lowth's *Short Introduction to English Grammar* appeared in 1762, it was becoming accepted throughout Europe that a child's first grammatical education should be that of his own language. By the end of the century, the normal age for starting Latin or second-language studies had slipped from about eight to around twelve, after first-language studies; this is still the situation today.[2]

## CÉSAR CHESNEAU DU MARSAIS

César Chesneau du Marsais[3] (1676–1756) was a widely respected French philosopher and grammarian. In 1722 he published his *Éxposition d'une méthode raisonée pour apprendre la langue latine* (Exposition of a Rational

Method for Learning the Latin Language) but we'll call it the Rational Method for short. As the title implies, it's more an essay than a textbook, explaining how Latin can be learned with the principles of general (rational) grammar that had been in vogue for half a century, thanks to Port-Royal.

At the end of the seventeen hundreds, when du Marsais's works were collected and published after his death, Jean d'Alembert, another well-known intellectual of the day, opened the collection with a lengthy eulogy in honor of du Marsais. Referring to the Rational Method, d'Alembert makes his case for philosophers as grammarians:

> All the principles of [language], we can say, belong to everyone, because they exist inside us; to find them, all we need is an exact and thoughtful analysis; but the gift of this analytical ability is not given to everyone.[4]

> One of the greatest efforts of the human spirit has been to subject language to rules. . . . It is up to philosophers to set the rules of language, and it is up to the best writers to establish their usage. Grammar is thus the work of philosophers. . . . Only the philosophical mind can discover the principles on which the rules are established.[5]

Du Marsais confined his book to a discussion of teaching Latin. Although most of the principles would be applicable to other languages, his Rational Method was designed specifically for Latin because of the language's very loose word order.[6] Learning Latin, said du Marsais, is based on the students' grasping (1) the meanings of Latin words; (2) the word order of Latin, which does not follow that of French; (3) the underlying words that are not expressed on the surface (that is, ellipses); and (4) the idiomatic usages of the language.[7]

The Rational Method describes two very different stages, what du Marsais called "routine" and "logic." Both cover all four points above; the first stage, though, does it without any mention of grammar, while the second focuses on a grammatical analysis of what the students have learned in the first stage. Du Marsais's method, he claimed, was a logical imitation of the way living languages are learned by children, who first acquire vocabulary and practice the language, and only later study the grammar.

Thus the emphasis of the initial or "routine" stage was acquiring vocabulary. This seemed obvious to du Marsais, who was puzzled that it was not the standard procedure, since "after all, knowing a language means understanding the words."[8] This stage is perfectly suited to the strongest ability of young children, which is their voracious memory. The common way to teach vocabulary in schools, he observed, was by reading classical texts. However, the content and the vocabulary were often over the heads of the students (certainly not the first time this was noted by a scholar), with predictably poor results. Instead, the vocabulary should be carefully chosen by the teacher; most of all, it ought to consist of words and phrases that are of interest to the children and are among the most commonly used.[9] This leads naturally to better retention. The children are "delighted" to learn these words and to be asked about them, accomplishing a double purpose: furnishing useful vocabulary and, as with the work of Comenius, providing ideas and knowledge about life. Later on, when students deal with classical texts, they are pleased to encounter familiar words.

The most distinctive feature of du Marsais's method was how he handled Latin word order. A word order that differs from that of the students' native language is the most troublesome aspect of language learning, he believed.[10] Even when children know the words, they are so accustomed to their first-language word order that they often cannot take in the meaning otherwise. Du Marsais advocated a form of interlinear translation, which just means writing a translation of each line of a text directly underneath it.[11] Traditionally, this meant placing a well-thought-out, natural version of the text in the translation, so that both language versions read equally smoothly. But in this method, argued du Marsais, students are overburdened: they have to know the meanings of the words, determine their grammatical roles, confront an unfamiliar word order, and be able to relate this to the often-loose French translation. Du Marsais, given his emphasis on vocabulary acquisition, approached interlinear translation in a novel way. He rearranged the words in the *Latin* text so that they were in the order that was natural to the students in their native language; this meant, for example, placing the subject before the verb, adjectives next to the modified nouns, and so on. The students then worked on a literal translation of each Latin word, so that the finished version, though perhaps not in the smoothest French, at least had the constituents in the "right" word order. "With the method that I make use of, they have but one thing to do: retain the simple meaning of the Latin words."[12]

Yet there was more to it than this. An essential concept of rational grammar was that sentences often have a longer, underlying form. The process of ellipsis, or leaving out implied words, is part of any language; it makes speech simpler.[13] As du Marsais said, "Language is merely the expression of thoughts. . . . Whether it is out of need or convenience, or even more likely, the eagerness of the imagination to convey its thoughts, we say in one word what could actually be said in several."[14] For example, prepositions are often not expressed in Latin; typically, the case ending of a noun indicates what the word's relationship is to the rest of the sentence. *Lutetiae*, ending in *-ae*, could mean "in the city of Lutetia" in the right context. Du Marsais would have added the words that are "missing" to a French or English speaker: *in urbe Lutetiae*, or "in the city of Lutetia."

To du Marsais, the practice of literal translation with elimination of ellipses was much more than a convenient and effective technique. The practice "greatly develops clear thinking, because it accustoms the children to putting order and clarity into their thoughts. They never encounter a truncated proposition; they always see the subject, the verb, the complement, and all the circumstances of it."[15] This clarity in thinking was not limited to Latin; one of the greatest benefits of this method was as a general skill that transferred to the students' first language.

All this meant that the students would have several texts to work with. The main one would be the artificial one, with the Latin words rearranged into the familiar French word order and the addition of all the implied words. On the facing page would be the original Latin text, and below that a more traditional, elegant translation in French.[16] Du Marsais gives an example of how he would exploit a lengthy poem by Horace using this method. Taking just the opening line, we have four versions of the line: (1) the original text, (2) the text arranged in English word order with missing words added, (3) a translation of the new word arrangement, and (4) an elegant translation of the original text.

(1) Phoebe, sylvarumque potens Diana; Lucidum caeli decus[17]
(2) (O) Phoebe, atque potens Diana sylvarum, (o vos) lucidum decus caeli
(3) Oh Phoebus and powerful Diana of-the-woods, oh you shining ornament of-heaven
(4) Phoebus and Dian of the woods . . . whose radiance all the heaven floods[18]

Du Marsais justified his approach:

> I know well that this literal translation is at first difficult for those who don't see the point; they fail to see that the goal that I propose by this manner of translation is only to show how one spoke Latin, something which can be done only by explaining each Latin word by the corresponding French word.[19]

Before reaching such sophisticated texts, though, du Marsais began with simpler readings, such as familiar Latin prayers and fables. There was, nevertheless, no talk of case, tense, or declension or any other grammatical terms, and there was no overt memorizing of the endings. Instead, students learned the meanings of whole words without breaking them down into roots and suffixes, just as young children do in learning their first language. For example, *amavi* was memorized simply as "I loved," not as the first-person singular of the perfect form of the verb *amo*, having the root *am-* and the suffix *-avi*.

Clearly the goal was not to create beautiful Latin compositions or to imitate the style of ancient authors, which had been major goals since Roman days. Instead, on the first page of his book, du Marsais states that the main objective of his method is to develop the mind. In fact, he doesn't even mention actually learning the language.

Only after the students had mastered the "routine" portion of the course did they move on to the second phase of the method, which was the study of grammar, or "logic." By the time they entered this stage, they already had an intuitive knowledge of the grammar, which suited du Marsais's belief that knowledge of grammar follows the acquisition of the language. The study of grammar involved the usual matters and rules. Nevertheless, there was a tremendous difference: in contrast to the traditional methods, the students not only knew most of the grammar (in the way a native speaker knows it without the terminology) but were now old enough to understand the reasons behind the rules. Du Marsais shared the disdain for mindless grammatical work in traditional classrooms that had been expressed by scholars from Saint Augustine to Locke. He quotes his scholar friend, Bernard Lamy, who recalled his own misery at school during grammar study:

> It seemed as though they had stuck my head in a bag and they were marching me along to the crack of a whip, punishing me each time that, not able to see where I was going, I wandered off the path. . . . I understood nothing of all these rules that they forced me to learn by heart.[20]

What a waste of a child's ability! As Du Marsais comments,

> If instead of this painful and useless exercise . . . one had spent half of these years in learning Latin words and studying authors using literal translation . . . isn't it obvious that one could translate French into Latin more easily and with greater success? Everyone agrees that the first Latin of children [in the old method] is nothing but bad French dressed up as Latin: really, can one pull out of his brain something that never even penetrated it?[21]

In spite of du Marsais's glowing reputation, there is no evidence that his method was put into widespread practice. No doubt the traditional methods of which he despaired continued in general use. But his initiative did not go unnoticed. The introduction and eulogy from his collected works in 1797 show that he created quite a stir, and in a fashion that is difficult to imagine today. The bitterness of the attacks from his rivals and du Marsais's replies to them can be compared only to a modern political campaign. The essential dispute, his biased editors said, was between prejudice and philosophical reasoning. In reality, his method was considered esoteric and unsuitable for the common class of students. His defenders, of course, dismissed this argument. The editors, for example, claimed du Marsais's critics were favored by the ignorant, and du Marsais by the great minds of the time. In conclusion, they asserted, who cares about second-rate opinions?[22] Unfortunately they do matter if there are enough of them, as the Rational Method's failure to revolutionize Latin teaching in France demonstrated.

# 19 Robert Lowth's Prescriptivist Grammar

## ENGLISH NEEDS A STANDARD GRAMMAR

Robert Lowth (1710–1787), an Englishman who was an expert on the Hebrew language, served a short time as a professor of that subject at Oxford University. Above all, though, he was a clergyman rather than a teacher, grammarian, or author. It's curious, then, that he ended up writing a grammar that was the most enduring book of its kind since William Lily's Grammar a century and a half earlier. Their situations were very different, though. Lily wrote for the traditional Latin curriculum, while Lowth was at the forefront of the movement to produce vernacular grammars. His book, *A Short Introduction to English Grammar* (1762), was used by generations of young English-speaking students before they proceeded to other language studies.

The starting point for Modern English is considered to be around 1500. When Lowth wrote his grammar in 1762, in his opinion English had been "cultivated . . . polished and refined" for about two hundred years, which would be from just before the time of Shakespeare. Nevertheless, in spite of the many improvements in the language during that long period, "it hath made no advances in grammatical accuracy,"[1] a rather startling charge against what many would consider the Golden Age of English literature. But "accuracy" is the key word here. If English was going to take its place as a leading international language, Lowth and others like him argued, it necessarily had to be standardized. Linguistic expression was either right or wrong, and it was up to grammarians to make the distinction. "The principal design of a grammar of a language is to teach us to express ourselves with propriety in that language; and to enable us to judge of every phrase and construction, whether it be right or not."[2] English was still awaiting the creation of one standard grammar that the entire nation could look up to and rely on. Lowth's came the closest to this goal.

## THE TROUBLE WITH ENGLISH

Lowth asserted that English was grammatically one of the simplest languages of all. Take verbs, for instance. In English, he said, there are only

*Figure 19.1*    Robert Lowth: the face of prescriptivism.

about six or seven forms for most verbs, compared to "some hundreds" in other languages.[3] Most duties of tense, aspect, and mode are handled by a few auxiliaries, instead of the more common affixes in other languages. He contended that presumably a standard grammar hadn't yet been written because English was so easy, in fact, "that our grammarians have hardly thought it worth while to give us any thing like a regular and systematical syntax."[4]

This simplicity, unfortunately, was also the source of the language's troubles, he claimed. Indeed, the fact that it was grammatically simple meant that its speakers believed that they didn't need rules, and so neglected their study.[5] The result?

The English language, as it is spoken by the politest part of the nation, and as it stands in the writings of the most approved authors, often offends against every part of grammar . . . and yet no effectual method hath hitherto been taken to redress the grievance.[6]

Lowth's grammar aimed to correct this situation.

"It is . . . expected of every person of a liberal education, and it is indispensably required of everyone who undertakes to inform or entertain the public, that he should be able to express himself with propriety and accuracy."[7] It was therefore highly distressing to Lowth that even the finest writers of the language could not write flawlessly. "Our best authors have committed gross mistakes, for want of a due knowledge of English grammar, or at least of a proper attention to the rules of it."[8]

It's not clear what Lowth's underlying motive was in pointing out the errors of the most illustrious writers. Was it to console the learner with the fact that even the mightiest are not perfect in their English? Or was it to promote grammarians like himself to positions of great authority that only a very few could ever hope to attain? In any case, one of Lowth's hallmark techniques was to point out such errors. "I am sure we have [no grammar book], that in the manner here attempted, teaches us what is right, by shewing what is wrong; though this may perhaps prove the more useful and effectual method of instruction."[9] And point out errors he did, from Shakespeare to the Bible.

## LOWTH'S GRAMMAR

One of the other novelties and secrets of the book's success was its use of footnotes. Although not a new device, Lowth used them extensively to add details and higher-level information; they typically took up one-quarter and sometimes even three-quarters of a page. The result was essentially a course that was suitable for audiences at two levels.

The content of the book was predictable. He opened with chapters on grammar, "letters" (i.e., sounds), syllables, and words, and then devoted one chapter to each of the parts of speech, most notably the verb. He concluded with a lengthy chapter on the sentence, which could easily have been entitled "Syntax," a section on punctuation, and a sample grammatical analysis (a "resolution," he called it) of a biblical passage. The ideas are familiar, the definitions are traditional; it's the clear explanations, the plentiful examples, and the optional, additional information in the footnotes that likely accounted for the success of the work, as well as its surprising brevity (about 130 pages). Perhaps the comments, both positive and negative, about famous authors appealed to readers in the way that celebrity news is popular today. It's fascinating nowadays to read Lowth's list of "errors" by Shakespeare, Pope, Sheridan, and others; it must have been even more interesting to readers who knew the cited works well from their studies.

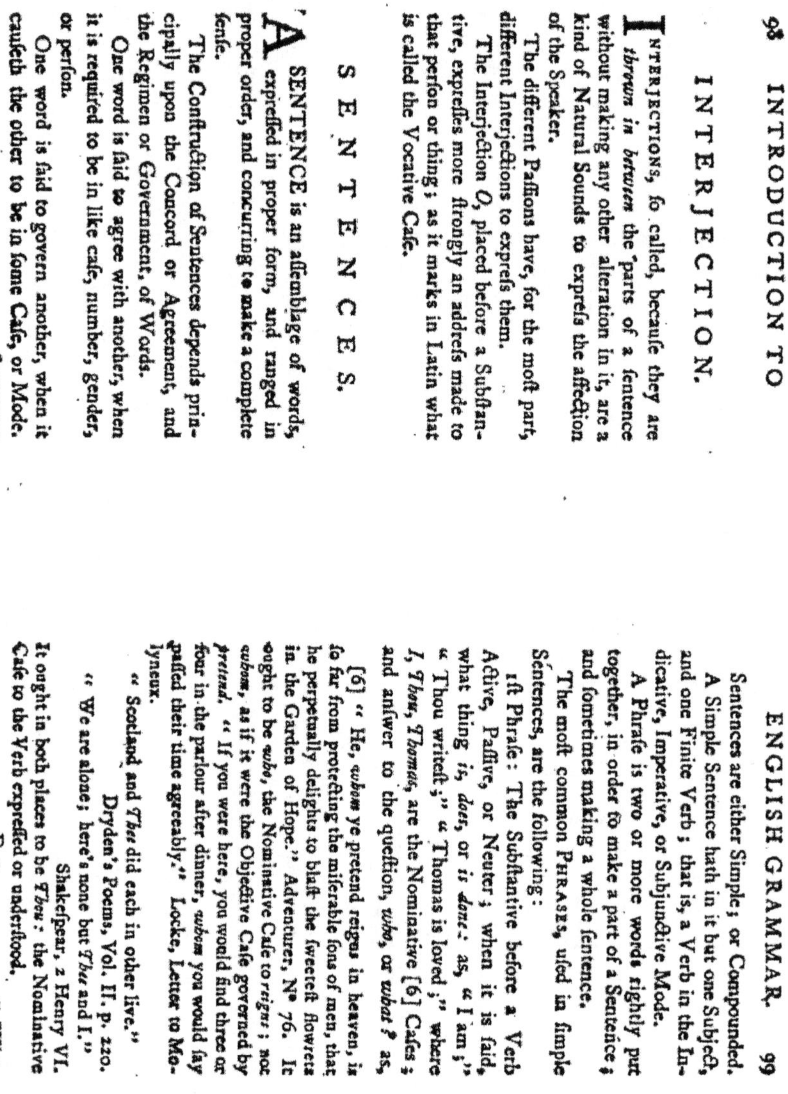

98   INTRODUCTION TO

## INTERJECTION.

INTERJECTIONS, fo called, because they are *thrown in between* the parts of a fentence without making any other alteration in it, are a kind of Natural Sounds to exprefs the affection of the Speaker.

The different Paffions have, for the moft part, different Interjections to exprefs them.

The Interjection O, placed before a Subftantive, exprefs more ftrongly an addrefs made to that perfon or thing; as it marks in Latin what is called the Vocative Cafe.

## S E N T E N C E S.

A SENTENCE is an affemblage of words, exprefsed in proper form, and ranged in proper order, and concurring to make a complete fenfe.

The Conftruction of Sentences depends principally upon the Concord or Agreement, and the Regimen or Government, of Words.

One word is faid to agree with another, when it is required to be in like cafe, number, gender, or perfon.

One word is faid to govern another, when it caufeth the other to be in fome Cafe, or Mode.

Sentences

---

ENGLISH GRAMMAR.   99

Sentences are either Simple, or Compounded.

A Simple Sentence hath in it but one Subject, and one Finite Verb; that is, a Verb in the Indicative, Imperative, or Subjunctive Mode.

A Phrafe is two or more words rightly put together, in order to make a part of a Sentence; and fometimes making a whole fentence.

The moft common PHRASES, ufed in fimple Sentences, are the following:

1ft Phrafe: The Subftantive before a Verb Active, Paffive, or Neuter; when it is faid, what thing *is, does,* or *is done:* as, "I am;" "Thou writeft;" "Thomas is loved;" where I, *Thou, Thomas,* are the Nominative [6] Cafes; and anfwer to the queftion, *who,* or *what?* as,

[6] "He, *whom* ye pretend reigns in heaven, is fo far from protecting the miferable fons of men, that he perpetually delights to blaft the fweeteft flowrets in the Garden of Hope." Adventurer, N°. 76. It ought to be *who,* the Nominative Cafe to *reigns;* not *whom,* as if it were the Objective Cafe governed by *pretend.* "If you were here, you would find three or four in the parlour after dinner, *whom* you would fay paffed their time agreeably." Locke, Letter to Molyneux.

"Scotland and *Thee* did each in other live."
Dryden's Poems, Vol. II. p. 220.

"We are alone; here's none but *Thee* and I."
Shakefpear, 2 Henry VI.

It ought in both places to be *Thou:* the Nominative Cafe to the Verb expreffed or underftood.

"Who,

E 2

*Figure 19.2*   Robert Lowth's highly successful *English Grammar* used footnotes to provide higher-level information and to point out errors of famous writers.

## PRESCRIPTIVISM AND THE ROLE OF LATIN AND GREEK IN GRAMMAR

Grammars from this era have been accused of several faults. The first is the sin of prescriptivism, or dictating which language forms are correct and which are not, according to the author's own prejudices. Given the context of a grammar such as Lowth's, the charge is baseless. The notion of a descriptive grammar of a European language, simply noting competing usages and alternative forms, would not have made sense at the time. In the seventeenth and eighteenth centuries, stability in the language was exactly what the public was looking for, and it was up to writers such as Lowth to set the standards. Some authors were undoubtedly better at it than others; Lowth's name naturally comes up because his book was the most successful for generations, even after the English language had settled down.

Another criticism is that the grammars tried to force modern languages into a Latin and Greek framework, as though grammarians of the day were somehow oblivious to the structural differences. This is most obvious in English, which, as Lowth noted, has fewer variations in word form than most other languages. Nevertheless, English verbs are still conjugated—*I look, you look, he/she/it looks, we look, you look, they look*—just like in Latin, which in turn had borrowed the pattern from Greek. It's often been said that ending a sentence in English with a preposition is wrong because it was not allowed in Latin—even though it simply was not possible in the latter.[10] But of course, eighteenth-century grammarians were aware of all this. The Abbé de Levizac tells us of an episode that took place in the Académie française, the body founded in 1635 to watch over the French language.[11] This problem of "learning French in Latin," said one esteemed member of the institution, was a remnant of the tradition of studying French only as an introductory means of learning Latin. The inadequacies of this system led to debates in the academy on what influence Latin should have. De Levizac says, "In one of their sittings, last year, they examined the following question: 'Are we, or are we not to admit *cases* in the French language?'" Two reports were prepared "in the most scientific and critical manner"; one argued for the existence of cases in all languages, and the other took the opposing stance. The reports were read to the assembly, and a lengthy discussion followed. Unable to reach agreement, they commissioned the Abbé Sicard, a respected scholar known for his grammatical work, to examine the question and write a report. His conclusion: "I have insisted in a strong manner, *with all the modern grammarians,* upon the impossibility of admitting *cases* [italics in the original] in those languages in which the nouns, adjectives and articles . . . have invariable forms." The academy therefore banned the teaching of cases for French in the public schools.

In spite of the opinion of "all modern grammarians," we nevertheless must consider the context and the audience for grammars such as Lowth's. Is it realistic to expect Lowth or any other grammarian of the seventeenth and eighteenth centuries to abandon the format that had been used for two thousand years? Moreover, it was just what was expected by the readers. After all, it wasn't only children who used these books. They were reference works of grammar, and in the mind of the public, grammar was to be done in the classic style, like Greek and Latin. Lowth was simply following tradition and meeting the needs of his audience.

# 20 Lindley Murray
## "The Father of English Grammar"

Following in the footsteps of Lowth came an American, Lindley Murray (1745–1826), who has been called "the father of English grammar."[1] He practiced law early in life before abandoning the profession and eventually moving to England after the American Revolution; there he devoted himself to intellectual pursuits and wrote on a variety of subjects, notably religion and grammar. In 1795 he published his *English Grammar,* a textbook that became the most successful first-language teaching grammar of its time and was used throughout the English-speaking world.[2] All together he wrote eleven textbooks and was the best-selling author in the world for a while: more than twenty million copies of his books were sold.[3]

## MURRAY'S ENGLISH GRAMMAR

Intellectually, his *English Grammar* is the successor to Lowth's famous work. Murray adapted Lowth's idea of creating a two-level course. Whereas Lowth accomplished this by using footnotes for higher-level information, Murray had a different idea. Footnotes are not as likely to attract the attention of young readers as a continuous text, he decided. Instead, he wrote a continuous text, but in two sizes. Larger print gave the more basic information, while the smaller print was intended for further study. You'd have, then, a paragraph or two in larger type that introduces a rule or grammar point, followed by several in the smaller print. He informs us that the reader has a choice: read only the larger print straight through for a continuous basic course or read the entire text for a complete course.[4]

Like Lowth's grammar, the content of Murray's book contains few surprises. Murray tells us that he painstakingly worked on the phrasing of the rules in order to make them as clear, brief, and "harmonious" as possible for easier learning by heart. The success of the book is a clear indication that deductive learning and memorization of grammar rules are firmly back as the accepted method. Like Lowth, he believed that teaching the language by presenting examples of real errors was a valuable tool, but instead of holding up the errors of the best writers, he was content to create

*Figure 20.1* Lindley Murray.

his own examples. A final point that strikes the modern reader is how much language education continued to be seen as an essential part of a youth's moral education. Murray, as a devout Quaker, assures us that he has been careful not to include any examples or other prose that "might have an improper effect on the minds of youth."[5] On the contrary, as had been done for centuries, his text provides useful values for his readers.

What *is* different is a clearly stated philosophy that indicates a break from the past. The rational grammar movement in the classroom had stressed the importance of a genuine understanding of grammar, but that was a historical anomaly. Learning grammar without formal study of the rules had been tried, but the method had lost out by 1800. For the most part, students in the past had, in one form or another, merely learned the rules and applied them to reading, writing, and speaking as best they could. Murray's book, though, reflected a new perception of what first-language study could accomplish. "Many of the notes and observations are intended, not only to explain the subjects . . . but also to invite the ingenious student to inquiry and reflection, and to prompt a more enlarged, critical, and philosophical research."[6] Furthermore, Murray quotes the Scottish scholar Hugh Blair (1718–1800), one of the earliest experts on the teaching of composition:

> All that regards the study of composition is intimately connected with the improvement of our intellectual powers. When we are employed in the study of composition, we are cultivating the understanding itself. The study of arranging and expressing our thoughts with propriety, teaches us to think, as well as to speak, accurately.[7]

We see why the study of foreign and classical languages was being pushed to a later age. It was a detailed knowledge of one's own language that laid the foundations for the intellectual skills that were required for an education. Although the study of Latin was still seen as beneficial for the training of one's memory and organizational skills, it was no longer a match for the study of a young child's first language.

Whether or not this goal of laying the intellectual foundations succeeded is not directly relevant to us. But language teaching itself, it seems, in spite of earlier enlightened talk from various scholars and experimental methods scattered here and there, was still very similar to what it had been throughout much of history: study the rules of grammar in order to communicate effectively and correctly. True, there was no longer an emphasis on imitating long-deceased authors and sometimes there was a concern whether students actually understood the rules. The measure of success, though, in language learning was shifting away from style to a stress on accuracy (expression "with propriety," as Blair said).

## THE FIRST PRACTICE EXERCISES

This need for correctness is demonstrated by another novelty from Murray. It was he who popularized the use of practice exercises for grammar. Until then, the better grammars contained plentiful examples but gave students no chance to work with this information. Two years after the introduction of his grammar textbook, Murray came out with *English Exercises Adapted to Murray's English Grammar* (1797), which quickly became a companion to its predecessor. It's exactly what it sounds like: nearly 150 pages of grammar exercises. Almost one-third are devoted to parsing, or identifying parts of speech. The first example gives an idea of the level of detail required: "Hope animates us." Here is the expected reply, just what a student a thousand years earlier might have had to know as well:

> *Hope* is a common substantive, of the neuter gender, the third person, in the singular number, and the nominative case. *Animates* is a regular verb active, indicative mood, present tense, third person singular. *Us* is a personal pronoun, first person plural, and in the objective case.[8]

Exercises on syntax made up the next part of the book. The favored procedure was to give a rule of grammar and follow it with a list of sentences to be corrected. Here, for example, is how the section opens:

> RULE I: A verb must agree with its nominative case, in number and in person: as "I learn; "Thou art improved; "The birds sing."

This was followed by the first few sentences to be studied under this rule:

> Disappointments sinks the heart of man; but the renewal of hope give consolation.
> The smiles that encourage severity of judgment, hides malice and insincerity.
> He dare not act contrary to his instructions.
> Fifty pounds of wheat contains forty pounds of flour.
> The mechanism of clocks and watches were totally unknown a few centuries ago.[9]

The rest of the book contains exercises on punctuation and review exercises to correct sentences on a given common fault. Notice that there is no logical connection whatsoever between the sentences. Each is an isolated example of the rule gone wrong. This sentence-based-exercise approach to teaching grammar was definitely a new way of doing things—and it was the wave of the future.

As testimony to the success of Murray's works, more than seventy years later a parody of his grammar was published anonymously in Dublin: *The Comic Lindley Murray; or, the Grammar of Grammars* (1871). Full of dreadful puns,[10] it follows the layout of its target, chapter by chapter, for seventy-two pages. "The well-known and useful work of the celebrated Lindley Murray has been generally regarded as a dry production,"[11] says the author at the start, but he soon admits that his purpose is not only to amuse his readers, but to provide "a graceful tribute to the memory of the gifted Grammarian."[12] What teacher could ever hope for anything better?

# 21 The Grammar-Translation Method
## It's Not What You Think

### THE NINETEENTH CENTURY

We saw in the previous chapter that matters had taken a modern turn in the seventeen hundreds, as learning a foreign language began to mean the study of one of the vernaculars (though often in addition to Latin or Greek). Unlike in earlier centuries, this started after children had studied their own language. By the end of the eighteenth century, Lowth and Murray had written highly successful and influential teaching grammars for first languages, and Murray created the first widely used exercises to practice grammar points. The nineteenth century witnessed the greatest changes in the development of language teaching of any century. It was indeed in the eighteen hundreds that language pedagogy earned the right to be considered a modern discipline with aspirations to a scientific basis. But before reaching that point at the end of the century, there was a tremendous amount of experimentation. Throughout the period, the quest for the one "best" method to teach a foreign language inspired several teachers to new levels of creativity (philosophers had retired from the game, we might say). The results always left the search unfulfilled, but their attempts are nevertheless worthy of study—maybe even to find some useful ideas to apply in today's classroom, or just as likely, some to avoid. We'll start with the much-maligned Grammar-Translation Method from earlier in the century and proceed eventually to the beginnings of truly modern language teaching with the Reform Movement.

### THE GRAMMAR-TRANSLATION METHOD

When you think of the Grammar-Translation Method, what comes to mind? Probably you have dark thoughts of endless, picky grammar rules and verb paradigms and silly sentences to translate. If you've ever studied or taught a language using the method, chances are high that you will not think kindly of Grammar-Translation. If you haven't, it's likely that you know its poor reputation and believe that it's a method to be avoided in the modern classroom. In this age of communicative methods, just the idea of working on a language merely by studying grammar rules and then translating sentences sounds hopelessly old-fashioned, even ignorant. You'll be hard pressed to find supporters, especially among those who suffered through perhaps years of dry memorization and odd, out-of-context sentences (we'll see plenty of examples in a moment).

Nevertheless, Grammar-Translation is a good example of why it's not fair to judge a piece of history by today's standards. It's not possible to evaluate this method from more than two hundred years ago by looking at what it has become: the method and the audience have both changed substantially since its beginning.

Few of us realize how old the method actually is. It's still in use today, which to most people indicates that its origins must not be so distant. In fact, though, we could have looked at Grammar-Translation in the last chapter, because it can be traced to a specific person (Johann Meidinger), a specific work (his *Praktische französische Grammatik,* or "Practical French Grammar"), and therefore a specific year (1770).[1] In the big picture, however, it was simply the forerunner of a movement that is more closely associated with the eighteen hundreds.

## THE BASICS OF GRAMMAR-TRANSLATION

The name "Grammar-Translation" is misleading because it gives the idea that studying grammar and doing translations can be attributed to this method. That of course is not true, as we've clearly seen. The difference between this and previous methods of study was in the way that the grammar and the sentences to be translated were presented to the students. In line with the developments of the seventeen hundreds, students no longer studied grammar with an aim to interpret and imitate classical literature, but with the objective of learning to use a language in real life.

Grammar-Translation as practiced in the early eighteen hundreds was really a simple method: at the beginning of a course, it consisted of presenting grammar *indirectly* in a graded order along with a few vocabulary items.[2] After that, there would be some sentences to translate, written by the author to illustrate the grammar under study and to use the new vocabulary. These sentences, as we've already seen with Murray's exercises for native speakers, were often completely unrelated to each other, though sometimes they were loosely associated in some sort of short narrative. What matters is that Grammar-Translation continued the new practice of sentence-based language study. In a word, the method considered language to consist of rules and vocabulary, and what was needed was just practice and more practice in applying these two components.

Let's look at two early Grammar-Translation advocates who wrote highly successful foreign-language textbooks and were the chief popularizers of Grammar-Translation in its early days.

## JOHANN FRANZ AHN

Johann Franz Ahn (1796–1865) was a German schoolteacher known for his innovative language-teaching texts, many of which had the words "practical" (meaning that it contained exercises for practice) and "easy" somewhere in the title. His works of interest to us date from 1834 and after. They were for teaching or self-study in numerous European languages. Some were translated into other languages, so that in the end he had German books for French students, French books for English students, and so on. They sold well for much of the nineteenth century.

His *Introductory Practical Course to Acquire the French Language* is an excellent example of Grammar-Translation in its simplest form. Divided into three parts, it's visually a strikingly uninspiring book, containing a monotonous stream of plain text.

The first part is the basic course consisting of 155 short sections, or lessons, some only a few lines long. The format is clear and consistent. In spite of the Grammar-Translation name and reputation, Ahn uses very little grammatical terminology and in fact has no grammar rules in the basic course! In a technique reminiscent of du Marsais's literal translation a century earlier, he doesn't list verb paradigms or all the relative pronouns, for example, or even talk about what the parts of speech do. Instead, he starts most sections by giving the students several vocabulary items (with approximate pronunciation) that may already be plural, or past, a phrase, a superlative form, or a relative pronoun, and so on. *Vous avez* ("you have," plural), for example, is given as one item without any other forms of the verb "to have." *Vu* ("seen") is another item. All these are learned as separate vocabulary items that are applied immediately to translating sentences that appear directly below. Thus, without discussing tense, students already can translate sentences with *vous avez vu*, or "you have seen." By the end of the second page (section 13), students are reading French sentences like "We have a father who is good" and even "Have you seen our little brother?"[3] From the fourth page (section 18), he includes English sentences to translate into French for extra practice. Verbs are always the biggest difficulty, so later he does in fact list verb paradigms, but in general there is little of what we think of as "teaching grammar." A student capable of keeping up with the course would eventually be able to translate from English into French this bit from section 102: "I loved formerly this young man, he was always so modest and sensible. He spoke little, but so well, and he always sought friends who loved better the books than the wine. We were often together, we never thought of the play (gaming)."[4]

The second section concentrates on verbs. After a lengthy list of paradigms of all the tenses, moods, and aspects, there are passages to translate; some are short, others long—*Beauty and the Beast* is an example of the latter. Most are to be done from the second language into the first, but not all. There is no explanation or comment on the grammar—just example lists of verbs.

The final section of the book is a collection of mini-glossaries, one for each of the translation passages of the second section. The inclusion of glossaries was still quite a novelty, but this format made it even easier, as the students did not have to thumb through one long list of all the words in the book.

Ahn's books varied somewhat over the years and according to the languages under study, but the contents remained essentially the same. The sections of the Italian book of a few years later are headed by labeled grammar points and the German book includes a smattering of grammatical "observations," for example, and has some "easy dialogues," but the books give the feeling of the same authorship and method. Detailed rules of grammar are avoided. They are surprisingly simple and, in spite of an unattractive layout, are actually quite interesting and "user-friendly," to borrow a modern term.

## HEINRICH OLLENDORFF

Heinrich Ollendorff[5] (1803–1865) was another German author who, like Ahn, wrote a series of successful language-teaching texts for a number of languages. Unlike Ahn, though, Ollendorff approached language teaching as a business. He created a method based on Grammar-Translation, and his books were essentially translations of each other. With usually only minor variations, they featured the same grammar, the same examples, and even the same translation sentences. He made the grand claim that his method could teach a language in six months, and in a spirit of showmanship, he even numbered and autographed each book.

The books all follow the same format: A lesson begins with grammar and vocabulary combined; that is, new words are learned through a generous number of examples. There are then the expected sentences to translate. Overall, his books are much longer (five hundred or more pages compared to barely one hundred for Ahn's) with more examples and more grammar. One distinctive feature of the books is Ollendorff's fondness for the question-and-answer format. In the preface to each of his books, his first sentence extols the benefits of studying questions: "My system of acquiring a living language is founded on the principle, that each question nearly contains the answer which one ought or which one wishes to make to it." That is, much of the structure of the reply to a question can be found in the question itself—a built-in hint for the student. The result is that questions and answers abound in the examples of each lesson and in the translation exercises.

any money ?—They have not any.—Who has their money ?—Their
friends have it.—Are their friends thirsty ?—They are not thirsty.
but hungry.—Has your servant a good dog ?—He has one.—Has he
this or that nail ?—He has neither this nor that.—Have the peasants
these or those bags ?—They have neither these nor those.—Which
bags have they ?—They have their own.—Have you a good servant ?
—I have a good one.—Who has a good chest ?—My brother has one
—Has he a leather or an iron chest ?—He has an iron one.

---

## THIRTEENTH LESSON.—*Leccion Décima tercia.*

| | |
|---|---|
| *How much?* | *¿ Cuanto ?* |
| *How many?* | *¿ Cuantos ?* |
| How much bread have you? | ¿ Cuanto pan tiene V. ? |
| How much money? | ¿ Cuanto dinero ? |
| How many knives? | ¿ Cuantos cuchillos ? |
| How many men? | ¿ Cuantos hombres ? |
| How many friends? | ¿ Cuantos amigos ? |

| | |
|---|---|
| | *Solo.* |
| *Only.* | *Solamente.* |
| *But.* | *No (v) sino.* |
| | *No (v) mas que.* |
| " have but one friend. | Solo tengo un amigo. |
| have but one. | Tengo uno solamente. |
| I have but one good gun. | No tengo mas que un buen fusil. |
| I have but one good one. | (Yo) tengo solamente uno bueno. |
| The book is not mine, but yours. | El libro no es mio sino de V. |
| You have but one good one. | V. no tiene mas que uno bueno. |
| How many horses has your brother? | ¿ Cuantos caballos tiene su hermano de V. ? |
| He has but one. | No tiene mas que uno. |
| He has but two good ones. | Él tiene solamente dos buenos. |

| | |
|---|---|
| *Much* | *Mucho.* |
| *Many.* | *Muchos.* |
| *A good deal, very much.* | *Muchísimo.  Muchísimos, (pl.)* |
| Much bread. | Mucho pan. |
| Many men. | Muchos hombres. |
| A good deal of good bread. | Muchísimo pan bueno. |
| Have you much money? | ¿ Tiene V. mucho dinero ? |
| I have a good deal. | Tengo muchísimo. |
| Have you much good wine? | ¿ Tiene V. mucho vino bueno ? |
| I have a good deal. | Tengo muchísimo. |

*Figure 21.1*    A page from Heinrich Ollendorff's Spanish course.

The preface to the American edition of Ollendorff's Italian textbook provides some useful and surprising information about how language-teaching methods were seen at the time. The preface is written by an Italian professor in the United States who was charged with making additions and corrections to the book. He notes,

> Scarcely a week passes among us that is not marked by the advent of one or more new books to facilitate the acquisition of foreign languages. . . . Each claims to be superior, in its method of teaching to all its predecessors, if not absolutely infallible in every important detail.[6]

Reviewing the current situation, he declares that there are just two methods of learning a language. The first goes by several names: the classical, scholastic, or scientific. It is, in fact, the method most commonly used since the ancient days: "In this the practice is almost entirely subordinated to abstract, formal rules, which are prominently brought forward and hold the first place."[7] Interestingly, this sounds like a condemnation today of Grammar-Translation. The other, and superior method, is the empirical or practical method. "Here a commencement is made with the concrete tongue: almost exclusive attention is given to the living practice, the grammatical principles of the language being either postponed or subordinated, or perhaps altogether neglected."[8]

Ollendorff's (and Ahn's) work falls plainly into the latter category of methods, claims the author of the preface, and the difference is great. With relatively little effort, students will be able to reach a complete knowledge of Italian "in a space of time that will be deemed incredibly short by those who have confined themselves to the tedious systems heretofore in use."[9] Here's the secret, as told by another professor in the preface to another of Ollendorff's works—compare this to Ahn's work as well as that of du Marsais:

> Instead of presupposing a familiarity with English Grammar in the pupil as is commonly done, [Ollendorff] begins apparently without any system, with the simplest phrases, from which he deduces [makes clear] the rules, until gradually and almost imperceptibly he makes the pupil master of the etymology and syntax of every part of speech. The rules are, as it were, concealed amid the multitude of exercises which are added to each lesson, and which serve to fortify the learner in the principles he has already acquired.[10]

This is not at all how Grammar-Translation is seen today. We think of it as the epitome of the deductive method, when in fact it was inductive.

One of the biggest criticisms of Grammar-Translation is that its sentence-based nature requires the use of isolated, artificial, unnatural sentences. That is not how it was viewed at the time. On the contrary, these sentences were the strong point of the method:

Another characteristic feature of the book, and one in which its practical merit chiefly consists is, that the examples on which the rules are based, and those which are intended to illustrate the rules, are not derived from the German Classics; they are neither the ideal language of Poetry, nor the rigorous language of Sciences, but of *life*—short sentences, such as one would be most likely to use in conversing in a circle of friends, or in writing a letter.[11]

That's right: these artificial sentences were seen as examples of real, everyday language, as opposed to the unhelpful prose learned from literature. It's a matter of the changing perspective over the course of two centuries.[12]

Ollendorff's tendency to self-promotion emerges in one of the final translation exercises. It can be found in both the German and Italian courses:

THE MASTER. If I were now to ask you such questions as I did in the beginning of our lessons, viz: Have you the hat which my brother has?—Am I hungry? Has he the tree of my brother's garden?, etc., what would you answer?

THE PUPILS. We are obliged to confess that we found these questions at first rather ridiculous; but, full of confidence in your method, we answered as well as the small quantity of words and rules we then possessed allowed us. We were, in fact, not long in finding out that these questions were calculated to ground us in the rules, and to exercise us in conversation. . . . At all events we should be ungrateful if we allowed such an opportunity to escape without expressing our liveliest gratitude to you for the trouble you have taken. In arranging those wise combinations you have succeeded in grounding us almost imperceptibly in the rules, and exercising us in the conversation of a language which, taught in another way, presents to foreigners, and even to natives, all insurmountable difficulties.[13]

Just imagine: students toiling over a translation of what amounts to an advertisement for their own textbook! This passage, though, addresses one of the other chief criticisms of Grammar-Translation: that it neglects speaking and listening. Even as explained here, it certainly doesn't fit modern ideas of what constitutes oral practice. But this must be compared to what was being done at the time. Compared to classical methods, this was surely a "conversational" course. In a tremendous break with the past, it taught students sentences that may seem odd to us, but were much closer to real life than what they encountered in literature.[14]

The idea of a series of language-teaching books was not unheard of in the mid-eighteen hundreds; we've already seen, as just one example, that Claude Lancelot of Port-Royal came up with textbooks for teaching several languages in the mid-sixteen hundreds. There was no attempt, however, by Lancelot to standardize the works; that is, using his original ideas, he simply applied his "new method" to the teaching of a few languages over a period of years, hoping, we suppose, that each was better than the previous one. It wasn't until the late seventeen hundreds that we begin to see a method as an intellectual property that one would today protect with a patent. Ahn and Ollendorff immediately come to mind. They developed new ways to teach languages and applied them with little change to a variety of languages. The commercial possibilities were obvious: then as now, if you gained a reputation for having an effective method of teaching a language, there was a lot of money to be made. A simple but nevertheless valid explanation of this respect for methods is that it was a sign of the times, one that reflected an admiration for the new world of science that had emerged in recent years. There may have been nothing truly scientific about Ollendorff's or Ahn's method, but they both demonstrated a well-planned process that removed some of the "art" of previous centuries. All the methods under discussion here had the facade of a new, modern way of doing things.

## THE GRAMMAR-TRANSLATION METHOD: IN MEMORIAM

If it's possible to feel sorry for a language-teaching method, the poor Grammar-Translation Method deserves sympathy. It started out with the best of intentions. It was supposed to lighten the burden of second-language study for students, to take them away from the drudgery of rule memorization and irrelevant readings. We've seen enough quotations from prominent scholars and authors telling us of their miserable experiences in the language classroom. Concern for the mental well-being of the younger student was a trend that had been developing for a few hundred years, and Grammar-Translation was another step. As represented by the works of Ahn and Ollendorff, it has a lot to recommend it—if we keep a historical perspective.

Inevitably, Grammar-Translation evolved over the years. One of the main purposes of the method was to create a more humane approach, but to some, still under the influence of classical studies, Grammar-Translation needed to be more rigorous. It became more and more laden with grammar rules in greater detail and with exceptions to these rules. That's a simplistic explanation, but the fact is that by later in the century it was indeed possible to find the type of out-of-touch Grammar-Translation course that ruined its reputation.

Overall, we can view Grammar-Translation as a positive step in the history of language teaching. As an attempt at a logical, caring approach to foreign-language learning, it marked one of the biggest breaks ever with tradition. It was hugely successful in its early format with authors like Ollendorff and Ahn. It was a simple course to implement in the classroom, so it did not require a good deal of skill or training. If we recall the plight of teachers such as Spoudeus in the seventeenth century, it's probably fair to say that such a system would have been quite a success with less educated and capable instructors.[15]

If you're ever asked about Grammar-Translation, reply with a question of your own: Do you mean the original Grammar-Translation from the first half of the eighteen hundreds? Or the later version that gave Grammar-Translation such a bad name? It makes a difference.

# 22  Two Diversions
## Prendergast and Gouin

Let's have an intermission between the two main acts of the nineteenth century and consider the efforts of two ambitious reformers. Neither proved to have the insights to revolutionize language learning, contrary to their high expectations. There were other hard-working, innovative souls during the century, but these two make for good stories. One, Thomas Prendergast, created an extreme but highly original sentence-based method, a development of Grammar-Translation. The other, François Gouin, devised a popular method unrelated to anything that had come before. Both were based on the way that children supposedly really learn their first language. Each man was convinced, like many others before and after, that only he had finally figured out the secret of foreign-language acquisition.

## THOMAS PRENDERGAST AND HIS MASTERY SERIES

Thomas Prendergast (1806–1886), a British civil servant, was the creator of the Mastery of Languages series, books intended for private study. In total, he wrote five courses between 1864 and 1872. The Mastery Series was a logical development of the Grammar-Translation era and sentence-based language teaching. Prendergast took these principles to an unexpected and certainly original extreme, one that foreshadowed the Audio-lingual Method of nearly a century later.

Prendergast approached language teaching with the assumption that he could create a method based on the natural way that children learn language.[1] He was certain that he knew what it was. Quite simply, Prendergast said, children learn not just isolated words but entire phrases and sentences. From these they work out the grammar of the language and build variations of these chunks of language. Prendergast's method, then, was based on learning carefully constructed sentences and sets of variations. A child's attempts are rather haphazard and often unsuccessful. The Mastery Series, on the other hand, improved on nature by streamlining the process. The word "method" in common language is vague, but in this case it couldn't possibly be clearer. Prendergast prescribed *exactly* how the book was to be used. Follow his rules and success was assured; woe be to those who ignored him.

A book consisted of a mere forty or so "Texts" (always capitalized by Prendergast, giving an air of authority), which were actually sentences that averaged about twenty to twenty-five words in English. It was useless to start with short sentences, he believed, because they didn't provide enough material for manipulation or illustration of grammar. The Text sentences were broken into two or three parts, and under each sentence were "Variations" in English, which were created from the new words of the sentence and from vocabulary of previous lessons. On a neighboring page all this was translated into the target language. In the entire course there were four or five hundred of these variations, or practice sentences.

6

THE MASTERY SERIES.

Text III.

41. Would not the messenger, if that villager had besought him, have hastened with thee to call back the master?

42. Would the villager, if thy servant, oh Martina, had besought him, have called back the rustic to me?

43. My friend has hastened, in order that he may chastise thy uncle's faithless messenger.

44. If thy cousin had entreated his friend, would he not have liberated the slave?

45. In vain Philip is beseeching my friend Martina that he may not wound the neighbour's servant with a sword.

46. Would not thy friend, oh cousin, have wounded the wolf with a sword, had he lacerated thee?

47. Did the neighbour beseech the messenger that he should not liberate that villager with me?

48. Did not Paul beseech Hortensius that he should not provoke the insane villager?

49. Let the messenger relate to thy cousin, not to thy uncle, that the servant is asking his master for this.

50. Oh master, stimulate Martina that he may wound the wolf and set free the villager.

51. Had thy uncle entreated him, would not that villager have hastened in order that he might call the doctor?

52. The doctor was relating to my uncle that the servant had liberated both me and my friend.

53. The rustic exclaims that a madman has wounded the master with thy sword, oh my son.

54. Would not that servant, if the doctor besought him, hasten with us to liberate the master's son?

55. Would not thy son hasten that he might liberate thee, if the panther were lacerating him?

56. Would not Manlius, if thy son called him, hasten with me to wound the wolf?

57. A neighbour exclaimed that the madman had hastened to wound the master with thy sword.

58. My friend announces that thou hast stimulated my cousin that he should hasten to liberate the rustic's son.

59. The rustic announces, oh master, that the tyrant was expecting thee and thy son.

60. The servant wounded the neighbour with thy sword, in order that he should not relate this to the lord.

LATIN MANUAL.

Text III.

41. Nónne nuntius, si pāganus istè eum ōrávisset, ād dóminum révocandum tēcum propērávisset?

42. Pāganusne, Martí, si servus tuus eum ōrávisset, rusticum ad me revocavisset?

43. Amicus meus properavit ut patrui tui infidum nuntium castiget.

44. Nonne amicus, si eum sobrinus tuus orasset, servum liberavisset?

45. Philippus amicum meum Martium frustra orat ne servum vicini gladio vulneret.

46. Nonne amicus tuus, O sobrine, lupum gladio vulneravisset, si te laceravisset?

47. Vicinusne nuntium oravit ne paganum istum mecum liberaret?

48. Nonne Paulus Hortensium oravit ne paganum insanum provocaret?

49. Narret nuntius sobrino tuo, non patruo, servum hoc dominum orare.

50. O domine, Martium stimula ut lupum vulneret et paganum liberet.

51. Nonne patruus iste, si patruus tuus eum oravisset, properavisset, ut medicum vocaret?

52. Medicus patruo meo narrabat servum et me et amicum meum liberavisse.

53. Rusticus exclamat insanum gladio tuo, mi fili, dominum vulneravisse.

54. Nonne iste servus, si medicus eum oraret, ad filium domini liberandum mecum properaret?

55. Nonne tu, si partim tua lacerraret, filius tuus properaret ut liberaret?

56. Nonne Manlius, si eum filius tuus vocaret, ad lupum vulnerandum mecum properaret?

57. Exclamavit vicinus insanum properavisse ut magistrum gladio tuo vulneret.

58. Amicus meus nuntiat te sobrinum meum stimulavisse ut ad filium rustici liberandum properet.

59. Rusticus nuntiat, O domine, tyrannum te filiumque tuum expectare.

60. Servus vicinum gladio tuo vulneravit, ne hoc domino narraret.

7

*Figure 22.1* A page from Thomas Prendergast's Latin course.

As with early Grammar-Translation, there was no explicit grammar; everything the learner needed to know was carefully illustrated in the sentences and could be worked out by the learner. This was aided by working with a "studiously limited" vocabulary to avoid confusion, but mostly by acquiring a thorough mastery of the sentences. And indeed, it would be hard not to master the sentences if one followed Prendergast's strict rules. The student was advised to begin by reading the text sentence slowly and carefully twenty times. All work, with never an exception, had to be done out loud—no silent reading. The next step was to read the sentence faster and faster until in the end the learner could recite it from memory as quickly as if it were in English (all his books were for English speakers). It was then time to tackle the Variations, one by one, using the same procedure. Prendergast was very upbeat about this: "The sudden Mastery of a complicated sentence of about 25 words will impart feelings of triumph and communicate an impulse which constitutes a broad distinction between the results of this and of all other methods."[2] Readers were warned absolutely not to proceed until this level of fluency was achieved.[3]

It sounds like an exhausting and deadening way to learn a language, but Prendergast was prepared for this objection. The timings for using the method were prescribed to the minute. The underlying principle here was that a person's memory works best when it is under pressure, but only for short periods. Prendergast made sure (or so he believed) that one's memory would never tire from his method. For the first two weeks the reader was to study the sentences for no more than ten minutes at a time, but exactly six times each day, with an hour or two separating each sitting. Thereafter, the sittings could be reduced to three, presumably of twenty minutes each. Students expected grammar, he knew, so if the promise of its acquisition through his innovative method was not enough for the reader, he gave his permission to investigate grammar on one's own after mastering the first hundred Variations, but only "if they are very anxious for it." He discouraged it in any case because the longer it was postponed, the easier he felt it would be to grasp the rules.

Prendergast urged the student to try his method for at least a month. He was confident, in fact, that just two weeks would convince almost anyone of its effectiveness. "It is impossible for anyone to make this experiment without arriving at the conviction that this is the veritable method of nature, and that it is incomparably superior to all others."[4] He seemed blissfully convinced that its results would be adequate compensation for all the necessary effort. Although indirectly acknowledging the amount of work and dedication that using his method would require, rather than view it as a drawback, he managed to profess it as a tremendous plus: "This system forms an admirable instrument for self-discipline and for acquiring and fostering habits of industry, of observation, of accuracy and of method, in the application of its principles to other studies and pursuits."[5]

It's not hard to see why Prendergast's Mastery Series had only limited success after the allure of its strict and novel method faded. Prendergast's conviction of the truth of his method blinded him to reality: almost no one has the time or the self-discipline to adhere to it. Most likely the results for those who courageously stuck with it were not as brilliant as promised, either. What is striking and impressive about Prendergast's insights, however, are their similarity to behaviorist principles in psychology of nearly a century later. Without getting ahead of ourselves, behaviorism when applied to language learning meant, above all, the formation of habits; that is, repetition and manipulation of carefully controlled material and vocabulary would lead to automatic responses. Prendergast, we can state with sympathy, was a man ahead of his time.

## FRANÇOIS GOUIN AND HIS ODYSSEY TO DISCOVER THE SERIES METHOD

Let's begin this section with a quote from the preface to a work by our next scholar.

> The world has this year seen a magnificent celebration of the grand services to the cause of education rendered by Comenius.[6] In spite of this we are still far from having definitely adopted in our school and college practice the now acknowledged principles perceived by Comenius that education must be organic[7] and not mechanical, that language teaching, modern and classic, should proceed by dealing with things and not with words and grammatical abstractions, and that before all else education should have direct bearing upon actual life.[8]

François Gouin[9] (1831–1896), like Prendergast and others, thought that he had found the genuine method of nature for learning a language, but it certainly didn't agree with that of Prendergast. A Frenchman, Gouin was a rather ordinary high school language teacher, well versed in Latin and quite proficient in Greek as well. Being the studious type, he decided to take some time off and go study in the fine universities of Germany to advance his education. There was one little problem, however: he didn't speak a word of German. He considered this to be only a minor difficulty, though, because he was, after all, a language teacher who had mastered the classical languages. Confident in his abilities, he allowed himself a few weeks or at most a few months in Germany to pick up the language before commencing his studies. Instead, Gouin embarked on a remarkable journey of linguistic discovery that led to the creation of a new method, one that was truly novel.

### Background

Gouin was understandably impressed by the technological achievements of the day, and in them he saw the promise of a bright future for humanity. In recent years technology had bridged the geographical gap among nations, mostly thanks to the development of the railroad. Now that this invention had made social contact so easy, there remained a key obstacle, that of language. If only people could learn to speak to each other, "the brotherhood of nations will cease to be a vain and empty word."[10] This high ambition needed a method that would enable students to master a language not in ten or twenty years, or even in six months, but one that could produce immediate results in communication. He liked to refer to this dream method as a "mental railway" among nations. But how, he wondered, could this happen? Can we really do better than the greatest minds who have come before us? But this was a defeatist attitude, he decided, one that would have prevented the development of many of the tremendous inventions that the nineteenth century had witnessed. No, it must be possible. And in fact, Gouin declared that he himself had discovered the way. Gouin wrote all about this process in probably the most fascinating account ever written by a language teacher. It's worth going into in depth not just for the interesting insights that he picked up along the way, but simply because it is such a great story. It takes up nearly sixty pages of his 407-page book, *The Art of Teaching and Studying Languages.*

Gouin came up this method when he realized the way it is done in children, in nature:

> This method, which, when perfected both by time and by practice, might well be called by the name of the 'Natural Method.' . . . Yes, Nature has already solved the problem that we are investigating, and she holds a permanent school for early infancy, in which we can, if we wish, at any time take part, and where we may be able to study her never-failing processes.[11]

No one had ever examined the process carefully, he decided; instead, language learning by children had typically been dismissed as occurring by chance or simply as a miracle of nature.

Of course, Gouin did not have this in mind when he headed off to Germany to study in Berlin. With the fervor of youth, he expected to speak the language as well as a child within a few weeks, given his determination. He had no plan in mind. "It seemed to me that a living language might be somehow assimilated in the very air of the country."[12] He stopped in Hamburg to take a few academic classes for practice and to assess the task before him. He signed up for some classes in an institution with able teachers and eager students. He wanted to see just how much he could understand by listening and observing gesture and accent. The result, to us at least, was predictable. He understood nothing—not one idea was conveyed. He realized he'd have to start from the beginning.

## The First Attempts

The obvious way to begin was with the classical method, and he had complete faith in it. After all, what else was there to do than to first learn words, then master the rules, and finally use them to put words into sentences? It was the product of centuries of thought and effort. It was how he had learned Latin and Greek.[13] But then, come to think of it, it had taken him years to reach a level that would not be adequate for a living language. This raised the first doubts that he could master German in a few weeks. The realization that German was a living language, however, that could be practiced with native speakers chased away these doubts.

Here we may be venturing into the realm of fable, certainly not for the last time in listening to Gouin's story. His solution was to devour the German grammar he had brought with him, with the help of a dictionary. In one week of obviously herculean effort, he assimilated the entire grammar—with the exception of the irregular verbs, which he set as his task for the next two days!

> In ten days I had mastered the grammar of the German language. This victory swelled my courage, and I hastened forthwith to the Academy in order to measure the extent of this first step and to realise the power acquired. . . . But alas! in vain did I strain my ears; in vain my eye strove to interpret the slightest movements of the lips of the professor; in vain I passed from the first class room to a second; not a word, not a single word would penetrate to my understanding. Nay, more than this, I did not even distinguish a single one of the grammatical forms so newly studied; I did not recognise even a single one of the irregular verbs just freshly learnt, though they must certainly have fallen in crowds from the lips of the speaker.[14]

This called for further reflection. He realized that grammar and 248 irregular verbs were insufficient. Thinking back to his studies of Greek, he had made considerable progress by memorizing two thousand Greek roots, the base of all conjugations and declensions. Very well, it was a dead language and had not worked to perfection, but the results in German may be superior. As he so interestingly put it, "A remedy which might be impotent upon a dead body may very easily produce an effect upon a living being."[15] After an arduous search he found just one book of German roots. He was disappointed that it contained only a thousand of them, but it was better than nothing. He memorized these in four days. He gave himself four more days to review his grammar and 248 irregular verbs and, hopeful that this was now sufficient, was prepared to launch himself again into the world. Unless his masters at school had been mistaken, he now possessed all that was necessary to communicate in German.

> Imagine then, if it be possible, the astonishment at first, then the stupefaction, then the degradation by which I was overtaken after the first quarter of an hour at the lecture I attended, when I had to submit to the evidence, and to confess to myself that I was, so far as regards

the spoken language, exactly in the same state as upon the first day; that I did not understand a word, not a syllable, and that all my efforts had been made in pure waste, or at least had produced no appreciable result.[16]

This time he sadly retreated to his lodgings, unable to explain his failure.

His next attempt, without genuine confidence, was to attempt to learn through conversation, a method he had avoided because of its lengthy trial-and-error nature. His landlord was a barber, so Gouin took to sitting in the salon, listening to customers. He even dared participate at times, but only after preparation. The results were not encouraging:

I attempted to follow the conversation, hazarding from time to time a sentence carefully prepared beforehand, awkwardly constructed with the aid of my roots and grammar, and apparently always possessing the property of astonishing and hugely amusing the customers.[17]

Weeks of this method gave him painfully limited conversational tidbits. Worst of all, for this systematic man, was the lack of organization and logic to what little he could produce.

He went back to the old tried-and-true classical methods, this time to straight translation of German works with the aid of a dictionary. He was yet again surprised that, in spite of his knowledge of the grammar book and sizeable collection of verbs and roots, he found it tough going. Even words that looked familiar, he lamented, were like faces a person knows he has seen before but is unable to place. But onward he went, with nowhere else to turn. All he had was faith that someday it would work, somehow it all would fall into place:

We must read, read, read, day in and day out; translate, translate continually; hunt, hunt a hundred times after the same word in the dictionary; catch it a hundred times, a hundred times release it; we shall finish by taming it.[18]

But Gouin, who had displayed superhuman abilities earlier, needed an entire week to translate just eight pages of Goethe and Schiller. Incredibly, it was only at this point that Gouin finally gave up on the classical methods, at least for learning a living language. After reaching this irrevocable conclusion, he noted with remarkable understatement, "My faith was beginning to be shaken."[19]

## Still Hopeful: If the Germans Can Learn German . . .

Searching for a new direction, he sought the advice of bookshop owners in Hamburg.

> I begged them to let me into the secret of the persons who learn German, or rather of those who had really arrived at learning it. They immediately offered me Ollendorff's book, and bade me pay especial attention to these words, 'fifty-fourth edition.' The whole world then studied this book! There was no doubt of it; it was certainly here that all the foreigners who spoke German had learnt that language. I bought the celebrated method; I read the preface attentively, then I meditated and I pondered for some time over this promise, 'German in ninety lessons.'[20]

Gouin knew of Ollendorff but had never tested his method. He was surprised to find much of merit in its pages. Unlike the useless sentences of literature, or the abstract grammar rules that required memorization, he found, as Ollendorff had promised, real language—language of everyday utility. Ollendorff himself could not have summarized the positive aspects of his work much better than did Gouin. Ollendorff, thought Gouin, had found the way of nature. And Ollendorff made a solemn promise of success to the reader, published fifty-four times in fifty-four editions, Gouin noted, without having been disproved. Fired up with rediscovered purpose, Gouin vowed to finish the course in thirty days instead of ninety.

It's highly unlikely that Ollendorff ever had such a determined and talented pupil. Gouin worked through the book right on schedule. For fear of a premature failure, he avoided contact with German speakers. At the end of a month, he had indeed mastered Ollendorff. But had he learned German? He wasn't sure . . . He had been quite pleased with his progress at first, but by the third week doubts were creeping in as he realized that the author had left out thousands of words and forms. The most harmful doubt arose when, near the very end of the book, Ollendorff confided to the reader that the course was incomplete, that the reader should himself continue to construct exercises of the type he had encountered in the book. It sounds harmless to us, but Gouin, perfectionist that he was, saw it as a betrayal. He had been promised the German language; instead, he himself was supposed to finish the job of learning a language he didn't know. Clearly, Gouin was a difficult and demanding man. "I understood that I had once more been deceived."[21] He'd been attracted by Ollendorff's refusal to follow the classical tradition, but in the end the results were poor. After blessing the book with such praise at the beginning, he finished with the judgment that it was nothing more than "a miserable compilation of words."[22]

To shorten the story, let's just say that he examined two other popular "methods" of the day by Joseph Jacotot and Thomas Robertson, and that although they were different in philosophy he rejected them before even starting them, sure that by now he was able to foresee their inadequacies.

At a loss for what to do next, he settled on a change of scenery and headed for Berlin, his original destination for university studies. His contacts in France had given him letters of introduction to several distinguished professors and he quickly made their acquaintance. They spoke to him in French (how had *they* learned a foreign language?) and encouraged him to associate with the students and learn through practicing conversation. But, as anyone who has been in such a situation will tell you, trying to learn a second language by speaking to natives who already speak your own language is extremely difficult, and in those days, any German university student spoke French much better than Gouin spoke German. He dutifully made the social rounds but found that he more often than not ended up speaking his own language. He therefore resolved not to speak any more French, but what was the result? No one wanted to talk to him anymore in his pitifully limited German.

## Desperation Sinks In

Nevertheless, he was still not ready to surrender. His next desperate step was to attend university classes for one week in the faint hope that at this point, with his knowledge of grammar and roots, he could slowly begin to make sense of the lectures, as a child somehow manages to make sense of the speech around him. For the entire week he sat in class, straining to make some sense of the proceedings, but at the end of the allotted time, "I had sat and watched for seven or eight hours a day, various mouths alternately opening and shutting, and this was all."[23]

There remained but one idea in his head—one that was so "heroic," so outlandish, that it required days for him to take the step. Finally, he knew what he had to do: he would memorize an entire German dictionary! He approached it with a self-discipline and methodology that would have made Prendergast proud. Let's see—314 pages, in thirty days—that makes ten pages each day. He found that he could accomplish this mammoth task each day from six o'clock until around noon. He reviewed the previous day's work in the afternoon. By the time he reached the middle of the dictionary his own doubts about this method had abated: "My courage was exalted, my confidence in the coming success was absolute; my happiness was complete."[24] When he finished this extraordinary feat, he felt as mighty as Caesar: "I came, I saw, I conquered."

That very evening he hurried to a lecture, full of enthusiasm and confidence, but was shattered to find that he understood not a single word, no more than he had understood upon his arrival in Hamburg months ago. With no other fresh ideas, he spent days reviewing the dictionary again and again in a desperate effort to absorb the words, until he could translate column after column as quickly as his eyes could process them. But the results were just as dismal. At this point, Gouin tells us, his eyesight began to fail from the prolonged strain, and he was virtually blind for a month. Fortunately his vision returned, apparently as good as new. By then it was nearing summertime, and he decided to return to France for a well-deserved break before heading back to Germany. He refused to give up.

## The True Way Is Revealed

It is impossible to judge how much of Gouin's story is actually true. Maybe it occurred as he recounted it; perhaps he indulged in a bit of artistic license. In any case, those who have spent countless hours, months, and years in a frustrating and vain attempt at mastering a foreign language will undoubtedly sympathize with the plight of this determined and capable scholar who wanted nothing more than to learn enough German to attend classes and further his education.

What happened next upon his return home sounds thoroughly plausible, however. When he had departed France ten months earlier, he left behind a nephew who, at the age of two, had barely begun to talk. When Gouin next saw him, he was both impressed and discouraged that this little creature was now able not only to understand speech but to express any idea or need that he required. What was it that allowed this mere child to acquire a language so easily? Why was learning a language seemingly impossible for Gouin, a man in possession of the rational and analytical abilities of an adult, a trained and superior memory, and a self-discipline completely alien to a three-year-old? Gouin resolved to observe the child. He had been pondering one possible clue. There are many things that a child of three has never encountered or experienced. One scientific way to investigate this question of language acquisition, then, was to observe the child (Gouin never gives him a name) in a new situation and discover how he turned it into language.

He found his chance soon afterward when the child's mother suggested that they visit a mill, a common and important structure in those days. It would be a completely new experience for the boy. As expected, the child was fascinated by the process of turning grain into flour. He watched every movement of the workers, examined every piece of equipment and each corner of the mill, and listened to the strange, impressive sounds of the machinery. He had a wonderful time. For an hour afterward he was quiet, assimilating what he had seen. And then came the language:

> He manifested an immense desire to recount to everybody what he had seen. So he told his story, and told it again and again ten times over, always with variants, forgetting some of the details, returning on his track to repair his forgetfulness, and passing from fact to fact, from phrase to phrase, by the same familiar transition, "and then . . . and then . . ."[25]

This storytelling seemed to help him consolidate his experience, to remove the superfluous, and to strengthen the key events in his mind. "He was still digesting, but now it was on his own account . . . he was conceiving it, putting it in order, moulding it into a conception of his own."[26]

At the boy's insistence, Gouin managed to build a miniature mill that even included a small channel of water and a mill wheel. The mother made him some sacks into which he could put sand in place of the flour. The boy recreated the work of the millers, complete with grunting sounds as he slung the little sacks of sand over his shoulder. In addition, he again and again narrated the experience, describing each action as he carried it out. The one constant in his narration, noted Gouin, was the verb. Suddenly, in a "eureka" moment, it came to Gouin: the boy's actions could be summed up by "I see, I hear, I know."[27]

Was this the secret of learning a language? Yes—that's what Gouin thought. He was thunderstruck, as the true way of nature was revealed to him. He summarized it in four insights:

1. A child first perceives something new, then reflects on it, and finally turns it into a conception. Thus, this novelty is turned into a fact that becomes part of one's individuality. The reflection and conception stages amount to putting the new information into its proper place. The child fits his perceptions onto the base of earlier knowledge; that is, he fits it into existing experience. "This alliance, this forced mixture of the old with the new . . . this grafting of the new upon the old . . . I saw that to express each new perception, it was necessary, so to speak, to employ the whole of the vocabulary already acquired."[28] Gouin compares the process to a botanist who ignores familiar plants while walking through a field, but who stops only before an unknown plant and attempts to classify it in relation to those he already knows.[29]

2. Any act of classification needs rules, so what are they for a child? Gouin believed that a child organizes his or her experience both by time and by cause and effect ("means to an end"). For example:

[The water] flowed along the mill-race [the channel for the water],
then fell upon the wheel,
then this wheel turned round,
then the mill worked,
then the mill ground the corn.[30]

Note how this matches his nephew's style of recounting the events, all of them connected by "and then . . ." This organization is assimilated by repetition over a period of several days.

3. Children learn through sentences, not words, which are mere abstractions. Gouin indicates that he means complete thoughts or propositions, not actual sentences. He now had an explanation for why he had failed so miserably in spite of his valiant efforts. Memorizing a dictionary was nothing more than memorizing thirty thousand abstractions, which had no reality. He had worked only with his eyes, not with his ears, which in fact were the primary organs for learning.[31]

4. The verb is the key to communication. Ollendorff and all the others had seen the noun as the most important part of speech, but it is the verb that expresses chronological order and cause and effect. In a passage that perfectly represents Gouin's passionate and florid style, he gives us what amounts to an ode to the verb:

> How shall I trace what this revelation was to me? The verb! Why, it was the soul of the sentence. The verb was the foundation upon which the child, little by little, built up his sentence. The verb was the germ from which, piece by piece, sprang and blossomed forth the sentence itself. The verb! Why, when we have this element of the sentence, we have all; when this is lacking, we have nothing. The verb! This, then, was the link by which the child attached sentence to sentence, perception to perception, conception to conception.[32]

Gouin then set out to break down human experience into hundreds of descriptive sequences that could be listened to, acted out, and repeated by the learner. The key, as Gouin described it, was to recreate the events that make up one's "individuality," that is, the formative experiences that teach a child about life. This would truly be a natural method. Gouin decided that approximately fifty broad *series* (note the terminology here) of sequences could accomplish this. Each sequence in the series was called a *theme*.[33] The verb was the key constituent of any sentence in the theme; it led the way, we can say, to the needed vocabulary. The idea was that once the important verbs for a theme were learned, other nouns could be used to expand vocabulary.

For example:

> In the history of a single tree I shall have the history of all trees, and in the expression of the development of a single plant I shall have the expression of the development of all plants. I shall have nothing more to ask of the dictionary than certain substantives, the names of certain species.[34]

Here is Gouin's theme on an oak tree:

> The acorn sprouts.
> The oak plant takes root.
> The shoot sprouts out of the earth.
> The sap rises.
> The sapling throws out leaves.
> The stalk buds.
> The stalk blossoms.
> The flower blooms.
> The fruit forms.
> The fruit ripens.
> The fruit falls, &c, &c.[35]

Gouin realized that there were actually two types of language. The first is the one that makes up his series; it perceives the phenomena of the external world. This language supplies factual information, so he called this "objective language." This is the language that is at the heart of the Series Method. The other, which he named "subjective language," is that which judges, evaluates, appreciates, blames, and so on—in other words, it expresses opinions and emotions.[36]

To make the story briefer (not one of Gouin's strong points), we can say that students listen to the lesson as it is read and acted out by the teacher; they then repeat the sentences and actions themselves. This supplies the objective language. As the students carry out this routine, the teacher comments on the actions with subjective language, such as "I hope that," "Try to," "It is difficult," "It is important to," and so on.[37]

The system is not as brief as our discussion implies. The task of summarizing human experience into fifty series of the type illustrated would be just as absurd as it sounds. What Gouin had in mind was that each series consisted of *fifty or sixty* of these little themes, or activity chains, which in fact typically consisted of about twenty-five sentences. Any series, as a result, was made up of at least 1,250 sentences.[38] All together, a course would therefore consist of between sixty thousand and one hundred thousand sentences. Unlike Prendergast's method, they were short and simple; like Prendergast's, they relied on frequent repetition of vocabulary.

According to Gouin, students are capable of doing five themes per hour. That's an impressive 125 sentences. In typical Gouin style, he started with the desired results and then worked backward to calculate how much time could be allowed, just as he had done in memorizing the dictionary. To complete a course in one year, studying every single day except five, would require two and a half hours each day. This should be done in two equal sessions. To finish the course in just six months would mean a commitment of five hours per day of two sessions of two and a half hours.

## Success at Last

Gouin's story requires that success followed, of course. He eagerly returned to Berlin to see what results his insights would bring. He lodged with a local family, where he spent weeks teaching French to the family's children. Using the system meant translating the French sequences into German as well, so Gouin became both a pupil and the teacher. Gouin reports that success was immediate. He began to understand conversations and speak in a week. In two months he was dreaming in German. And within three months—so claims Gouin—after so many miserable experiences, and heroic but pathetic attempts at just trying to get a start in the language, Gouin was standing in front of a crowd of students *debating in German!* But it wouldn't be a Gouin story if it were only that . . .

The subject proposed (I can never forget it) was the comparison of the formula of Descartes, "Je pense, donc je suis," with the formula of Hegel, "Das reine Nichts und das reine Sein sind dentisch."[39] After a long and lively debate (in German, be it understood), the French student [Gouin, referring to himself] was proclaimed victor. I knew German![40]

It's a warm and happy ending to a story that would have revolutionized language teaching if its claims had stood up to scrutiny.

Whether we believe the entire story or not, we can surely identify with his odyssey in search of the best method to learn a foreign language. It's reassuring to hear that it happens to others; on the other hand it's discouraging to read of yet another "can't fail" method that supposedly unlocked the secrets of the mind but in the end couldn't live up to its promise. Gouin's tale also points out the failures of standard methods in the early days of the modern era. In a time of closer international relationships and increased immigration, a method that aimed to teach real language for practical purposes was required.

There is much to recommend Gouin's Series Method. He realized the primacy of speech and the importance of learning through listening.[41] He understood the validity of connecting language with personal experience. He was one of the very first to grasp the importance of the new science of psychology (another of the many scientific advances he admired from his day) and its support for using movement and actions to reinforce learning.

Looking back we can, at our peril, try to find echoes of earlier scholars. He reminds us of Comenius in the choice of an empirical approach that involves as many senses as possible, as well as the creation of materials that follow the course of a lifetime. His notion that all knowledge can be described in a limited number of categories was the foundation for the universal language of John Wilkins. Indeed, Gouin was a dreamer who would have been at home in the sixteen hundreds. His goal was to promote peace among nations through universal communication—the method was a variant of Wilkins's means, but for the same end.

Gouin was fortunate enough to see his method achieve considerable success. His story took place in the early 1850s, but it wasn't until 1880, when the method had slowly gained a favorable reputation, that he wrote *L'art d'enseigner et d'étudier les langues,* the complete guide. The method had several things going for it, being new, a genuine method (that is, having the necessary scientific aura) that met the new needs of the time while being really different from anything that had come before. Gouin set up a language school in Geneva and the method was widely used in other schools throughout Europe for several decades.

It's also not hard to find fault with the Series Method. It relies heavily on first- and third-person singular verb forms, for example. It's also difficult to imagine that everything can be reduced to a series, or that it can teach language that handles all the functions one needs in daily life. More important,

Gouin is painfully vague about how to teach advanced language, which reminds us of his own impatience with Ollendorff, who had not finished the job, Gouin asserted. The novelty of the Series Method itself was probably a drawback eventually; adult learners who were looking for a quick way to engage in daily life in a foreign country were unlikely to recognize the benefits of the method. However, the biggest obstacle was probably the time commitment. Like others before him who were so absorbed in their own methods, he seemed oblivious to the time and dedication required. The idea of a two-and-a-half-hour session that meant listening to, acting out, and repeating more than three hundred sentences cannot be the attractive prospect for a typical learner that Gouin imagined it was.

# 23 Esperanto
## A Successful "Constructed Language"

François Gouin was interested in the role of language as a means to promote international communication in Europe in the late eighteen hundreds. His solution was to find that one elusive way to make foreign-language learning easier in order to produce a world of polyglots. But there was another possibility from this hopeful period of history. Even if you could successfully study another foreign language or two, it still would leave you out of touch with all those in the rest of the world who didn't speak your several languages. The answer? Create a simple, easy-to-use language that can be learned everywhere.

It wasn't a new idea, as John Wilkins demonstrated in the seventeenth century. It's been speculated for centuries that the world would be a better place if we all had one common language: the ability to communicate with anyone and everyone, many believe, would lead to universal understanding and peace. It would allow more efficient transmission of ideas, leading to more balanced development throughout the world. It also would have the advantage of not being associated with any particular nationality. Intuitively, it just seems a great idea.

Esperanto was the creation of Ludwik Zamenhof (1859–1917), a Polish eye doctor born in the ethnically divided city of Bialystok:

> In Bialystok the inhabitants were divided into four distinct elements: Russians, Poles, Germans and Jews; each of these spoke their own language and looked on all the others as enemies. In such a town a sensitive nature feels more acutely than elsewhere the misery caused by language division and sees at every step that the diversity of languages is the first, or at least the most influential, basis for the separation of the human family into groups of enemies. I was brought up as an idealist; I was taught that all people were brothers, while outside in the street at every step I felt that there were no people, only Russians, Poles, Germans, Jews and so on.[1]

Zamenhof began work on a constructed language as a teenager and published his efforts in 1887. He called his language Esperanto, from the Latin word *spero*, the verb "to hope." The name means "one who hopes/is hoping" in Esperanto itself.[2] The language has several advantages compared to nature. It's perfectly phonetic, with fixed stress rules, so even a novice can sound out any word. And for people in Europe in 1887, a great deal of the vocabulary was recognizable, as the majority came from Latin and the rest from Germanic and eastern European languages. The grammar is simple and predictable, with all irregularities removed. Here are just a few examples:

1. Any verb in the present tense ends in -*as*; in the future, -*os*; and the past, -*is*.
2. Word order is generally subject-verb-object, but is fairly flexible because word functions are indicated by suffixes. All nouns end in -*o*, adjectives in -*a*, and adverbs in -*e*. When a noun is an object an -*n* is added.
3. Plurals add -*j* (pronounced like the letter *y* in English) to the end of the word, giving the suffix -*oj* (pronounced "oy"), or -*ojn* for plural direct objects.
4. There is a considerable list of prefixes and suffixes that affect the meaning of a word. The suffix -*et* serves to make a diminutive, or a smaller version of a noun: *domo* is "house," so *dometo* is a small house, or a cottage. The prefix *mal-* indicates the opposite of an adjective. *Varma* is "hot," so *malvarma* means "cold."
5. Yes or no questions begin with the marker *ĉu*, (*ĉ* = English *ch*, so it's pronounced as "chew").

Using the words *vi* ("you") and *paroli* ("to speak") and applying just some of these rules, we can see that *Ĉu vi parolas Esperanton?* is inquiring whether the listener speaks Esperanto.

Since the late eighteen hundreds, many artificial languages have been invented, but Esperanto is still the most successful. It's all relative, though. Very possibly you've heard of Esperanto, but chances are slim that you speak or read Esperanto or know anyone who does, which is good evidence that it was never able to assume its intended role as a truly international language.[3] It's impossible to pinpoint a single reason for the failure of any of the planned languages to conquer the world. Some obstacles are political, others are cultural or practical; in any case, it's a good idea that has simply never found enough supporters. Nevertheless, Esperanto has hundreds of thousands of devoted fans around the world, many clubs and organizations, an annual international conference, and an abundant literature. It certainly shows no signs of fading away.

# 24 Natural Methods
## Learning Like Children

The Series Method of Gouin was based on the supposedly "natural" way that everyone learns a first language. It wasn't the ultimate solution, of course, but it's indicative of the direction that *some* language teaching was heading. Many shared Gouin's opinion that in a modern world with increasing contact among nations, the need for spoken communication was more pressing than for the written. The conviction that the best way to acquire a new language should be based on nature continued to be productive. The natural methods, as developed by Lambert Sauveur, Maximilian Berlitz, and others, filled this need in the United States for some. Sauveur, with hope for reforming language teaching at all levels, aimed his materials at young educated learners. Berlitz, in contrast, directed his method at a wider population, especially a new class of language learners: immigrants, who were pouring into the United States and other countries. These learners, typically neither students nor well educated and older than the target audiences of the past, were concerned above all with plain oral communication.

## LAMBERT SAUVEUR

Biographical information on Lambert Sauveur (1826–1907) is sketchy.[1] A language teacher, he was born in France but lived and worked in Belgium before emigrating in the 1860s to the United States, where he met a German educator named Gottlieb Heness. Years before, Heness had spent time with the famous Swiss educational reformer Johann Pestalozzi,[2] whose ideas were strikingly reminiscent of Comenius. Pestalozzi preached a gentle, hands-on approach to learning that shunned routine memorization and stressed proceeding from the known to the unknown. Heness had experimented with these ideas while teaching German in the United States and was ready to open a language school. He recruited Sauveur to be the French specialist for the new school, which became a success after opening in Boston in 1869. Sauveur wrote several books for the school and talked at length about its philosophy.

Our system of teaching consists of learning to speak a living language without the aid of the grammar, and without a single word of English ever being spoken.[3]

The fundamental principle of the method is that one must always proceed from the known to the unknown, making the new words understood by using the ones that the student has already acquired, and without ever resorting to the English language.[4]

This admirable goal was achieved by a simple technique: conversation. The original textbook written by Sauveur for the school was called *Causeries avec mes élèves,* or "Chats with my students." And that's what it is—two hundred pages of imaginary conversations. Sauveur said it was easy to write; he simply imagined his students in front of him, and the questions and answers that would arise poured out onto paper.

In the following example showing the first part of the seventh lesson, note the friendly tone; nothing said is meant to be taken very seriously.

The meals are so important for conversation!—*There is no conversation at the table, monsieur.*—Excuse me, my friend, in France we speak a lot at the table. We enjoy the conversation more than the food.—*Do you speak French at the table?*—Of course, we speak only French.—At what time do you have breakfast, madame?—*I have breakfast at half past seven.*—And you, mademoiselle?—*I have breakfast at seven.*—And you, my friend?—*I have breakfast at half past nine.*—That's very late. You must get up late as well.—*I get up at nine.*—Oh! Lazybones, you lose the best and most precious hours of the day.—*No, monsieur. I get up earlier than mademoiselle.*—What?—*Mademoiselle has breakfast half an hour later than I do.*—I think that there is a misunderstanding. Show me with your fingers at what time you get up. [The student holds up several fingers.] Ah, there we are. You are showing me six and yet you are saying nine.[5]

Lessons lasted two hours. Sauveur claimed that in the very first lesson, before the textbook was used, students assimilated through demonstration and question-and-answer more than one hundred words.[6] By the time students were ready to make use of the textbook, a conversation such as the one above was practiced only after many hours of preparation. Conversations, then, were intended primarily as reinforcement rather than as a means to introduce material.

At a glance, it's not easy to find logic in the titles of the forty-nine lessons. The first few are on the parts of the body (easily demonstrated and acted out), while the rest are a mixed lot. For example, lesson twenty-seven is entitled "God," followed immediately by lesson twenty-eight, "The Cricket." But in fact, each is actually more of a starting point than a restricted topic. "The Cricket," for instance, which tells the story of an insect envious of a butterfly, veers off to a brief discussion of suicide, among other matters: Is the cricket in despair?—*Yes.*—Aren't you afraid that he will commit suicide?—*No, man alone kills himself.*—Alas, yes! It's a strange sign of his superiority.[7]

What's a teacher to do with such a method and material? In a lengthy, oddly placed footnote in the middle of lesson five ("Hair"), Sauveur answers a teacher who had asked him just before the book went to press if his texts wouldn't be too much, too soon for the students. His reply tells us a great deal about how he envisioned that the book be used.

> One must not lose sight of the fact that I always assume that the student is led by an attentive and intelligent teacher. No book can replace oral practice completely. Moreover, my work is but a portion of the lesson that is to be given: it can guide the teacher, suggesting ten questions for each one that I ask, as well as inspire the pupil, prompt him to ask questions, and awaken his curiosity. It is all the Socratic system. If the teacher spends eight hours on one of my lessons, it will be time well spent. I am also asked if the student must read my book with the teacher. My dear teaching colleagues, I have neither the right nor the conceit to dictate anything to you. Put your experience alongside mine, and do what you judge to be best for your pupils. However, if you wish to follow my advice on this point, do this at the beginning: give the book to your students to read at home in preparation of your teaching, but in the classroom forbid them to open it: their ears alone should be occupied. When they are before you, ask them a hundred questions on the lesson, and if you want, read them a page of the book, but make them understand all of it without ever speaking one word of English. Therein is the secret and the condition of success. It is a revolution in teaching, but it is necessary.[8]

Nevertheless, grammar and translation, those two activities that seemed out of place in this natural and conversational system, were in fact welcome at higher levels. Sauveur even wrote a book on grammar,[9] but managed to model it on his other works. Instead of the expected isolated list of dry rules, it contains conversations about grammar that give traditional information. Full of examples from literature, it's like attending an informal lecture by a favorite teacher. It's a big step from the "catechistic" (question-and-answer format) pseudo-conversations of Donatus and his successors. Sauveur's main concern was student comprehension; as many scholars before him had noted, grammar was often something memorized but not understood. Sauveur, on the other hand, once again saw his students in front of him in his mind and simply imagined when they would ask for clarification.

Sauveur was responsible for the success of the Natural Method, as it became known, but he preferred to give credit where it was due, to his colleague Gottlieb Heness, to whom he attributed its creation.[10] Sauveur also cited several historical inspirations for his teaching, including Montaigne's experience as a child, the question-and-answer method of Socrates, and even the Port-Royal schools.[11]

Sauveur and Heness did very well in their business and their Natural Method became widely known within a decade.[12] But it wasn't the only "natural" or direct method of the day, and it wasn't even the most successful. That claim belongs to the work of our next personality.

## MAXIMILIAN BERLITZ

Suppose you had to learn a new language and you had to learn it as quickly as possible. Among your several options, chances are good you would consider a name that is synonymous with foreign-language teaching and learning: Berlitz. The company founded by Maximilian Berlitz in 1878 is thriving today with more than 470 centers in over seventy countries.[13] At the risk of sounding like paid advertising, we would almost certainly agree that Berlitz is the most famous name in the history of language teaching.

First, just a little background on the man himself.[14] Maximilian Berlitz (1852–1921) arrived in the United States in 1870 from his native Germany. Already an experienced language instructor, he planned to find work teaching the several languages that he knew, in the only way that he knew: Grammar-Translation. Eventually he was the proprietor (and sole faculty member) of a little school in Rhode Island. When he advertised for a French professor, he chose a young man named Nicholas Joly.[15] The official version is that Joly arrived just at the time that Berlitz fell ill from overwork. Berlitz was dismayed to find that Joly spoke no English (his hiring was based on a beautifully written letter of application in French), but unable to go on, Berlitz reluctantly left the French lessons in the charge of Joly after telling him to just point and get by any way he could. When Berlitz at last returned six weeks later, expecting to find the school in turmoil, he was astonished to find the students engaging in lively question-and-answer sessions and expressing themselves with surprisingly good accents. He realized in fact that they had accomplished more than they would have under his own guidance. And he understood that here was the inspiration for a new (to him, at least) method of teaching a foreign language: no translation, minimal grammar, just spoken communication in a pleasant environment.

It's a good story (and mercifully short after Gouin's tale) and there is no real need to question it. However, it does have a certain fanciful ring to it: Berlitz was completely out of touch with his own school for *six weeks*? We get the point, though. Just like his contemporaries Sauveur and Heness, who were active just up the road in Boston, and Gouin in France, Berlitz thought that he had found the superior method of teaching a new language by resorting to the way of nature.

The fundamentals of Berlitz's method are really almost the same as those articulated by Sauveur, so there is no need for much elaboration.[16] As with others who advocated a natural method, it was justified as being the way that a child learns to speak. The starting point was "a constant and exclusive use of the foreign language and direct association of perception and thought with the foreign sound and speech."[17] This meant that vocabulary was taught solely through demonstration and dramatization. Abstract terms were no exception; they had to be communicated through actions or previously acquired vocabulary. The focus was on speaking and aural comprehension, and grammar was taught through examples, usage, and analogy. The vocabulary and grammar points were carefully chosen to enable the learner to proceed from the known to the unknown.[18] Written materials were not used to introduce information but only to reinforce and review what had been covered in class. They presented the information in new contexts.[19]

Much of his success resulted from his ability to meet the needs of the immigrant population with a somewhat less sophisticated approach than Sauveur's. What *was* genuinely different and innovative about Berlitz's method was how he systematized it. Like Gouin (and unlike Sauveur), he had the vision and business talents to turn his method into a lasting enterprise. Unlike Gouin's venture, Berlitz's has lasted well over a century. The Berlitz method, we might say, took the "art" out of teaching: the system itself was the secret of success, not the instructor. His young teachers were typically transient; that is, they tended to be just passing through. Nevertheless, they were educated native speakers (an absolute requirement) who received training in the method and were expected to adhere to a detailed and carefully laid out program at all times. The result was a true system; a student could stop his or her lessons at one center and pick them up at another without any confusion or interruption. We've seen how the public liked language learning to be systematic; Ollendorff is a perfect example. Berlitz's system gave the undertaking a veneer of respectability to the public. It was reassuring. And clearly it works in many situations.

## SUMMARY

Gouin, Sauveur, Heness, and Berlitz all had success with methods of teaching that were supposedly based on imitating a child's learning. Each thought it was an original insight, and Gouin's at least was indeed innovative. But if we look back to Holyband in sixteenth-century England, we see an example of essentially the same thing. Inspired by a wave of immigration, Holyband and others came up with conversation manuals and used a direct method that forbade the students' language in the classroom. Sauveur even duplicated the lighthearted nature of Holyband's conversations.

Natural or direct methods worked relatively well for their audiences in reaching the goal of spoken communication. Why didn't they spread to the schools? For the methods of Sauveur and Gouin, a major reason is that they required a lot of work and a special talent in the teachers. For the Berlitz method, native speakers were required. Several other factors were in play, all based on expectations. First, the audiences were different. The written form of a language has almost always been more respected than the spoken, so families continued to expect their children to be taught the "proper" form of the language. Related to this was the notion that learning through often playful conversation was not rigorous enough; it seemed unacademic—a prejudice as old as Aristotle, who, you may recall, had claimed that "amusement does not go with learning—learning is a painful process."[20] This has been called the "trivialization" factor.[21] In fact, these methods went squarely against the intellectual current of the latter half of the eighteen hundreds. In an age where science and system were held in the highest regard, the success of natural methods was ironic. The rational grammarians such as du Marsais and the Port-Royalists, or even the Modistae from the twelve hundreds, were arguably more scientific than our scholars here. Psychology was emerging in the late eighteen hundreds, yet there was no mention of it in these methods. Gouin, Saveur, Heness, and Berlitz, in contrast, emphasized that their ways were really just common sense. The fact that Berlitz alone turned his method into a true system undoubtedly explains his lasting success compared to the others.

# Part III
# Modern Times

# 25 The Reform Movement
## The Start of Modern Times

A great deal was going on in the field of language teaching around 1880. We've just looked at the natural or direct methods. We now come to the Reform Movement, and with it, the dawn of a new era—a cliché, but descriptive in this case. For more than four thousand years, we've been able to look upon our ancestors' efforts as curious, inspiring, misguided, strangely uninformed or illogical, or even remarkably insightful; in any case they most likely strike us as one thing: quaint. They were definitely the old days, and we view them as we do any period of long-ago history—with emotional detachment. The Reform Movement marks the early days of the modern era; from here on it will be much more familiar to us.

Actually, the Grammar-Translation Method was reformist, but the term is reserved for the early "modern" scholars. It could also include the Natural Method proponents more deservedly than Ahn and Ollendorff, but again, the term "Reform Movement" refers properly to a specific shift that began in the 1880s, whose key points were an emphasis on the study of connected texts and the use of an oral approach. The former point was inspired by the new science of psychology and the notion that items having a logical connection are more easily remembered. The oral approach was supported by the budding linguistic branch (that is, "science") of phonetics. Once again, it's essential to keep in mind the position that science in all its guises held in the minds of people in the eighteen hundreds, because admittedly it is difficult today to see how phonetics could play such a role and have such an influence. The new sciences of psychology and phonetics gave reform efforts a credibility that would otherwise have been lacking.

There were several scholars (and for a change, we really do mean scholars—they were affiliated with universities) who can be given credit for this movement. They came from all over Europe, but an Englishman eventually became the face of the movement. Henry Sweet (1845–1912), the leading figure in phonetics of his day, was the inspiration for the character of Professor Henry Higgins in George Bernard Shaw's play *Pygmalion*, better known in its film adaptation, *My Fair Lady*. Higgins bets that he can teach a poor, young working-class woman the speech and manners of a member of the upper classes (and succeeds, of course). We'll come back to Sweet later, but for the moment it's sufficient to note that he wrote some pioneering works in phonetics and phonetic transcription in the 1870s and believed that language teaching had a lot to learn from this field.

## VIËTOR'S PAMPHLET: "LANGUAGE TEACHING MUST START AFRESH"

It's rare that one can find a precise starting point of a historical shift, but we can say that the catalyst for the Reform Movement was a German pamphlet published by language teacher Wilhelm Viëtor in 1882.[1] Language teaching was in need of updating; that much was clear. Viëtor expressed the dissatisfaction of the day. It was widely lamented then that German students were being given too much work, and Viëtor laid most of the blame on language study, which he felt took up a disproportionate amount of time. If the results had at least been satisfactory, it might have been considered a necessary hardship, but in fact, after years of study, students were woefully ignorant of the workings of their native language and incapable of functioning in a foreign one. That certainly sounds familiar. So do the reasons given by Viëtor. Study of one's first language in Germany in 1882 typically began with the parts of speech and moved on to memorization of useless vocabulary and grammar rules that meant nothing to the students.[2] We don't need to go into details because by now we understand. This was no way to learn a language. Nevertheless, this same tired, ineffective way of teaching the first language was somehow thought to be the best way to teach a foreign language as well—and the results were predictable. "And even if you actually succeeded in stuffing the pupils' heads with the best grammars and the most comprehensive dictionaries, they still would not know the language!"[3] (We can't help but wonder if he knew the story of Gouin's travails.) Success, said Viëtor in a clear reference to the Grammar-Translation mania, will not come until it is realized that language is not just letters and words and isolated sentences. The foundation of any language is its sounds, and the first step is their mastery. Thus, what was new in Viëtor's book was the emphasis on pronunciation. The poor standards were shocking enough for him to devote quite a few pages to pointing out examples of the errors that students made; his point ultimately was that one cannot learn correct pronunciation from a book. "As Sweet said in the Preface to his *Handbook of Phonetics* (1877): 'If our present wretched system of studying modern languages is ever to be reformed, it must be on the basis of preliminary training in general phonetics.'"[4]

In a remarkable statement that shows how little language teaching had advanced in real-life classrooms in fifteen hundred years, Viëtor compared the typical methods of 1882 to those of our old friend Donatus of the fourth century. Current methods used in the language-teaching classroom were no better than the "Donatus approach," whose goal was above all the learning of grammar and vocabulary. As described by an 1881 pamphlet cited by Viëtor,[5] think of a cabinetmaker teaching an apprentice how to make a cabinet. First, he would lay out all the types of wood used by a cabinetmaker and classify them according to everything from color to hardness. Then he would assemble all the woodworking tools, and again sort them by function, size, and so on. The apprentice would eventually become expert in describing all the essentials for constructing a cabinet, but all without ever having made a single mark on a piece of wood. Thus, instead of engaging in real language use, students memorized grammar and vocabulary, and then translated dozens of illogical, irrelevant, silly sentences on the same grammar point. The rallying cry, Viëtor said, becomes "Death to rules and isolated sentences! The basis of all language teaching must be the connected text!"[6]

Yes, connected text, no matter what that might be: it could be a story, a rhyme, a puzzle, or a song for instance. Here is an example of a lesson plan:

1. There is no preparation needed by the students.
2. With the students' books closed, the teacher reads the text as many times as needed and makes any desired translations.
3. With books open, either the teacher or a student reads the text.
4. With books open, the teacher asks questions on the text, even in the students' own language if necessary. Students answer these in complete sentences.
5. Students try to retell the story orally in the target language.
6. In writing, students answer the same questions as before, first on the board, and then copied into their copybooks.

The lesson should have no written translation from the first into the second language, and there should be no explicit grammar. Only the foreign language is to be spoken in class. There is to be no written homework at all; the only work for the home is perhaps a poem or other short piece of prose to learn (to be performed at home in front of the mother or sisters, interestingly).

Perhaps it's fair to look at it this way: until the early nineteenth century, connected texts had been the rule, but this involved using authentic classical texts, such as a letter by Cicero, and the consequent study of grammar rules and peculiar vocabulary. This gave way to Grammar-Translation, which solved the problem of irrelevant sentences (that is, those that were out of date and on topics beyond the grasp of the students) and, despite the method's name, grammar overload. But Grammar-Translation had eventually returned to the ageless concern for grammatical minutiae. Reform in the later eighteen hundreds, however, was based on emphasizing oral work, either through conversational natural methods or through controlled oral work, based on phonetics. As different as they were, they had strong philosophical similarities.

An English teacher in Germany named Hermann Klinghardt put some other new ideas to the test in a year-long experiment with a group of fourteen-year-old boys in 1887 and 1888.[7] Using a Henry Sweet textbook and a controlled oral approach based on Sweet's suggestions of using phonetic transcription, the first ten hours of class time focused exclusively on pronunciation and the learning of Sweet's phonetic notation system. The class then went on to one of the many texts by Sweet. After one semester, Klinghardt switched the students from the phonetic notation to the real spelling. They managed the transition just fine. They continued in their new reader, and by the end of the year they were making excellent progress in their writing activities, but were especially strong in oral work, just as had been expected and desired. The experiment was an unqualified success. It's clear that they preferred this to their French studies, in which they were using a textbook by the internationally known Karl Ploetz, author of Grammar-Translation books of the worst kind.[8]

## HENRY SWEET AND THE PRACTICAL STUDY OF LANGUAGES

But let's get back to Henry Sweet. Giving just a summary of the Reform Movement leaves out many worthy scholars, but Sweet's career epitomizes it all the way through. In 1899, he published *The Practical Study of Languages: A Guide for Teachers and Learners*, a landmark work in the teaching and studying of languages. Its fame rests more on its content rather than the effect it had; it was not the catalyst for radical change that Sweet perhaps hoped for, but it had a ripple effect through the work of others in the new century.

For us, though, what matters most is how the book signals the onset of modern times. It's very easily and quickly seen: all we have to do is compare its contents with any of the other works we've looked at until now, even (or maybe we should say "especially") those of Sweet's contemporaries, like Gouin or Sauveur. It was an ambitious work that covered a very impressive array of topics, not simply classroom procedures. It even included such high-minded matters as deciphering unwritten languages and writings in unfamiliar scripts. The book was an attempt to give a comprehensive view of the entire field of language study, with an audience ranging from travelers to missionaries to self-study students. Starting with Sweet's description of the purpose of the book, the difference between this approach and what has come before is like comparing an automobile with a horse and buggy:

> This book is intended as a guide to the practical study of languages. Its object is, first, to determine the general principles on which a rational method of learning foreign languages should be based, and then to consider the various modifications these general principles undergo in their application to different circumstances and different classes of learners.[9]

*Figure 25.1* Henry Sweet: leader of the Reform Movement and model for Professor Henry Higgins of the film *My Fair Lady* and the play *Pygmalion* by George Bernard Shaw.

My object is both to show how to make the best of existing conditions, and to indicate the lines of abstract research and practical work along which the path of progress lies.[10]

That last phrase is a novelty—abstract research? It's not a theme we'd expect from earlier writers, who were always looking for that magic method that would end the debate and solve the problem of language learning forever.

Sweet realized the foolishness of this quest. It's not a matter of finding the secret; it's a question of using logic, psychology, and science to establish the foundations of methodology. Only then is it proper to focus on specifics.

> In the present multiplicity of methods and text-books, it is absolutely necessary for real and permanent progress that we should come to some sort of agreement on general principles. Until this is attained—until every one recognizes that there is no royal road to languages, and that no method can be a sound one which does not fulfill certain definite conditions—the public will continue to run after one new method after the other, only to return disappointed to the old routine.[11]

Of course, by "this multiplicity of methods" he meant, above all, the works of the leading figures of the eighteen hundreds. Sweet had a lot to say about them, and it wasn't very collegial.

> Ollendorff, Ahn, Prendergast, Gouin—to mention only a few—have all had their day. They have all failed to perform what they promised; after promising impossibilities they have all turned out to be on the whole no better than the older methods.[12]

His main complaint was their reliance on discontinuous sentences, which violated the learning principle of associationism that was preached by psychology.[13] It's ironic, really, that this fundamental technique of the Grammar-Translation Method, which had been introduced as a way to promote authenticity, was now condemned as conveying silly and irrelevant language. He had especially sharp words for Prendergast, giving several examples of Mastery Series sentences that he found absurd.[14] Furthermore he found the variety of language to be restricted, no matter whose method it was. The constructors of artificial sentences like Ahn, Ollendorff, and Prendergast neglected idiomatic language and relied on repetition of specific grammar points.[15] Ollendorff received the curious honor of having an insulting adjective formed from his name: Sweet dismissed with disdain an example of another author as "Ollendorffian."[16] Sweet called the practice of teaching through endless exercises and translations into the second language (a skill that requires a high level of expertise) the "arithmetical fallacy," that is, merely accumulating information without knowing its proper usage, which in the end adds up to nothing. As for Gouin, a fellow advocate of an oral approach, he created a method that was heavily dependent on concrete words in severely limited grammatical situations. "In its present form the Gouin method is incapable of teaching the pupil to say, 'I think so,' or 'I would rather not do it,' or, indeed to express anything that falls under the categories of emotion or intellect."[17]

What Sweet called for was a more orderly and systematic approach, proposing the following requirements for the foundation of a rational method:[18] (1) a careful selection of the language to be used in the materials, (2) a limitation of the amount of the language, (3) an arrangement of the materials for the four skills, (4) a logical order of presentation of the materials in terms of difficulty. If we compare any of the previous methods, whether the literature-based classical method, or Grammar-Translation, or the natural methods based on conversation, we find them lacking in at least one of these points. Grammar-Translation seems to come the closest to passing the test, but its flaw lies in the first requirement; although the language was indeed carefully selected, its artificiality causes it to fail.

While Sweet agreed with other reformers in rejecting the complete methods derived from Grammar-Translation, he disagreed with them on the role of grammar. He realized that the situations of a young child and a school-age learner are not the same. The young child's learning is a slow and often inefficient process that starts with a blank mind. He or she is also learning the concepts of language at the same time, an utterly different situation from that of a second-language student. On the contrary, an older learner has analytical abilities that can be exploited with grammars and dictionaries. He or she also has powers of concentration unknown to an infant. He certainly was not promoting the study of grammar rules in the way favored historically. In his view grammar was an aid to forming psychological associations: "The sole problem of grammar is to make these unconscious associations into conscious and analytic ones by defining and analyzing them, and stating them as briefly and clearly as possible by means of a suitable terminology."[19]

For Sweet, the practical study of languages has to be scientific—a combination of psychology and phonetics. Psychology is obvious to us; his emphasis on phonetics is somewhat puzzling today, however.[20] He points out rightly that subtle sound differences within a language can be significant (compare, for example, *sheep* and *ship*); nevertheless, he believes that learning by imitation doesn't work, and that unfamiliar sounds are better learned by analysis. Transcription leads to better pronunciation, especially in languages written nonphonetically, which in turn leads to better aural comprehension. Experience shows, he adds, as do experiments such as Klinghardt's, that students learn to read and write the real spelling without any problem when transcription is abandoned. In other words, it's easier to learn the written form of a word you already know orally than to learn the pronunciation of a word whose spelling you have memorized. It's the way children do it: speak before spelling.[21]

His other recurring emphasis, as we read in Viëtor, is on the need for materials to be presented in connected texts.

> The main foundation of the practical study of language should be connected texts, whose study must, of course, be accompanied by grammatical analysis.[22] . . . It is only in connected texts that the language itself can be given with each word in a natural and adequate context.[23]

But what kinds of connected texts? Sweet believed that students find the new more interesting than the familiar, but that linguistically it's better to deal with the familiar, so it's a balancing act. The best are

> texts in which the meanings of words and their constructions unfold themselves easily from a simple context of progressive difficulty, in which there is repetition enough to help the memory, and yet variety enough to keep the attention on the alert.[24]

In advice that only Sweet could have given, he says, "be dull and commonplace, but not too much so."[25]

There are three types of text: (1) descriptions, which are the easiest because they generally use present verbs in the third person only, and tend to be of familiar things; (2) narratives, which also are in the third person, but most commonly use the past tense; and (3) dialogues, which are the most difficult because they use more colloquial language, include all persons and tenses, and show less logical continuity.[26] Examples of topics for descriptions include nature (earth, sea, sun, seasons, months, days, and colors), and humans (races, tools and weapons, food, houses, clothes, and language). Narratives can be anecdotes, biographies, or tales of daily life, for example; the essential requirement is that they not be too long. Riddles and proverbs, commonly found in textbooks of the day, are to be avoided for lack of connectedness; moreover, proverbs frequently use archaic language.

Was Sweet being revolutionary? We might say that in fact he was advocating a middle way between the uncontrollable natural methods and the more traditional and artificial methods. What was indeed revolutionary was that language teaching was finally being transformed from an art to a science.

# 26  Two Reports on the State of Language Teaching

## THE TWENTIETH CENTURY UNTIL 1950

The introduction to the early twentieth century was, we dare say, written at the beginning of the chapter on the Reform Movement. In just a few years, language teaching emerged from its ancient past as an art into a modern discipline striving to be a science. We'll begin with two reports from the United States on language-teaching practices. One reason is that they provide a picture of the state of the field (in one place, at least). The more important reason they're discussed here, though, will be seen in later chapters, in which we'll move to the esteemed Harold Palmer, then look at the curious case of Basic English, and follow with the Second World War and some of its effects on language teaching.

## THE REPORT OF THE "COMMITTEE OF TWELVE" (1898)

In the United States, a distinguished group of scholars from the Modern Language Association carried out a study in 1898 at the request of the National Educational Association, which was gathering recommendations on the teaching of all academic subjects. The Committee of Twelve, as they called themselves, was asked to create guidelines for courses in French and German at the high school level. Reflecting the changing state of language teaching, it's an impressive and sober work of about one hundred pages that quickly states its purpose, considers the options, and sets objectives. Briefly, the Committee considered the following methods in use at the end of the nineteenth century to be their options, noted along with a summary of their remarks. These comments take into consideration the situation of the typical American student and teacher at the end of the nineteenth century.

1. The Grammar Method:[1] This was what they called Grammar-Translation. By 1898 it was still to be found in a few classrooms, but it was generally looked upon with disfavor, they said. Nevertheless, the Committee was impressed by certain aspects, such as its benefits for training the memory

and the improvement of young persons' reasoning skills. Unfortunately, it neglected to broaden the students' minds, especially because of the lack of literature. Moreover, it was simply boring, thus disregarding the decree of "modern pedagogy" that the best work in any field was achieved only with the goodwill and interest of the learner.

2. The Natural Method (The Direct Method):[2] The Committee conceded that oral work most readily aroused interest in a foreign language. However, they sniffed, the Natural Method was not worthy of consideration as a method: "It is a principle, an impulse, rather than a plan," whose success depends excessively on the personality of the teacher. "Too often the results . . . are a rapid, but unintelligible pronunciation, the fluent use of incorrect forms, and, worst of all, a most discouraging self-complacency." They also criticized the assumption that an infant's way of acquiring a first language was applicable to students, given their more developed reasoning skills and greater life experience. That's enough abuse to direct against anything, but the Committee *really* disliked this method Additionally, they charged,

> It provides little discipline for the intelligence; it affords only the poorest kind of mnemonic [i.e., memory] training; it favors vagueness of thought and imprecision of expression, and, finally, it sacrifices the artistic interest of language study to a so-called 'practical' one.[3]

The one kind comment they made noted that it unquestionably held the attention of students. It's easy to see what the committee valued in the classroom. They at least allowed that it might be useful in the future as an enlivening technique in a classroom, but certainly not as a method.

3. The Psychological Method:[4] This is Gouin's Series Method with some improvements from Victor Bétis, who had co-translated Gouin's book into English. This method, surprisingly, found considerable favor with the Committee. The most attractive to the students, it trains the memory and gives the students a considerable vocabulary in a relatively short time. Its drawbacks are a reduced attention to judgment formation, reading (i.e., literature), and pronunciation.

4. The Phonetic Method:[5] This method was proposed by the Reformists, including Viëtor in his famous tract. The Committee praised its scientific approach to the subject. However, noting the realities of living in an isolated nation where few people traveled abroad and the majority of students studied a language for a shorter time than in Europe, it regretfully concluded that there simply was not enough time in American schools for the method to fulfill its potential. Moreover, it neglects the essential component of literature.

5. The Reading Method:[6] The Reading Method is, well—the Reading Method. "The title explains itself." As uninspiring as it may seem to us, it was the answer to the Committee's quest, fulfilling the needs of the average American secondary school student better than the other methods reviewed. The most important need perceived, as is clear by now, was literature. The greatest value in studying a foreign language, given the situation of the United States, was in learning about people of another country as well as their literature.[7] The method as seen by the Committee called for reading plenty of texts from the beginning, accompanied by "abundant" translation practice. It differed from more traditional times, though, because grammar was seen as a tool for understanding the reading rather than as a mental exercise.

> The great advantage of the [Reading Method] is that it quickly enables the student to read French and German literature—not with the complete appreciation that only an all-around command of the language can give, but with the same kind of intelligence and enjoyment with which good classical scholars read Latin. Indirectly, it helps the pupil to form a good style, and to increase the volume and precision of his English vocabulary; it cultivates the taste by dwelling upon delicacies of expression; it exercises the memory through the enforced retention of words and idioms; it trains the linguistic sense by calling attention to the points of resemblance and difference in various tongues; and the exact fitting of phrase to thought forms an excellent discipline for the judgment.[8]

The drawback of the Reading Method was its lesser appeal to students, especially compared to oral methods. Just as important, probably, was that for the teachers it eventually became quite dull: according to the Committee, it was too easy!

The Committee envisaged a three-level system that could be taught in a period of two to four years. The levels were simply elementary, intermediate, and advanced. Objectives were set for each level, as this example demonstrates:

> At the end of the advanced course the pupil should be able to read at sight, with the help of a vocabulary of special or technical expressions, difficult French not earlier than that of the seventeenth century; to write in French a short essay on some simple subject connected with the works read; to put into French a passage of easy English prose, and to carry on a simple conversation in French.[9]

A more advanced ability to speak the language would be commendable, no doubt, but would require far more time in the classroom than was practicable. Therefore, the spoken language was subordinated to the goal of reading.[10]

## THE COLEMAN REPORT (1929)

Another study on foreign-language teaching in the United States was carried out between 1924 and 1927 by a group of academics led by a Professor Coleman; the report informally took his name. This work examined more aspects of teaching than did the Committee of Twelve: it considered "the objectives of teaching, the content of the courses, the organization of classes and the methods of instruction."[11] The Coleman Committee had one singular advantage over the Committee of Twelve: the twentieth century brought with it much better recordkeeping, so the group was awash in statistics. As a result, the report was full of tables and charts, and three times as long as the report from 1898.[12]

The Coleman Report is actually much better known than the work of the Committee of Twelve (it's all relative, of course—the former is usually summarized in a sentence or two and the latter is more or less forgotten), but three hundred pages instead of one hundred simply meant that they had more arguments for the same conclusions: "It is obvious that practice in hearing, in speaking, and in writing the foreign language in most classrooms during the first two years must be regarded as ancillary to the development of reading ability."[13]

Two years was the standard amount of time spent studying a foreign language in high school,[14] and in those days the great majority of students didn't pursue university studies. The Coleman Committee commented again on the isolation of the United States and the difficulty of traveling abroad. In fact, "a very large majority of the modern language teachers in the United States have neither traveled nor studied in countries where [their specialist] languages are spoken."[15] To be precise, 71 percent of foreign-language teachers surveyed had never been to *any* foreign country.[16]

As did the Committee of Twelve, the Coleman group acknowledged that the trend had for several years been moving toward a more direct approach in which students "are trained to understand the foreign language through the eye or through the ear or through both, without the interposition of the mother tongue."[17] Unlike their predecessors, the Coleman group praised the results of oral work, but nevertheless reiterated that it was not practicable: the principal reasons were a lack of trained teachers, class sizes, uneven results among classes, difficulties in testing, and of course, the inevitable neglect of reading.[18]

The conclusions of both the Committee of Twelve and the Coleman Report are certainly understandable, given the realities of early twentieth-century America. Within a few years, however, this emphasis on reading abruptly ceased to meet the needs of American education. The Second World War changed everything. But we'll come back to that at the proper time.

# 27 Harold Palmer
## A Modern Teacher

## HIS LIFE

Harold Palmer (1877–1949) may receive high praise from historians, but he's generally not a household name among language teachers today. His is another interesting life story, but unlike that of Comenius, has a happy ending, and in contrast to Gouin's, doesn't need artistic license and tall tales. Palmer was simply a successful, widely traveled, and influential scholar of language teaching.

Just a few years earlier, in the days of Gouin and Berlitz, a language scholar's academic output was, we might conclude, rather limited in focus. It typically consisted of a book or two or three all based on a method (usually "the" method that would solve forever the problem of learning a foreign language), or perhaps a work presenting the author's thoughts on the best educational practices. It's not until we arrive at the Reform Movement that we find authors who produce multiple works on various aspects of language teaching. Nevertheless, their concern was frequently phonetic or historical, and of limited interest today.[1] With Palmer, in striking contrast, we find a long list of titles that shows precisely how far the field had progressed in just a few years. Among them are *The Scientific Study and Teaching of Languages, The Principles of Language-Study, The Teaching of Oral English, The New Method Grammar, English Intonation with Systematic Exercises, A Grammar of Spoken English, Colloquial French: Fluency Exercises,* and *A Beginner's English-French Dictionary.*

Palmer's father was a teacher before establishing himself as a local businessman and newspaper publisher in a town in Kent on the southeast English coast. Palmer's grandfather had also been an educator.[2] As a young man, inspired by his love of languages and desire for adventure, Palmer moved to Verviers, Belgium, in 1902, where he took up the teaching of English. His first job was with a school whose methods were Berlitz in all but name. This was Palmer's first encounter with the Direct Method, and he was tremendously impressed. Soon he established his own school in Verviers, where he became deeply interested in experimenting with a variety of methods. He and his teacher friends read and discussed the works of contemporary scholars, including Sweet. Palmer made extensive use of phonetic transcription and became a prominent member of the International Phonetic Association. He also developed the idea that language teaching could be more effective with a carefully controlled vocabulary; this was to remain a fundamental interest throughout his life. In the following years he devised lists of essential English vocabulary that he applied to writing materials, and he started a dictionary that used only the most common words of the language.³ Within a few years, Palmer and his friends realized that the search for the "'one true standard and universal method' was misguided, and that what was needed instead was a principled basis for the (selection of) methods, in other words a 'science of linguistic pedagogy.'"⁴

By 1914, Palmer had a Belgian wife and a young daughter. Much to the surprise of the residents of Verviers, the Germans invaded their town at the outbreak of the First World War, making it one of the earliest casualties. After a frightful six weeks in hiding (the Germans were arresting British citizens and sending them off to prison camps), the family managed to escape to England with only the clothes on their backs.

Palmer found work at local universities in London, where his work in phonetics led to an interest in intonation and substitution drills. In 1917 he published a landmark work, *The Scientific Study and Teaching of Languages*. Four years later, there appeared a less academic, more accessible version of his ideas, *The Principles of Language-Study*, which we'll look at in detail in a minute. Thanks to his growing reputation as an innovative expert in language teaching, he received an exceptional invitation. He was offered a position as a "linguistic adviser" to the Japanese Department of Education, with the emphasis on reforming methods of teaching English in Japanese middle schools. This was a wonderful opportunity for Palmer. He accepted and ended up staying in Japan for fourteen productive years, during which he wrote dozens of works. Probably his most significant achievement was the creation of a series of materials that made use of his extensive research into vocabulary frequency.

Palmer stayed on in Japan until 1936, when he returned to the United Kingdom as a well-known figure in applied linguistics. The language-teaching research institute he founded in Tokyo in the 1920s is still going strong.⁵ Very early on, Palmer had founded a journal for the institute, probably inspired by late nineteenth-century journals for the Reform Movement. The *Bulletin*, as it was simply called, was certainly one of the very first periodicals devoted to everyday language pedagogy, though its content and readership were firmly based in Japan. When Palmer left the country, editorship was taken over by A. S. Hornby, another distinguished scholar in our field who spent much of his career in Japan. Immediately after the Second World War, Hornby founded what became the premier language-teaching journal internationally, *English Language Teaching*, which is known now as *ELT Journal*. Thus, Palmer played an indirect but very influential role in the journal's creation.[6] Palmer's health deteriorated during the last decade of his life, but he remained active in writing and lecturing until his death in 1949.

## THE PRINCIPLES OF LANGUAGE-STUDY: SUMMARY

*The Principles of Language-Study,* published in 1921, is an easy, pleasant book to read, which was exactly what Palmer had in mind. It was only forty years since Gouin had written about trying every language-learning method known to civilization, it seems, in his quest for the true way to acquire a foreign language. In contrast, the ideas contained in the *Principles* sound as though they were written only recently. Although we may not agree with all of it, it's not difficult to imagine that this is the work of a recent author.

Palmer is utopianly optimistic about the course of language teaching. Inspired by the events of recent decades and the dawn of a scientific approach, he takes it for granted that foreign-language teaching will evolve and improve.[7] He compares language-teaching methods to common products like bicycles and typewriters, whose forms gradually have converged, so that it's no longer possible to distinguish one brand from another at a glance. In a similar fashion, teachers will learn from their predecessors and contemporaries until eventually there will be a blending of methods and an agreement on the best way to teach foreign languages. Whatever the results eventually are, success presumably will include certain principles:

1. Training the students' "spontaneous capacities" in the early stages:[8] Learning a foreign language, for Palmer, is above all a matter of learning the spoken form: "We are considering language as manifested by the normal colloquial form as used by the average speaker in ordinary circumstances."[9] He makes the distinction between two types of abilities in a language learner. First, there are one's "spontaneous capacities"—these are the abilities a person (most often a young child) utilizes in a natural language-learning environment. These are opposed to one's "studial capacities," which are the rational and analytical abilities that are applied to learning a language in a classroom or through self-study. It may sound similar to the learning/acquisition debate from much more recent work, but it's not exactly the same. Whereas later scholars (especially Krashen) disdained classroom "learning," Palmer asserts that the less natural studial capacities are just what are needed to master reading and writing, which are themselves "unnatural" activities.

Language learning is based on habit formation, and it is practice that allows the formation of new habits. This makes use of one's spontaneous capacities. This is obvious in children, but evidence is found in adults as well. With the exception of a gifted few, success in foreign-language learning is best achieved by living in an environment that provides everyday practice, requires the use of one's ears rather than eyes, does not demand attention to details and analysis, and above all, allows the learner to speak only when he or she is ready. What happens is the "reawakening" of the spontaneous capacities in the adult. It makes sense, then, that the most efficient way to teach a language in the classroom is through exercises that help to reawaken these capacities. In Palmer's words, these include the following:

(a) Ear-training exercises, by means of which he may learn to perceive correctly what he hears.

(b) Articulation exercises, by means of which he may cause his vocal organs to make the right sort of muscular efforts.

(c) Exercises in mimicry, by means of which he will become able to imitate and reproduce successfully any word or string of words uttered by the native whose speech serves as model.

(d) Exercises in immediate comprehension, by means of which he will come to grasp without mental translation or analysis the general sense of what he hears.

(e) Exercises in forming the right associations between words and their meanings, by means of which he will become able to express his thoughts.[10]

2. Understanding the importance of habit formation:[11] Language study as habit formation is a fundamental principle for Palmer. The first stage in a language course therefore is the most important, because bad habits learned in the early stages (bad pronunciation, overuse of translation, for example) risk becoming permanent—and it's harder to unlearn something than to learn it, he warns.

You cannot truly speak a language until you can do it automatically. "Few people (if any) have ever succeeded in speaking the language by a series of mental gymnastics; our progress is to be measured only by the quantity of language-material which we can use automatically."[12] However, Palmer notes that adults don't like the work involved in learning new habits, thinking it tedious. He promises that there are ways that are not boring: "There exist many psychologically sound repetition devices and varied drills intended to ensure automatism and interest."[13] Palmer was a firm believer in the efficacy of drills, convinced that they didn't have to be tiresome.

3. Avoiding the acquisition of bad habits:[14] It's very simple—bad habits can best be avoided by making sure that students are not forced to produce language until they have had sufficient preparation.

4. Ensuring progress through gradation of the work:[15] Materials should be presented in a logical order, "passing from the known to unknown by easy stages." But Palmer was explicit about the requirements:

(a) "Ears before eyes": Students should hear the material before seeing it, even phonetically.

(b) "Reception before reproduction": Students should hear the material before producing it.

(c) "Chorus work before individual work": There should be group repetition before individual repetition.

(d) "Oral repetition before reading": Students should repeat the material before reading it.

(e) "Immediate memory before prolonged memory": Students should have numerous opportunities to practice new material through repetition and immediate memory (what we would now call short-term memory) before being expected to produce it on their own without prompting.

(f) "Drill-work before free work": There should be extensive drilling before free conversation, composition, and translation.

5. Maintaining a balance in the aspects of the language that are taught:[16] This means, simply, that there must not be excessive emphasis on any one skill. The teacher should avoid the temptation to focus on his or her area of interest.[17] This of course must keep in mind the goals of the class.

6. Presenting materials in as concrete a way as possible:[18] A few examples of the right kind are superior to a detailed description or an accurate definition. There are four ways of giving the meaning of a foreign language unit: (a) by direct association, such as pointing at an item or acting out a verb; (b) by translation; (c) by definition; and (d) by using it in context. Some tips for putting this into practice include giving many examples when possible (too often the teacher thinks that one is enough), presenting concrete examples for nouns and acting out verbs when possible, using gestures to reinforce meaning, illustrating with real people and situations, and finally, giving the students the chance to practice what has been taught.

7. Securing and maintaining the students' interest:[19] As we've pointed out, drills that could create habits through rapid response form an essential part of Palmer's classroom. In his mind, it is a misconception among students that drills have to be dull. He humorously acknowledges that some believe that he wanted to make foreign-language learning boring by avoiding activities and topics of interest to students. How nice it would be to employ only activities and topics that would amuse the class; however, the fundamental point is this:

> We readily plead guilty to a firm insistence on habit-forming exercises and drills, but continue to urge in mitigation that the practical study of language, the mastery of any form of actual speech, is a habit-forming process and little else. We must have the courage and honesty to face

facts as we find them: a language cannot be mastered by learning interesting things about that language, but only by assimilating the material of which that language is made up.[20]

This of course doesn't mean that student interest should be ignored. It should in fact be of high importance—so long as it does not cause the core principles to be violated. Indirectly he makes the distinction between what we now call intrinsic and extrinsic motivation.[21] "Few people learn anything well unless they are interested in what they are learning. Hope of reward and fear of punishment are certainly stimuli to work, but very poor stimuli compared with that represented by interest."[22]

The six chief points in creating or maintaining interest (if not enthusiasm, he adds realistically) are the following: (a) the elimination of bewilderment: "There is an immense difference between difficult work and bewildering work; of difficulties there must necessarily be many, but of bewilderment there should be none";[23] (b) a sense of progress achieved; (c) competition ("a stimulus not to be despised"); (d) game-like exercises, when used cautiously and as long as they promote habit formation; (e) a mutually respectful relationship between the teacher and the students; and (f) variety in the classroom activities.

8. Using speech psychology to dictate the logical order of progression:[24] Here Palmer is referring not to the gradation of materials, but to decisions in planning the curriculum. Should students work with written or spoken language at the beginning? Should a phonetic alphabet be used? Is it wise to introduce exceptions early on? And so on—he carefully and honestly gives both sides of each question according to the traditionalists versus the modernists. There is little suspense, of course, regarding the outcome of each mini-debate. The modernists with their new ideas based on psychology prevail each time, with the following results: (a) begin with the spoken language before the written; (b) incorporate listening and pronunciation exercises from the beginning; (c) use phonetic transcription; (d) work on intonation from the start; (e) consider the sentence to be the basic unit of speech, not isolated words; (f) introduce common irregularities as needed, even at the beginning; (g) start with rapid and fluent oral work rather than with artificially deliberate and exaggerated pronunciation.

9. Using eclecticism in language teaching:[25] What do you think when you hear that someone uses an "eclectic" approach (i.e., drawing from various sources)? Do you think it indicates a wise decision to adopt a variety of techniques? Or do you assume it's an evasive term used by someone who really has no clear ideas? We sometimes hear that we are teaching in a "post-methods era," resulting in widespread eclecticism. Yet listen to what Palmer had to say about the same question in 1921: In one sense, eclecticism "suggests unoriginality, a lack of a coherent system, a patchwork

of other people's opinions."[26] However, Palmer was a strong advocate of eclecticism. The way Palmer intends it is in the positive sense:

> It implies the deliberate choice of all things which are good, a judicious and reasoned selection of all the diverse factors the sum of which may constitute a complete and homogeneous system. . . . It stands as the antithesis of prejudice, of faddiness, of crankiness, and of fixed ideas.[27]

> The cumulative effect of approaching the difficulty from different and independent angles will certainly secure the desired result.[28]

> Eclecticism, in short, is "the complete method."[29]

10. "Memorized matter" and "constructed matter:"[30] Palmer concludes with a discussion of what he calls "memorized" versus "constructed matter." He sees it as an important topic that one day, when more is known about it, will be incorporated into his principles.

When we speak, we produce "speech units"; these are everything from words to phrases to complete sentences. At our command we have a number of memorized units. Most are single words, but we also have as unanalyzed units some common short sentences such as "I don't know," "Pick it up," or "Just come here." On the other hand, most of what we produce consists of sentences made up of memorized smaller units that have been assembled into new and larger original units that have been constructed by a rapid and unconscious process. These longer units could not possibly have been memorized. In fact, it is a simple matter to compose a normal sentence that "millions of chances to one is an entirely original sentence."[31]

With that in mind, Palmer poses a question: in the classroom, what should be the proportion of memorized to constructed language production? Palmer, keep in mind, repeatedly emphasizes the role of habit formation in learning a foreign language. Another way to put this is to ask whether priority should be given to controlled production using memorized units or to creative production of original sentences. Obviously, "construction" is the goal of language—one cannot go through life uttering nothing but single words and short, memorized sentences—but Palmer considers unrestricted attempts at it to be contrary to the ultimate goal. "Too large a proportion of constructed matter will certainly result in an artificial sort of speech or a pidgin form, with all its evil consequences."[32] Remember his warning that it's more difficult to unlearn something (an erroneous language form in this case) than it is to learn it. The prevailing practice of the day was to encourage construction at the expense of memorization. He was indirectly referring especially to the Direct Method and all its forms that required students to speak in any way possible from the beginning.

We've spent so much time on Palmer because he represents the transition to a modern profession perfectly. It's not simply that he relied on scientific principles (Sweet and other Reformers had done that), but because he spoke with the voice and authority of an actual teacher of foreign languages. Here, after several thousand years, is someone who indeed seems to be a colleague with an understanding of what a classroom of today is like. It's a mistake to claim that he has been forgotten, but his contributions to the teaching of foreign languages deserve to be more widely known.

# 28 The Controversy of Basic English

## THE BACKGROUND

The background to the next episode we'll look at in the history of language teaching was laid out in the story of Harold Palmer. In the 1930s and 1940s something called Basic English caused quite a controversy among academics and attracted a lot of interest from the general public. Though generally forgotten today, it's still quite a tale. It concerns, yet again, a favorite old topic that we first saw with John Wilkins: the creation of an international or universal language. Beyond that, though, it involves egos, turf battles, and politics—not unfamiliar concepts to teachers, no doubt, but it's rare to think of them played out internationally in the field of language teaching.

Imagine a language—a very useful language—that you can learn in one month. In fact, you can learn the basics in a week because it has only a few grammar rules and a vocabulary of 850 words. This language is capable of expressing just about anything of a general, everyday nature. It certainly sounds wonderful. These were the claims made by Charles Ogden, a Cambridge philosophy professor and the creator of Basic English. Instead of a truly artificial language, he devised a simplified version of English in the late 1920s, and for more than a decade it was quite a success—that is, before abruptly losing favor in the 1940s. Basic English was promoted as a true international language, a tool for international peace, indispensable for science and trade. Winston Churchill, Franklin Roosevelt, and H. G. Wells all showed considerable interest. So what happened? How could something that sounds so good and which had no shortage of keen supporters fade away so quickly?

Let's start with some thoughts by I. A. Richards, one the most noted supporters of Basic English, from 1943:

> Basic English is English made simple by limiting the number of its words to 850, and by cutting down the rules for using them to the smallest number for the clear statement of ideas. And this is done without change in the normal order and behaviour of these words in everyday English. This is the first point to make clear. Basic English, though

it has only 850 words, is still normal English. It is limited in its words and its rules, but it keeps to the regular forms of English. And though it is designed to give the learner as little trouble as possible, it is no more strange to the eyes of my readers than these lines, which are in fact in Basic English.[1]

That's impressive. That a learner could within a few months be able to understand this paragraph is a powerful argument in favor of Basic English.

Remember that Palmer had, since the 1920s, been convinced that a key element to success in language teaching was the careful selection of vocabulary, which had been an essential part of his materials writing. Recall also that one reason for his admiration of the Berlitz method was its use of this technique. In any case, innumerable enlightened authors had for years noted the absurdity of teaching useless and difficult vocabulary. All this is to say that although it was not a new issue, the study of word frequency and vocabulary selection in the teaching of foreign languages was a hot topic in the 1930s. Palmer was a leading figure in this field but not the only one (Michael West was another). Basic English was a radical but logical development of this movement.

The original purpose of Basic English, however, was not to be an international language for general usage. It was created as a tool specifically for international science and commerce. In fact, "basic" is an acronym: British American Scientific International Commercial English. It was only with initial success that ambitions for it increased.


## HOW IT WORKED

Ogden's premise was straightforward: create as short a list of English words as possible that will allow you to express any common concept or thing.[2] In contrast to work being done in vocabulary research at the time, this didn't mean just taking the most frequently used words of English; the fact that a word occurs frequently among native speakers does not mean that it can't be expressed using other words. In the end, his list consisted of 600 things and 150 qualities. By "things" Ogden means nouns,[3] while "qualities" refer to adjectives. That's 750 words. The heart of the list, though, what makes the language work, and the ingenious aspect of Basic English, is the list of one hundred "operations." After nouns and adjectives, we still need adverbs, prepositions, and above all, verbs. Ogden's list of verbs is an astonishingly small fourteen words: *come, get, give, go, keep, let, make, put, seem, take, do, say, see,* and *send.* These verbs, plus the two auxiliaries *be* and *have* and the modals *will* and *may* can, he claimed, express any desired action. It's a nearly incredible claim—remember that he also said that it would result in perfectly normal-sounding English. He managed to do this by combining verbs with other words from the list to create verb phrases that took the place of thousands of English verbs. English already has a huge list of what are called "phrasal verbs" (verb + preposition or adverb) such as *get off, take out,* or *come in.* In Basic English these can replace common verbs like *descend, remove,* or *enter.* There are other tricks as well that allow us to dismiss many other verbs. For example, instead of *succeed* we can use *do well;* rather than *pay* we can *give money.* Sometimes it's just a matter of substituting a word in a common phrase, so instead of *paying attention,* you *give your attention.*

It's obvious, though, that such a system cannot handle areas dependent on jargon and less common vocabulary. Ogden's proposal was that after acquiring the core 850 words of Basic English, students could learn additional items specific to their field of expertise. In his opinion, this should require no more than an extra 150 words, making a maximum of one thousand words for any specialization. Take economics, for example. On top of the 850 starting words, a student learns another one hundred needed for general business, and then finally, fifty words specific to economics.

Let's examine a translation to see how successful it can be. You can decide how effective and natural it sounds. Here's a paragraph on economics, in its original form:

> The classification of incomes which is found most convenient for purposes of economic exposition naturally does not remain always the same. It changes with changing social conditions. That which was convenient in England in the eighteenth century would not have been very enlightening in India at that time, and is not very suitable for English use in the twentieth century. But tradition connected with it still plays such a large part in forming the thought of the present time that it would be useless to ignore it.[4]

Now here it is in Basic English:

> The grouping of incomes which is of most use for purposes of economic theory is naturally not the same at all times. It has to be changed with the changing times. It has to be changed with the changing conditions of society. That which seemed best in England between 1700 and 1800 would not have been much help in India at that time and is not very much good for English use at the present day. But in view of the connection it has with ideas which still have an important part in forming the thought of the present time, it is necessary to take it into account.[5]

Let's consider another translation using the core 850 words. Here is an excerpt of original text from *Little Women* by Louisa May Alcott:

> "Jo! Jo! Where are you?" cried Meg at the foot of the garret stairs.

"Here!" answered a husky voice from above; and, running up, Meg found her sister eating apples and crying over the "Heir of Redclyffe," wrapped up in a comforter on an old three-legged sofa by the sunny window. This was Jo's favorite refuge; and here she loved to retire with half a dozen russets and a nice book, to enjoy the quiet and the society of a pet rat who lived near by, and didn't mind her a particle. As Meg appeared, Scrabble whisked into his hole. Jo shook the tears off her cheeks, and waited to hear the news.[6]

In Basic English, notice in particular how the less common words are dealt with:

"Jo! Jo! Where are you?" came Meg's cry from the foot of the narrow steps going up to the top floor of the house.

"Here!" said a voice from overhead, sounding strangely thick, and running up, Meg saw her sister with an apple in her hand and a warm coat round her, crying over a book on an old three-legged seat under the window. This little room right under the roof was where Jo went most frequently to be by herself; and here her happiest hours went by, with six or seven apples, a good book, and the company of a rat living there, which by this time was used to her and had no fear of her at all. When Meg came in, Scrabble went quickly into his hole, and Jo, brushing the drops from her eyes, put down her book, waiting for the news.[7]

Ogden unveiled Basic English in 1930. It quickly drew interest and support because of its novelty, its claim of being easy to learn, and the reputation and status of its creator. Basic English really was a topic of common conversation for a time, not just among teachers and linguists but among the general public. It was an exciting idea, one that was too important to overlook.


## UNDER ATTACK

But the smooth debut of Basic English didn't last long. As supporters pushed for Basic English with great enthusiasm, others took a hard look at the language and began to realize that it didn't live up to all its claims. Michael West and Harold Palmer became leading opponents. Over the next few years, the arguments heated up and some nasty words were exchanged.

With the aid of a bit of hindsight, here are some criticisms of Basic English:

1. Ogden's claim to a vocabulary of 850 words was naive and highly misleading. In fact, considering how many words are formed by adding suffixes or by linking to create compounds, and all the verbs that have to be expressed as phrasals like *get off, come across*, and so on, it's not hard to argue that the vocabulary load is heavier than in other artificial languages.

2. Ogden's assertion that the vocabulary could be learned in a week and put to use in a month will strike most of us as extremely unlikely. Maybe Ogden could do it, but certainly not the average student sitting in a classroom anywhere in the world in who-knows-what circumstances.[8]

3. And who's going to teach this Basic English? Think about it—as teachers we'd have to know how to write and speak Basic English. Imagine giving a class using only the words from Ogden's list. Maybe it's a problem for you, maybe not. But when applied to thousands of teachers around the world, it becomes obvious that the logistics of launching Basic English as a viable international language are overwhelming.

4. Finally, a big problem for many people was simply that Basic English did not, as promised, produce natural English. Without the expertise and skill of a Cambridge professor, the results could be less than satisfactory.

Michael West came up with a simple but extreme example of Basic English's inability to handle every situation smoothly: "The priest thanked the ladies for their help in making the party so successful" becomes the awkward "the servant of the church said it was very kind of the women of good birth to help him in making the meeting of friends come off so well."[9]

Something else that riled the language-teaching community was the fact that Ogden was an outsider. To those who had devoted their lives to teaching languages, it must have been galling to see this Cambridge philosophy professor, who'd never taught a language lesson in his life, become the guru of language pedagogy.

Actually, the biggest failure of Basic English was an inability to keep to its intended purpose. As an instrument for international communication in science and commerce it might have had a future, but its popular appeal (and Ogden's resulting unrealistic hopes) stretched it beyond its capabilities into a failed artificial language for all purposes.

## THE DEMISE OF BASIC ENGLISH

The end of the debate came with the conclusion of World War II. As the Allied victory became apparent, the question arose of the role of English in the post-war world. Winston Churchill was intrigued by Basic English and its potential as an international language. Nevertheless, dictating language-teaching methodology was not among the responsibilities of the British government. In the House of Commons in 1944, Churchill expressed his hopes for Basic English but insisted that its use was an issue for the new British Council to resolve. It had been formed just four years earlier to promote British culture and the English language. The British Council diplomatically but ominously promised to promote it when realistic to do so but declared itself neutral in such matters.[10] Without the explicit support of this organization, Basic English was doomed. Within a very few years Basic English did indeed fade away as a tool for fundamental change in foreign-language teaching.

Nevertheless, the appeal of Basic English is undeniable. It just seems common sense that a simplified version of a language—any language—can be created and taught as a shortcut to international communication. And in fact, today it continues to have a small but enthusiastic group of supporters. Look on the Internet and you'll find several sites extolling the merits of Basic English. Perhaps it's the appeal of nationalism that keeps it going— the chance to have English as an international language. More likely it's just the lure of an international language itself—the same dream that many people have had for centuries: peace on Earth achieved through the ability to communicate freely with anyone.

# 29 World War II and the Army Specialized Training Program

## STRUCTURALISM

Read this carefully: "A language is primarily a system of vocal symbols and of devices for indicating grammatical structure: it is only secondarily a collection of words."[1] Think of the implications of this for language teaching. The spoken language takes precedence over the written, and learning vocabulary is not the most important part of studying a foreign language—learning structures and patterns is. This is essentially the structuralist viewpoint made famous by the Swiss linguist Ferdinand de Saussure at the end of the 1800s and in the early 1900s. It's quickly apparent that if we think of language as a collection of structures and patterns, we will be moving away from traditional teaching approaches based on studying literature and such popular conversational "natural" methods as the Direct Method. Palmer held a similar view—remember that his goal of habit formation relied heavily upon pattern practice and drills with carefully chosen vocabulary.

Structuralism was not limited to linguistics, however. As a theory that an area of study can be broken down into its components and understood by how they interact, it was applied to a number of widely different areas, from architecture to anthropology. In fact, the interests of anthropology and linguistics coincided at this time, when there was a tremendous interest in Native American languages, many of which were unwritten and on the brink of extinction. Investigating these languages in a systematic way was an important step to recording them. Franz Boas and Leonard Bloomfield pioneered a technique that was widely used to study unwritten languages (not just Native American). It required gathering large amounts of data on the spoken language through carefully directed conversations with native speakers, or "informants." It was the job of the linguist to sort, transcribe, and study this information, and with the help of the native speakers, eventually to come up with a phonological and grammatical analysis of the language. This provided not only a detailed description of the language, but information from which one could create materials for studying the language. The grammatical and phonological differences between the target language and English were of particular interest, as these were considered to determine the difficulty and sequencing of the materials.

## AN UNFORTUNATE OPPORTUNITY[2]

In the years just before World War II, a few people with an eye on the political situation realized that the United States had a shortage of speakers (sometimes none at all) of certain critical languages such as Thai, Burmese, Vietnamese, Russian, Dutch, and Japanese. An organization called the American Council of Learned Societies received a substantial grant in 1941 to establish what was known as the Intensive Language Program to create materials and courses for these less commonly taught languages.[3] Unlike the scholars responsible for the Coleman Report, these were linguists in charge, who now applied the methods that had been developed through years of fieldwork to the study of languages. Dozens of well-known linguists of the day were engaged in this activity.

> The courses were built on a triad of premises well known to us linguists but still unfamiliar to a distressingly large proportion of the general educated public: (1) the primacy of speech over writing, which means the learner must hear, imitate, and understand native (or near-native) speakers of the target language; (2) intensive concentration—as many hours per day as possible; and (3) guidance by someone trained in linguistic analysis, in order to focus on the real differences between the learner's native language and that being acquired and to avoid the multitudinous time-wasting traps that arise from popular misconceptions about the nature of language.[4]

This was, in brief, the opposite of the recommendations of the Committee of Twelve and the Coleman Report. The consequences of a reading approach for an isolated nation were soon apparent. When the United States joined the war shortly afterward, the American military entered the picture, determined to develop an expanded and improved program.

The Intensive Language Program was folded into the military effort, as part of the Army Specialized Training Program (ASTP), a selective program that taught crash courses in everything from engineering to the mechanics of combustion engines.[5] Still, for the first time ever, linguists and anthropologists were in charge of a major language-learning endeavor. It was an exciting time. One of the principal players called it "a fabulous civilian-military cooperation [for producing language teaching materials] on a scale not only never realized before, but hardly ever dreamed of."[6] The ASTP eventually engaged in the instruction of fifteen thousand students in courses in thirty languages at fifty-five universities.[7] Not unexpectedly, there was no uniform approach among all these courses. What was actually recommended by the Army was instruction for fifteen to seventeen hours per week for nine months (a total nearing six hundred hours); this was to be led by two instructors: a linguist trained in the ways of language analysis and a native informant to practice with the students.[8] Typical classwork, in line with habit formation and structuralist principles, consisted of mimicry/memorization, pattern drilling, role-playing, translation, and basic oral language practice. Phonograph records, quite a novelty, were commonly used to provide additional aural input.

## EVALUATING THE PROGRAM

It was indeed an impressive effort, one that could have revolutionized the teaching of foreign languages. How did it do, then? Unfortunately, it's not easy to say. The biggest problem is that the ASTP lasted only a few months before it was abandoned because of a manpower shortage among the troops. The ASTP overall (that is, not just in languages) was training one hundred fifty thousand of the brightest soldiers, which eventually put an untenable strain on troop numbers.[9] The ASTP had been approved in September 1942, began actual operations in December 1942, but was "virtually liquidated" by February 1944.[10] It was truly a sad ending: according to one participant, many of the language materials, developed with so much labor, love, and excitement, were simply and abruptly stored in a freight car in a railroad yard outside Washington, DC, where they remained for years. "I have never heard how they were disposed of."[11]

In appraising the Army Specialized Training Program, the first question anyone wants answered is simply whether it worked or not. But how can you judge the results of a program that lasted barely a year? What do you compare them to? In fact, assessment was not a major concern. If you're trying to create a massive program such as this one in as short a time as possible, you focus on the materials, syllabus, and activities before all else and postpone the testing procedures until later. Unfortunately, the end arrived sooner than expected and no specific procedures were ever developed. Instead, evaluation was often done informally. Until something better comes along, someone said, "the best tests have been found to be the standard devices: retelling or paraphrasing a spoken anecdote, situation, or description; impromptu responses to questions on familiar subjects, dictation."[12] In a case like this, then, success or failure is anecdotal rather than statistical; that is, it's defined by those who actually take part or observe the results. If they claim it is successful, then it is. And generally, the consensus was that it worked quite well.

The program had received considerable publicity. For example, in 1943, *Reader's Digest*, that enormously popular record of modern events, ran an article entitled "Teaching Languages in a Hurry" that featured high praise for the program and its results. It gave the impression that at last scientific method had found the way to teach a foreign language in a few weeks.[13]

Negative reactions were not hard to find, either. Experienced teachers (and learners) know that language that is learned quickly is also forgotten quickly when there is no opportunity to practice it. The entire way of doing things was so different for most people that it was unsettling to many. There was the inevitable resentment among language teachers that language teaching had been reformed, corrected, made scientific—however you wanted to characterize it—by university linguists and anthropologists. Their solutions were alien to most language teachers. And therein lies another major objection. Even if the program does work—even *if*—what is the use of it in real life? What school can be expected to adopt this approach?

> The school, after all, is not a training camp, working under high pressure, with intensive methods, designed to equip trainees with an immediately usable skill, but an educational institution organized to develop character, build character, build citizenship and transmit the cultural heritage of the race. Its major interest must remain life values.[14]

It's an old, old idea that the main objective of a classroom in a typical school is not to teach a working knowledge of the subject, but to turn the students into better citizens. Clearly that idea was still alive in the 1940s. But there were also more modern and relevant objections, and not just from "outsiders." A prominent linguist of the day was also not impressed:

> [Mario] Pei decried the Army Program's neglect (or, more exactly, postponement) of the study of writing, its preference for 'colloquial' speech, the difficulties of phonetic transcription for the beginning learner, the failure of the linguists to acknowledge Berlitz as the source of their approach, the sentence-level introduction of language units, and the 'hodge-podge of methods' into which the Program had evolved as methods chiefly applicable to 'exotic' languages were applied to the teaching of commonly-spoken ones.[15]

There's no room for reconciliation here, for criticisms like these went against the very heart of the program.

Whether or not the ASTP was a success has no real answer. Nevertheless, it most certainly was not a failure—if you overlook its original goals. It brought into the American classroom the notion that the spoken language was to be the emphasis in the future and that the best way to teach it was through the study of language structures and the formation of habits. Accompanying this were the first uses of audio-visual materials, particularly phonograph records. The question, then, was just how to apply all this to the ordinary classroom.

# 30 After the War

Following the Second World War, the structuralist-inspired approach continued its dominance. It was developed from the principles of structuralism, which we've discussed, and behavioral psychology. In its very simplest terms, behaviorism sees human behavior as being shaped by the process of conditioned response—that is, habit formation as a result of reward and punishment. This explains, then, the concern with common grammatical structures, habit formation through imitation and controlled practice, and carefully chosen vocabulary. We'll first examine the situation in North America, where the Audio-lingual Method (ALM) was the great hope for achieving the long-sought-after breakthrough in the language-teaching classroom. Then we'll turn to Europe and two variations on this same theme: the Situational Approach in the United Kingdom and the SGAV Method in France. We could go in any order, really, because understanding one means understanding the others. Nevertheless, we'll start with Audio-lingual because it's a continuation of the previous section. To keep repetition to a minimum, though, we'll start by focusing on the factors common to all three methods.[1]

1. Lessons are based on the procedure of presentation, practice, and production.
2. Lessons revolve around a dialogue at the beginning; the dialogue is worked over thoroughly, with repetition in chorus and individually, until it is memorized. Pronunciation and intonation are carefully monitored.
3. Use of the students' native language is strongly discouraged during the lesson.
4. Error correction is of the highest importance. All three methods recall Palmer's statement that a habit is easier to learn than to unlearn.
5. Although all four skills are addressed, the spoken language takes clear precedence.
6. A fundamental principle is that comprehension precedes production. Speaking and writing are controlled activities.

7. Grammar is taught inductively through the dialogue and by analogy in the follow-up exercises, which reinforce the grammar and sentence structures of the lesson. The exercises are of several types, but fundamentally amount to variations of a few types that involve repetition, substitution, and manipulation of forms.
8. All three methods stress the use of technology (that is, audio-visual aids) in the classroom.

## AN ASIDE: FOND MEMORIES OF YET ANOTHER WAY

I began my studies of French as a child in 1964. Our little blue textbook, entitled *Cours de langue et de civilisation françaises* (Course in the French Language and Civilization), was written by Gaston Mauger[2] and published in 1953.

The preface informed the reader that it was created at the request of the Alliance française, which is essentially the Gallic equivalent of the British Council. It grudgingly acknowledged that French after World War II was no longer the premier international language, and this book was a contribution toward maintaining the high status of French. There was no mention of dramatic changes in language teaching; in fact, the word "modern" was never used regarding the course's content. Even more noteworthy is that the term "method" was never used, either. Instead, it praised the role of tradition. And traditional it was, in outlook at least. The goal of the course and of the acquisition of the French language, one that the Coleman group would have approved of eagerly, was not to assist the student as a tourist but "above all to enter into contact with one of the richest civilizations of the modern world, to cultivate and enhance one's spirit through the study of splendid literature, and to become, truly, a person of distinction."[3] The book's intention, in contrast to the current of the times, was to allow the teacher a considerable amount of freedom. In a statement that seemed jarringly out of place in the post-war period, the Alliance française claimed that "pedagogy for us is as much an art as a science. . . . In our opinion, there are as many ways to teach as there are classes to be taught or even students."[4]

I was fascinated by this utterly alien textbook, written entirely in French. It was full of amusing drawings in an inexplicably foreign style that I remembered for years afterward. Even the layout was exotic, with its use of multiple fonts and lines and boxes everywhere. There were no dialogues, just short reading passages once we had reached an elementary stage. Each chapter opened with a very specific grammar point. Our class proceeded very slowly but I don't remember ever being bored by the material. I can't really say how much French I learned in just over two years, either, but in the end I had a wonderful impression of France and a desire to learn much more of the language. Years later I bought a copy just for sentimental reasons.

But then I changed schools, where I had to start French again from scratch—and there I encountered the Audio-lingual Method.

32

LEÇON 13

| Verbes en IR | Les saisons |

Le professeur commence la classe à 9 heures. Il finit la classe à midi.
Nous fin[issons] la classe à midi. Vous fin[issez] la classe à midi.
ou : Les classes commencent à 9 heures. Elles fin[issent] à midi.
Commencer est un verbe du 1er groupe : 1er groupe .... er
Finir est un verbe du 2e groupe : 2e groupe .... ir (-issons).

L'année a quatre saisons :

le printemps        l'été (m.)        l'automne (m. et f.)        l'hiver (m.)

● AU printemps le ciel est bleu, le soleil brille, [Il fait] beau (= le temps est beau).
Les arbres ont des feuilles vertes. Le printemps est la saison des fleurs.

En Europe :
le printemps commence le 21 mars     et finit le 21 juin.
l'été        commence le 22 juin      et finit le 22 septembre.
l'automne    commence le 23 septembre et finit le 21 décembre.
l'hiver      commence le 22 décembre  et finit le 20 mars.

● EN été, quel temps [fait-il] ? — EN été, [Il fait] beau et [Il fait] chaud (chaud ≠ froid).
Déjà les fruits grossissent. Sont-ils bons ? — Non; pas encore.

● EN automne le ciel est gris, [Il fait] du vent. Les feuilles des arbres (m.) tombent.

● Quel temps [fait-il] ? EN hiver, [Il fait] froid
La neige tombe, et la terre est blanche.

Je fais du feu
dans la maison.

Il pleut.
J'ai un parapluie.

Verbe faire :
Je fais, tu fais, il fait,
nous faisons [nu fəzõ],
vous faites, ils font.
[Le maçon fait un mur, les maçons font des murs.]
En été [Il fait] jour tôt. [Il fait] nuit tard. — En hiver [Il fait] jour tard. [Il fait] nuit tôt.

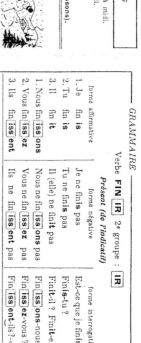

GRAMMAIRE

TREIZIÈME LEÇON

Verbe FIN [IR]   2e groupe : [IR]

Présent (de l'indicatif)

| forme affirmative | forme négative | forme interrogati[ve] |
|---|---|---|
| Je fin is | Je ne finis pas | Est-ce que je finit |
| Tu fin is | Tu ne finis pas | Finis-tu ? |
| Il fin it | Il (elle) ne finit pas | Finit-il ? Finit-e[lle] |
| Nous fin [iss] ons | Nous ne fin [iss] ons pas | Fin [iss] ons-nous |
| Vous fin [iss] ez | Vous ne fin [iss] ez pas | Fin [iss] ez-vous ? |
| Ils ne fin [iss] ent | Ils ne fin [iss] ent pas | Fin [iss] ent-ils ?- |

On conjugue comme finir :
blanchir (blanc)   rougir (rouge)   jaunir (jaune)   grandir (grand)   grossir

ATTENTION au v. Commencer : Je commence, tu commences, il commence, nous commen[ç]ons, vous commencez, ils commencent

☆ PRONONCIATION
Je finis [ʒə fini]   nous finissons [nu finisõ]   ils finissent [il finis]   il fait froid en hiver [il fe frwa ãnivɛːr]   il fait chaud en [...]
le printemps [lə prɛ̃tã]   l'automne [lotɔn]   l'hiver [livɛːr]   la feuille tombe [la fœj tõːb]   il fait jour tôt [il fe ʒuːr to]   il fait [...]

► EXERCICES ◄ I) Conjuguez aux trois formes (affirmative, négative, interrogative).
Commencer la classe à 9 heures. Finir la leçon à midi. Faire l'exercice de gram[...]

II) Répondez et écrivez : De quelle couleur est le ciel au printemps ? De quelle cou[...]
en automne ? De quelle couleur sont les arbres au printemps ? En quelle saison [...]
les feuilles ? De quelle couleur est la neige ?

III) Mettez l'article indéfini devant : beau printemps, long été, automne chaud, hiver [...]
bleu, feuille verte, fleur rose, petit oiseau, fruit rouge, neige blanche, terre brune, gra[...]

IV) Répondez : Quand grossissent les fruits ? Quel temps fait-il en hiver ? Fait-il froi[...]
d'école en Europe ? Fait-il chaud en été ? Quand pleut-il ? Quel temps fait-il aujourd'hu[...]
fait-il jour en hiver ? Quand fait-il jour en été ? Quand fait-il chaud ? Au mois d'août ?

V) Mettez le nom d'une saison : Au ... il y a des fleurs. En ... il fait beau. En ... il fait b[...]
les feuilles des arbres tombent. En ... la terre est blanche. En ... il fait chaud. En ... il fai[...]

VI) Quand commence le printemps en Europe ? Quand finit l'été ? Quand commence[...]
Quand finit l'automne ?

PRON. nous faisons : j'ai comme[nc]é dans fenêtre. Bon ≠ mauvais (méchant), en parlant des [...]
Je fais ou j'allume du feu (fe ≠) j'éteins le feu (tu éteins, il éteint, n. éteignons, v. éteignez, ils [...]

*Figure 30.1*   A page from Gaston Mauger's *Cours de langue et de civilisation françaises*, a traditional textbook in the post-war world (by permission of Librairie Hachette).

## THE AUDIO-LINGUAL METHOD

The Audio-lingual Method, or ALM as it is usually referred to, was the ultimate attempt at turning language teaching into a science.[5] There was no room for "art" in the ALM classroom. This was to be modern linguistic pedagogy at its best. It was, simply but truthfully, a refinement of many of the activities put into practice by the Army Specialized Training Program.[6] ALM is often associated with the launching of Sputnik, the first satellite in orbit, by the Russians in 1957. This unwelcome surprise, seen as a significant threat to United States security, spurred the American government to pass the National Defense Education Act the following year to bolster education in crucial areas. Sputnik may have been a threat, but it was good for language teaching. A major provision of the act was funding to develop and promote the teaching of foreign languages in the country. Apparently, the lessons of World War II regarding linguistic isolation had been quickly forgotten, but here was a new chance to tackle essentially the same problem with essentially the same answers. This time, though, it was a long-term project to develop language teaching in the schools.

The key concept of ALM is "over-learning" through repetition and practice—the formation of habits so strong that one can produce the desired language automatically and spontaneously. More than in the other two methods, speaking and writing are therefore controlled to make sure that the students use only language forms that they have learned and practiced. Writing, even later in the course, tends to be guided—answering specific questions to form a composition, for example. ALM also relies heavily on the practice known as contrastive analysis, in which equivalent language forms are compared for degree of similarity; the greater the difference between a language form in the student's first language and in the language under study, the more difficult the target form is assumed to be and the later it is taught. Finally, ALM was a pioneer in the use of technology. A language laboratory was a featured part of the program, if possible. This meant, of course, more practicing of pronunciation through imitation and replying to more grammar exercises.

The Audio-lingual Method is one of the most interesting chapters in the history of language teaching. No other method was so carefully thought out or had so much science behind it. To those who had complete faith in behavioral psychology and structuralism, it was logically the key to the ancient puzzle of second-language acquisition. It was brilliantly planned in excruciating detail. Focus on the most important and most common sentence patterns of the target language, practice them repeatedly (with limited vocabulary) until they become automatic—then just add more vocabulary, and there you have it! On paper it should have worked.

It didn't. What does not come across in any list of ALM procedures or principles is the extent to which the psychological element was overlooked. It sounds odd, considering that one foundation of the method was current psychology, but language learning was somehow regarded as a deadly serious business. Most students found ALM to be very, very boring.[7] That was the most easily verified and most obvious disadvantage to the method. There was more, though. There was no evidence that it achieved its goals. The ability to respond spontaneously in a transformation drill did not necessarily carry over to the real world. The fatal blow, though, came with the demise of behaviorism. It had been under attack since the late 1950s, especially from linguist Noam Chomsky, who was on the verge of bringing about a revolution in the field of linguistics. Behaviorism's insistence on examining only observable behavior led to a language acquisition theory based on a baby's imitation of speech around him or her. When a child's imitation of language forms is successful, goes the reasoning, communication occurs and the child feels rewarded. Unsuccessful imitation results in no communication and no positive reinforcement. It was pointed out, though, that an infant frequently produces ungrammatical and seemingly illogical utterances that he or she could never have heard. This fact alone is strong evidence against first-language acquisition as nothing more than early habit formation. Instead it suggests, as Chomsky says, a biologically determined behavior that develops on its own through an innate ability. A child cannot learn to speak without hearing language around him or her, but it is not needed for imitation. Thus, without an accepted scientific theory to back it up, the Audio-lingual Method rather quickly faded away, just another sure-fire method that failed to live up to its promise.

History should be impartial, but I lived this chapter, so I feel entitled to confirm the common opinion. After more than two years of my Mauger and its busy, visually entertaining contents and its continuing story of the life of a French family, I was presented with the ALM textbook for beginning French students. It was disturbingly thin. Inside there was page after page after page of nothing but text. And plain text, at that. A little bold print here and there, an occasional heading, and plenty of white space, but nothing more. There wasn't even any color. It was visually the dullest book any of us had ever seen.[8] And then came the lessons. We repeated the dialogues so many times that I still to this day remember some lines about meatballs in the cafeteria and a proposed trip to the seaside. The exercises afterward were certainly not an improvement. There was more repetition and hours of mechanical manipulation of sentences. We were treated as little machines that took in the language, processed and assimilated it, and spit it back out. Yes, it really was boring. If it had been my first experience in studying a foreign language, it might well have also been my last.

The last ALM materials were published in the early 1970s.

## THE SITUATIONAL APPROACH/THE ORAL APPROACH

In the United Kingdom, there was a less artificial and much more successful evolution of the principles that had been laid down long before the war and long before ALM. Structuralist-influenced interest in sentence patterns and in vocabulary frequency (especially Palmer and Hornby for the former and Michael West the latter) combined to create what was originally known as the Oral Approach for its emphasis on the spoken language. Eventually it became known as the Situational Approach, reflecting the insistence that everything, whether a sound, a word, or a grammar point, had to be introduced in some kind of context or situation. This usage of the term must not be confused with a specific "situation" such as asking for directions or introducing someone; it simply means that language, as communication, had always to be learned in a communicative context, which could mean with the use of objects and pictures (realia) or even gestures.

On paper, the differences between this approach and ALM are difficult to realize. Nevertheless, they were considerable. If you've used the *Access to English* series featuring the adventures of Arthur and Mary (*Starting Out, Getting On,* etc.) or L. G. Alexander's New Concept English books (*First Things First, Practice and Progress,* for example), you've seen what the Situational Approach had developed into by the 1970s—by the time ALM had more or less disappeared. It contains the vital human element that was absent in ALM: a sense that language learning can be fun, even funny, and that the language can even be used for genuine communication, not just robotic production of memorized patterns.

As with ALM, however, the theoretical basis for this approach was undermined by developments in linguistics in the 1960s and 1970s. Nevertheless, the intuitive appeal to both teachers and students of the materials such as those just mentioned (certainly the opposite of the reaction to ALM) and its unquestioned success in many situations ensured its popularity through the years.

## THE SGAV METHOD/ST-CLOUD METHOD

By now one may have the impression that developments in the teaching of English as a foreign language were taking over the post-war world. The French certainly felt that way. We'll try to dispel that notion by examining a parallel development in France that began in the 1950s. Recall earlier that the Alliance française had voiced a similar concern about English and the precarious state of the French language on the international stage; their answer was a charming but traditional work by Mauger. Others in France, more in tune with the times and linguistic advances, independently came up with another method that, in the end, looks an awful lot like the Situational Method and ALM. It was simply a product of the times.

Let's clear up the matter of the name first. French sources refer to it as *la méthode SGAV*, which even in French hardly rolls off the tongue, but that's the most common term for it. SGAV stands for *structuro-globale audio-visuelle*, which indeed means "structural-global audio-visual." A more attractive name for it is the St-Cloud Method, after the school at which it was developed.[9] It also is sometimes called the "Audiovisual Method."

The approach is associated with a widely used course called *Voix et Images de France* (Voices and Images of France), which debuted in 1961. In the early 1950s, as had been done in the UK, there was a project to devise a list of words that should be featured in teaching materials. The result, a three-thousand-word list called *Français Fondamental*, was another significant achievement in vocabulary selection in language pedagogy. It differed from the usual word-count lists because it took into consideration vocabulary that may not include the most common words, but which was felt to be useful to learners in common situations.

All the post-war methods under consideration here were quite regimented in their presentation, but the SGAV exceeded the others in this regard. Whereas ALM and Situational were also firmly guided by the materials, SGAV was envisioned as a system that required teacher training. The most distinctive feature of SGAV was its incorporation of technology into the lesson. In fact, it was essential. In the days when machinery was expensive and hard to come by, SGAV made use of more attainable equipment: a tape recorder and a filmstrip projector. The dialogues that formed the foundation of each lesson were presented in pictures with spoken accompaniment.[10] This was of supreme importance because SGAV, even more than the other two methods discussed here, stressed the overall presentation of the spoken language. The preface to *Voix et Images* says as much: "We have sought to teach the language from the beginning as a means of expression and communication, appealing to all the resources at one's disposal: attitudes, gestures, mimicry, intonation and rhythm of spoken dialogue."[11] Beginners, in fact, used a textbook that had nothing but pictures for the first sixty to seventy hours of instruction, so that students could focus strictly on modeling and practicing the spoken language.[12]

SGAV had a lengthier list of prescribed activities for students than did the other methods. These can be grouped into seven categories:[13] (1) theater, or acting out memorized dialogues; (2) questions about the pictures, instituted by the teacher and among the students themselves; (3) structural exercises similar to those of ALM and Situational; (4) directed conversation based on themes introduced in the dialogue; (5) conversion of a brief narrative passage into a dialogue; (6) finishing an interrupted dialogue or story in groups and comparing the results; and (7) free discussion.

SGAV had a long and distinguished career, but eventually was retired like the others by the late 1980s.

# 31 The 1970s and Beyond

## CHANGING TIMES

The Situational Approach and SGAV were highly successful, but by the 1970s their days were coming to an end as behavioral psychology and linguistic structuralism were pretty much discredited. As we noted, the methods continued to be popular for years afterward, but among the experts, language teaching was heading in a new direction. A dominant theory of psychology or language learning or any branch of knowledge stays on top only as long as a newer and better one doesn't come around. For our purposes, "the new kid in town" was cognitive psychology. Sometimes the new theory is just a development of the previous one, but at other times, as in this case, it marks a clear break. It doesn't really make sense to talk about one form of psychology as being the opposite of another, but cognitive psychology was very different from behaviorism. The latter, in its quest for scientific respectability, had firmly limited itself to describing behavior that could be observed and measured; there was simply no speculation about what went on in the mind. Cognitive psychology took as its objective the study of "cognition," defined as "the mental process of knowing, including aspects such as awareness, perception, reasoning, and judgment."[1] None of these processes could have even been discussed by behaviorism. Of course, both branches of psychology are much more complex than is suggested here, but it's safe to say that behaviorism is well defined with clear limits. In contrast, the nebulous nature of mental processes means that cognitive psychology, while maintaining a scientific pedigree whenever possible, is open to intuition and more tolerant of ambiguity. Most of all, it allows one a degree of freedom that was missing in behaviorism.

Without the restrictions of the preceding decades, language teaching gleefully took advantage of its new-found freedom. The 1970s saw a string of novel and imaginative methods that intrigued everyone in the field.[2] With names like the Silent Way, Total Physical Response, and Suggestopedia, it was hard for even the most jaded teachers to ignore them. They're sometimes referred to as "designer methods," perhaps because as in fashion, each depended heavily upon the personality and interests of its creator.

Coincidentally or not, they also suffered the same fate as most displays on a fashion catwalk: they were eye-catching and great for discussion, but it was unlikely that you ever met anyone who actually used them. Nevertheless, they presented new ideas that have indeed influenced our field, and some of these methods have a devoted following to this day. Caleb Gattegno, creator of the Silent Way (discussed below), in discussing his own work, but also aptly describing the efforts of the other "designer" methods of the era, said, "The most important contribution of this work is the opening of new vistas in education that should excite a new generation of people to experiment with what they find behind the doors that are now put ajar."[3] He and his peers were unquestionably successful in this regard.

Let's look at them briefly. The details are deliberately quite sketchy because a full description of each would require more space than is merited here, and information is readily available in libraries and online.

## TOTAL PHYSICAL RESPONSE (TPR)

Consider the lucky situation of young children just starting out in their language-learning careers. The language they're exposed to is simple and doesn't require much action on their part. True, a lot of it is commands, but by indicating comprehension and by following a few orders, they're not pressured to produce language until they're ready. James Asher (born 1929), an American psychologist, took this idea and created Total Physical Response, usually known as just TPR. The key pedagogical concept, based on left-brain/right-brain studies, is that a foreign language is more easily absorbed when introduced to learners who are using movement as well as listening and speaking. The basic activities in the classroom are responding to the teacher's commands and carrying out actions of increasing complexity. An example for a beginner: "Stand up and walk to the sofa"; for an advanced student: "Maria, if Jeffe moved a chair under the window, raise your hand, but if he moved the chair next to the table, make a funny face."[4] An example of teaching the simple past: "Alicia, stand up, go to the chalkboard, write your name, and sit down. (PAUSE) Alicia *stood* up, *went* to the chalkboard, *wrote* her name, *went* to her chair, and *sat* down."[5] Students build up comprehension and begin to produce language only when they are comfortable.

There are in fact some superficial similarities to learning theories of the 1960s. We could say that TPR is based on the stimulus-response pattern of behaviorism (a correct response to a teacher's verbal stimulus leads to praise), but it's not with any behaviorist philosophy in mind. It also clearly follows the maxim that comprehension precedes production. Unlike in the past, though, what is going on in the TPR classroom is a supreme concern for the psychological well-being of the students. Following commands is a clear, playful way to acquire language, and the lack of pressure to perform is not to avoid the formation of irreversible bad habits, but to put the students at ease.

There is no standard textbook or syllabus for TPR; some teachers will appreciate this, while others will feel awkward. There is no obsession with the grammar and pronunciation. The goal is effective communication at a comfortable pace for each learner.

It is often overlooked that Asher himself realizes that, however enjoyable TPR may be (and any demonstration shows how fun it can be), it is not a method for the complete mastery of a language.

> No matter how exciting and productive the innovation, people will tire of it. They no longer respond. It is important to neutralize adaptation by switching continually from one activity to another. . . . The tool [TPR] can be used at all levels to help students internalize new vocabulary and grammatical features. But, this requires a conservative application of this powerful tool.[6]

Total Physical Response sounds easy to implement, but there is one complication. To work well it needs to be a fast-paced, scripted activity. In other words, it requires more preparation than one might suppose. In fact, Asher recommends that it be practiced in a course under the supervision of an experienced teacher.[7]

In the end, TPR does not claim to be a complete method but one that is supplemented with other activities. It's still going strong, though, and when used correctly, can be a profitable and enjoyable activity.


## COMMUNITY LANGUAGE LEARNING

A few people are never afraid to talk, even when they possess only the most rudimentary elements of a foreign language. Almost everyone else, though, knows well the feeling of shyness and embarrassment that afflicts the typical language learner. Community Language Learning (CLL) introduced a new approach to this obstacle, one based on counseling theory. Students are seen as "clients" and the teacher as a language "counselor." Usually seated in a circle, the students from the beginning engage in conversation on a selected topic or just speak about points of personal interest. A student who wishes to participate says in the students' first language what he or she would like to contribute. This ensures that the entire group will understand the exchange. The teacher then gives the language to the student in the target language, and the student now presents the language as his or her own to the group. The instructor continues in this way, going around the outside of the circle to assist and translate for any student. The conversation, usually recorded, can be written on the board to be reread, translated, and analyzed grammatically. As the students progress, they rely less and less on the teacher, but are reassured by his or her constant presence. The spoken language takes precedence, though writing activities can be based on the conversations.

Community Language Learning was the creation of Charles Curran (born 1934), an American psychologist and theologian. The goal is to promote a warm, safe, supportive environment for language learning, one in which a student feels a part of a team effort. The method is by nature highly unstructured, which makes it difficult to evaluate and generally unsuitable for traditional academic environments. Nevertheless, it represents perfectly the experimental nature of the so-called "designer methods."[8]

## THE SILENT WAY

The name of our next luminary is well known in language-teaching circles, but in fact he was above all a mathematician. Caleb Gattegno (1911–1988) led a fascinating life.[9] He was born in Egypt, descended from a family of Spanish merchants who had emigrated there many years before.[10] He studied in France and Switzerland and later worked in countries all over the world. His interest in learning theory in general is what led to the Silent Way, whose learning principles he had first applied to mathematics and first-language reading and writing.[11]

Popular history tends to give Noam Chomsky all the credit for pointing out the problems with the behaviorist theory of first-language acquisition through imitation and practice. Nevertheless, this wasn't so. Gattegno, in the early 1960s, had objections as well and saw language acquisition more as a process of a child's experimentation and revision of conclusions. He viewed first- and second-language learning as barely comparable, because after a person has mastered the native language, he or she brings different knowledge to the task of second-language learning. The "natural way" made no sense. Neither did learning through memorization and practice of patterns.

Along the way, Gattegno had encountered a Belgian schoolteacher named Georges Cuisenaire who had devised a way of teaching mathematics using small rectangular, colored rods of varying lengths. Gattegno came up with a novel way to use these Cuisenaire rods, named after their inventor, in the language classroom. In doing so, he could very early on in a course "transfer the responsibility for the use of the language to my students, so that I became able to teach using fewer and fewer words."[12] It's from this that he coined the name. However, "The Silent Way" doesn't mean that the teacher never speaks.

Gattegno claimed that even knowing the vocabulary and syntax of a foreign language did not assure understanding it. This is because an essential aspect of any language has usually been overlooked. It's what he calls the "spirit" of the language. An important part is the "melody"—the intonation, the speed, even the breathing that varies subtly from language to language.[13] The Silent Way prefers to focus on this aspect of language at the beginning by exploiting a restricted number of words and grammatical structures. At the end of four or five English lessons, the students are working with only about twenty-seven words: just one noun (*rod*), several colors, a few numbers, the definite and indefinite articles, some personal pronouns and adjectives, the adverbs *here* and *there*, the preposition *to*, the conjunction *and*, and two or three verbs (*take, give, put*) in the imperative.[14]

Most of the work in the method rests on the Cuisenaire rods, which can be used to create a surprising number of situations for students to describe. An extremely simplified account of the first lesson has the teacher taking a rod and through mime, inducing the students to repeat the few words uttered. More mime and work with the rods quickly leads the class to the basic vocabulary and structures mentioned above. Errors, which are gently pointed out by modeling of other students, are to be expected. "To require perfection at once is the great imperfection of most teaching," in Gattegno's words.[15] This kind approach to errors is vital because the method requires uninhibited student participation.

Another key tool in the Silent Way is the wall charts that list previously covered vocabulary items. In one example of their use, the teacher (or a student, for that matter) gives "visual dictation" by pointing to words either individually or in succession. The wall charts also serve as references for written work because the charts are displayed permanently.

Many other supplementary activities build on these tools. Gattegno lists the complete set of materials needed for all of them:

> (1) a set of colored wooden rods, (2) a set of wall charts, (3) phonic code charts, (4) tapes [or CDs today], (5) drawings and pictures and a set of accompanying worksheets, (6) transparencies and a second set of worksheets, (7) three texts: sentences to be read separately; sentences to be read consecutively; a Book of Stories, (8) worksheets on the whole language, without any restrictions, (9) three anthologies, and (10) films.[16]

Gattegno promises results in the first few lessons:

> The students will be astonished to find that their teacher stands through much of the lessons, that he keeps them concentrating all the time, that he says less and less and they more and more, that he neither approves nor disapproves but throws them back upon their own tools of judgment, indicating that they must listen better, use their mouths differently, stress here or there, shorten one sound and prolong another.[17]

The Silent Way still has its practitioners, but it's not hard to see with even a superficial summary that to do it properly requires training and practice, thus limiting its spread.

## SUGGESTOPEDIA

Lowering the psychological barriers of foreign-language learners was commonplace by the 1970s, but Suggestopedia took this idea into new territory. Dr. Georgi Lozanov[18] (1926–2012) was a Bulgarian psychiatrist, psychotherapist, and practitioner of Suggestology,[19] one tenet of which is that the brain has unused resources that can be tapped for greatly increased learning efficiency.

> The main obstacle encountered in teaching is memorization, automation and the assimilation of the material presented. Teaching methods have so far been in accordance with the accepted "restricted" capacities of the human personality. . . . One of the most important tasks of suggestopedy has been to free, to desuggest and to explain to all students that human capacities are much greater than expected, and to provide liberating-stimulating methods to bring these locked-up human resources into play. . . . It must be underlined, however, that suggestopedy stimulates not only the memory, but the whole personality—its interests, perceptions, creativity, moral development, etc.[20]

The key to developing this potential is relaxation. Lozanov applied this to language teaching and named it Suggestopedia.[21] The method presents us with a classroom unlike any other. Students are seated in comfortable reclining armchairs; classical music plays softly in the background as they listen to the teacher read a long dialogue, the voice rhythmically matching the music. The result, Lozanov claimed, is a method that can teach languages faster than any other.

The aim of Suggestopedia is rapid learning, especially vocabulary acquisition, thanks to a hyper-receptive state created by a combination of physical and mental factors. We've just mentioned the comfortable reclining chairs and the classical music. That sets the stage for the best-known feature of the method, the presentation of the dialogue at the beginning of each lesson. The content, according to Lozanov, should be communicative, motivational, entertaining, interesting, and light-hearted.[22] A Suggestopedia dialogue is long—about ten pages and twelve hundred words. The translation is right there in a parallel column, and there are notes on grammatical points. In the first presentation, the students and teacher go through the dialogue together, following closely for meaning and pronunciation. Questions and comments in the students' first language are welcomed. The second time through, the class follows as the teacher reads the text in rhythm with the music, which has been "specially selected as suitable and experimentally checked. . . . The teacher must be able to modulate the tone and pitch of his voice to be in harmony with the particular features of the music."[23] Then comes the third and final reading, in which the instructor reads the dialogue yet again, this time in a normal voice but always with music in the background. The students are required to reread the text just before retiring at night and once again as soon as they get up the next day. In fact, no other homework is given, and they are even discouraged from additional self-study of the material.

The follow-up activities include imitation of the text, questions and answers, original and creative language production, study in an extra text, conversation on given themes, and voluntary role-playing.[24] Error correction plays an important role in Suggestopedia, but it must be done carefully and correctly in order not to embarrass the student. Ideally, errors are not pointed out directly; instead, the teacher either uses the correct form in another context or devises a situation for another student to give the proper language.

The relationship between teacher and students is crucial for establishing the necessary state of relaxation and trust; the goal for the students is a condition referred to as "infantilization," in which they willingly accept information from the teacher, who assumes a sort of parental role. The instructor is seen as a knowledgeable authority figure, serious but caring. This air of professionalism and seriousness is stressed from the very beginning: Lozanov counsels staff to be restrained, polite, confident, and discreet even when prospective students show up for information and course registration.[25] In the classroom, students assume new identities and fictional biographies.[26] All this is intended to give them a sense of freedom in their classroom behavior and a strong trust in those responsible for their language instruction.

There's a lot more to it, though, than dreamy-eyed students leaning back and listening to music. In his 1978 book, *Suggestology and Outlines of Suggestopedy*, Lozanov needed 390 pages to deliver the background and details of the method. And to be a teacher in Suggestopedia requires certification after weeks of training. It's no wonder, then, that in spite of its claims and testimonials, it's not an everyday solution to language pedagogy.

Nevertheless, interest around the world ran high in the 1970s and 1980s—partly because it was unique and for many, exotic (a method from *Bulgaria*?), but mostly because of its remarkable claims about accelerated learning and the potential applications of its principles to learning.

The courses are still available; until his death, each graduate received certification signed by Lozanov himself.[27] However, the effectiveness of the method is open to debate. According to an extensive study in Canada that compared Suggestopedia to an SGAV-inspired course,[28] the method did obtain superior results in the spoken language, though not as striking as those claimed by its supporters. Perhaps its strongest point was the exceptional enthusiasm produced among the students and their desire to communicate in the language, which, the report noted, is not a characteristic that can be measured.

## COMMUNICATIVE LANGUAGE TEACHING

The "designer methods" associated with the 1970s were a welcome change, but not long-term solutions in themselves. We mustn't be fooled into thinking they represented mainstream language teaching during this time. However, another, much more important result of the break with the past was the success of Communicative Language Teaching (CLT), the dominant theme in language teaching to this day. Unsurprisingly, it represented a pendulum swing away from learning through structures and controlled vocabulary. One reason is a subtle change in audience. In the 1960s and 1970s, European integration proceeded at an impressive pace, giving rise to demand for an improved way to teach languages. Although the emphasis for years had been on a practical oral approach, it was increasingly felt that language teaching needed to focus more on language in its wider contexts and varied uses: functions such as giving and asking directions, shopping, or telling time, for example, and notions like quantity, location, size, and so on. Another factor was the influence of current linguistics. Noam Chomsky, while knocking off structuralism, had revolutionized the study of language—among linguists, at least. Chomsky was not concerned with teaching foreign languages; he was interested in investigating the abilities of native speakers to create language to express their thoughts. Neither was he concerned with the social aspects of communication; it was enough for him to theorize an "ideal speaker" in isolation, one who represented all speakers of the language. This was criticized by more practically oriented scholars, who complained that Chomsky was ignoring the true purpose of language: communication. However, there was no single catalyst for CLT. It was simply a philosophy into which language teaching had grown.

We sometimes use the terms "method" and "approach" haphazardly because it can be hard to draw the line between them. But Communicative Language Teaching is definitely an approach rather than a method. It has no set guidelines, no special textbooks, and not even a guru associated with it. Anything goes, really, as long as it develops the ability to communicate, to perform the variety of functions needed in real communication. Success in communication is what counts, so error correction is not of primary importance. The ultimate aim is "communicative competence," a phrase that describes what abilities a successful speaker of a language should possess. A useful categorization divides this into four types of competence:[29]

1. Grammatical competence: This is pretty self-explanatory, but note that it includes vocabulary as well as the rules of syntax, morphology, phonology, and so on.
2. Sociolinguistic competence: This deals with the social or nonlinguistic aspect of communication—knowing what topic or degree of formality is appropriate in a given situation, for example.

3. Discourse competence: This is knowledge of rules governing cohesion and coherence.

4. Strategic competence: This refers to the ability to use both verbal and nonverbal strategies to make up for breakdowns in communication because of performance variables or insufficient competence.

CLT, in brief, is all about meaningful communication and communicative competence. It is believed that language is more easily learned in meaningful and realistic situations. It's very similar to the goals of the Situational Approach and SGAV, but in a looser, more realistic and less controlled environment. As an approach rather than a method, the class objectives often depend on the needs of the particular students, and the range and variety of exercises and activities is limited only by the teacher's imagination.

## STEPHEN KRASHEN

Stephen Krashen, an American linguist (born 1941), has the honor of being the final personality in our historical survey. For many teachers, especially outside Europe, Krashen was the dominant figure in applied linguistics in the 1980s and afterward. No other linguist achieved such a level of popularity. What endeared him to so many was a clear and simple theory of language acquisition. It consists of five hypotheses of varying fame:

1. The Acquisition/Learning Hypothesis: There is a distinction between language *learning*, which is a conscious process, and language *acquisition*, an unconscious process. Learning is what traditionally goes on in classrooms: it means studying rules, memorizing vocabulary, and taking tests, but it rarely produces an ability to communicate well. Acquisition, on the other hand, is what we think of as truly knowing a language and is the real goal of any student. Acquiring a language can occur only through constant meaningful communication.

2. The Natural Order Hypothesis: There is a natural order of acquisition of grammatical structures for any language. Most students will learn them in this natural order, regardless of first language, age, or other personal factors.

3. The Monitor Hypothesis: Most of us know the feeling. Despite knowing countless rules of a foreign language, in practice it just doesn't magically turn into smooth communication, because we're having to think about form every moment as we go along. The Monitor Hypothesis says that the rules and grammar that one has learned in the classroom (the learning system) serve only to monitor, or edit, the language produced by the acquisition system. This is successful only when there is enough time to think (which rarely

happens in real communication), the speaker is focused on form (which is possible only with adequate time), and he or she knows the relevant rule. Unfortunately, these conditions are rarely met. The degree to which a person uses the monitor is principally a function of personality type.

4. The Input Hypothesis: A learner progresses best by receiving comprehensible input that is slightly beyond his or her current level of knowledge. This is usually represented as $i + 1$, where $i$ represents the current level of knowledge and 1 is one step beyond that. Anything more difficult will lead to frustration from lack of comprehension.

5. The Affective Filter Hypothesis: The last hypothesis addresses psychological factors. Low motivation, anxiety, and low self-esteem, for example, can create a mental block, what Krashen calls an affective filter[30] that interferes with the comprehensible input needed for acquisition. This is why a positive, relaxing environment will greatly improve success in the classroom.

There is actually little in the theory that is new, from a historical point of view. No matter; it was seen as good advice that many found helpful. Teachers liked Krashen. However, experts in applied linguistics generally did not.[31] The complaint most often heard was that his theory simply was "unverifiable," and an unverifiable theory is a dead end. As one scholar has said in evaluating any theory, "The value of a scientific theory . . . normally lies in its explanatory power, its capacity to predict, and in the direction it gives to empirical research. . . . In short, a good theory stimulates research."[32] Although a lot of teachers found Krashen's hypotheses to be useful, in the end the theory could not serve as a means to advance language learning theory. How can you manipulate and measure inherently vague concepts such as learning versus acquisition, monitoring, and affective filters? Nevertheless, Krashen remains a popular and influential figure for many teachers, and has never stopped being active. These days he's a leading promoter of free voluntary reading in the classroom.

# 32 Conclusion

Instead of summarizing the entire history of language teaching in a few paragraphs, I direct the reader to the summary of each chapter in table form at the end of the book.

I hope that you have found something of benefit and interest in this book, and that you will recognize the significance of studying the history of our area of expertise. Before beginning this book, I distributed a questionnaire online and at work directed at teachers of English as a foreign or second language. I received 106 replies from a sample made up mostly of native speakers of English. I gave a list of twenty names and terms throughout history, both famous and obscure, and asked respondents to choose from the following: (1) I'm not familiar with this name or term; (2) I've heard of this name or term; or (3) If I had to, I could say a few words about this person or term. The only pre-1970s items that were even slightly familiar to more than half the audience were behaviorism, structuralism, and the Grammar-Translation Method. The big "winners," not surprisingly, were Krashen, Chomsky, all of the 1970s methods discussed in Chapter 31, and the Audio-lingual Method and Oral Approach. When questioned about names discussed in this book, 57 percent were not familiar with Harold Palmer, 66 percent with Henry Sweet, 59 percent with Jan Comenius, and 89 percent with Donatus. This of course was an informal survey that makes no pretense of scientific accuracy, but I believe the results were generally valid, at least in terms of the relative rankings of awareness of the names and terms.

My hope is that having read this far, you will agree that it is a pity that some important and interesting figures are forgotten today. I would like to see history become an accepted subfield of language-teaching education someday. Who knows? Eventually perhaps there will even be an association or two devoted to the topic.[1] On a smaller scale, I simply hope that I've stimulated some interest in the topic and provided some knowledge. As Montaigne said, "Make use of it as you wish."

I welcome comments from readers at garonwheeler@gmail.com.

# Appendix I

## SUMMARY OF CHAPTERS

Keep in mind that this is a summary of the people and events featured in the book. It is not intended to be a comprehensive overview of the history of the teaching of foreign languages.

| Chapter | Date | Key Names | Key Works and Events | Comments |
|---|---|---|---|---|
| Mesopotamia | c. 3300–2000 BC | Sumerians | First writing system, approximately 3300 BC: history begins | |
| | | Akkadians | Learned Sumerian, approximately 2000 BC. | They were the conquerors, but Sumerian was a more prestigious language. |
| Egypt | c. 1000–500 BC | | Study of texts in an older form of the language that was no longer intelligible. | Studying an older form of one's own language can be like studying a foreign language. |
| The Greeks | c. 500–100 BC | | Complete system of education; development of language description. | Studies were of their own language only. |
| | | Homer (700s BC) | Wrote the *Iliad* and the *Odyssey*, stories loved by all Greeks. | The works were studied in the original archaic form of Greek. |

*Continued*

Continued

| | | | | |
|---|---|---|---|---|
| | Dionysius Thrax (100s BC) | One of the first detailed grammars. | His description of Greek set the standard for language description up until today. | |
| The Romans | c. 500 BC–500 AD | | Adopted the Greek systems of education and language description. | They were fond of all Greek learning and the Greek language. |
| | *Hermeneumata* | Latin/Greek books for the school. | The works consisted of dialogues, readings, word lists, etc. They could be used to teach either language. | |
| The Middle Ages | 500–1500 | Most education in Europe was done through the Church. | | |
| | Donatus (400s) | The *Ars Minor*. | His Latin book, based on Roman and Greek technique, was the main grammar book in schools for more than one thousand years. Latin was eventually a foreign language for all students. | |
| | Priscian (c. 500) | *Institutiones grammaticae* (Grammatical Foundations). | A lengthy work, it was the most important Latin grammar for centuries. It was not intended for the classroom. | |
| William Lily | English, 1468?–1522 | | *A Short Introduction of Grammar*, more commonly known as Lily's Grammar (1540). | This was the official Latin text for English schools, used by generations. It was heavy on grammatical rules. |

| | | | |
|---|---|---|---|
| **Erasmus** | Dutch, 1466?– 1536 | *De ratione studii* (On the Method of Study, 1511). | This was an early example of proposed educational reform: inductive learning, proper presentation of materials. |
| **Roger Ascham** | English, 1515– 1568 | *The Scholemaster* (1570). | The book advocated double translation and called for considerate treatment of students. |
| **Claude Holyband** | French, active in England in 1500s | *The French School-master* (1573), *The French Littelton* (1576). | He owned successful language schools in London. The books relied heavily on entertaining dialogues. |
| **Michel de Montaigne** | French, 1533– 1592 | | Credited with originating the essay as a literary form, he described being raised as a native speaker of Latin, a dead language. |
| **John Brinsley** | English, born 1564 or 1565, active in early 1600s | *Ludus Literarius, or the Grammar Schoole* (1612). | The book described the ideal classical method in the classroom and compared it with the reality of the day. |
| **Eilhard Lubinus** | German, active in early 1600s | Preface to an edition of the New Testament of the Bible; republished in English (1614, 1621). | Learning should involve the senses, not just the study of rules and words on a page or their repetition. He was a great influence on Comenius. |
| **Jan Comenius** | Moravian (Czech), 1592– 1670 | *The Great Didactic* (1632), *Janua linguarum reserata* (The Gate to Languages Unlocked, 1633), *Orbis pictus* | "The first [person] to conceive a full-scale science of education" (Piaget). Learning involves all senses. Psycho- |

*Continued*

| | | | (The Visible World in Pictures, 1658). | logical factors are of the highest importance in the classroom. |
|---|---|---|---|---|
| **Port-Royal Community** | France, mid-1600s | | | They saw language learning as a means to better understanding of religious teaching, helping to save students' souls. |
| | | Claude Lancelot, grammarian (1616?–1695) | *Nouvelle Méthode latine* (New Latin Method, 1644). | This was one of the first teaching grammars in the students' own language. The rules were in rhyme. A main focus was on the visual presentation of the material. |
| | | Claude Lancelot, Antoine Arnauld, philosopher (1612–1694) | *La grammaire générale et raisonée* (The General and Rational Grammar, commonly known as the Port-Royal Grammar, 1660). | This was an early look at universal grammar: principles of language that are independent of time and place. Chomsky acknowledged it as a forerunner of his grammatical theories. |
| **John Wilkins** | English, 1614–1672 | | *An Essay towards a Real Character and a Philosophical Language* (1668). | The best-known attempt to create a universal language, it was based on a complete categorization of all knowledge and not derived from any language, living or dead. |
| **John Locke** | English, 1632–1704 | | *Some Thoughts Concerning Education* (1693). | Dismissing the need to study Latin and grammar rules, he focused on the needs of children inside and outside the classroom. |

| César Chesneau du Marsais | French, 1676–1756 | | *Éxposition d'une méthode raisonée pour apprendre la langue latine* (Exposition of a Rational Method for Learning the Latin Language, 1722). | He advocated rearranging Latin texts into French word order, with the emphasis on vocabulary acquisition. As with children, grammar study came only later. |
|---|---|---|---|---|
| Robert Lowth | English, 1710–1787 | | *A Short Introduction to English Grammar* (for native speakers, 1762). | He was the leading figure in prescriptivism: a language form is either right or wrong. He pointed out errors from the Bible to Shakespeare. The book made extensive use of footnotes to create an essentially two-level course. |
| Lindley Murray | American, active in England, 1745–1826 | | English Grammar (for native speakers, 1795), English Exercises Adapted to Murray's English Grammar (1797). | He believed that a detailed knowledge of one's own language laid the foundations for the intellectual skills required for an education. His grammar was a two-level course using fonts of different sizes for basic and advanced information. He created the first grammar exercises, heralding sentence-based language study. |
| Grammar-Translation | Originated in Germany in late 1700s, common in 1800s | Johann Franz Ahn (1796–1865), Heinrich Ollendorff (1803–1865) | Numerous books for teaching or self-study in various European languages. | It was intended as a kinder method that used realistic sentences instead of literature. The original method had very little explicit grammar. The method |

*Continued*

| | | | | deteriorated through-out the century until it became associated with the detailed study of rules. |
|---|---|---|---|---|
| **Two Diversions** | Mid to late 1800s | | | |
| | | Thomas Prendergast (British, 1806–1886) | Mastery Series of self-instruction for several languages (1864–1872). | The method was based on learning long, carefully constructed sentences and sets of variations. It was inspired by children's learning language in context. Instructions for study had to be followed exactly. |
| | | François Gouin (French, 1831–1896) | *L'art d'enseigner et d'étudier les langues* (The Art of Teaching and Studying Languages, 1880). | He created the Series Method, inspired by the author's observation of his nephew learning his first language. The verb is central as actions are broken down into a series of smaller actions. Gouin recalled his search for the best way to learn German in a long, somewhat improbable story. |
| **Esperanto** | 1887–present | Ludwik Zamenhof (Polish, 1859–1917) | | This is the most successful created or artificial language. Largely based on Latin and European languages, it has many fans even today. |
| **Natural Methods** | Late 1800s | | | This meant learning a language the way children do: |

| | | | |
|---|---|---|---|
| | | | through usage, without translation or grammar. The term includes the Direct Method. |
| | Lambert Sauveur (French, active in the United States, 1826–1907) | *Causeries avec mes élèves* (Chats with My Students, 1874), *Causeries avec les enfants* (Chats with Children, 1874), *Introduction to the Teaching of Living Languages without Grammar or Dictionary* (1875). | The teaching texts relied on imaginary, realistic conversations to be assimilated after extensive preparation. He used the term "Natural Method." |
| | Maximilian Berlitz (German, active in the United States; 1852–1921) | The Berlitz Method, adapted to books for many languages. | He founded a highly successful chain of language schools. |
| **Reform Movement** | Late 1800s | | It combined the new sciences of linguistics (especially phonetics) and psychology to turn language teaching into a modern discipline. |
| | Wilhelm Viëtor (German, 1850–1918) | *Der Sprachunterrict muss umkehren!* (Language Teaching Must Start Afresh!, 1882). | This influential pamphlet pointed out the lack of progress in foreign-language education and called for modern solutions. |
| | Henry Sweet (British, 1845–1912) | *The Practical Study of Languages* (1899) and many others. | This was a complete and modern guide to studying all aspects of a foreign language. |
| Two Reports | | | The reports focused on the state of |

*Continued*

*Continued*

| | | | | language teaching in the United States |
|---|---|---|---|---|
| | 1898 | | The Report of the "Committee of Twelve." | Noting the geographical isolation of the US, it reviewed current methods and recommended an emphasis on reading |
| | 1929 | | The Coleman Report. | It was a bigger report but reached the same conclusion: reading is the obvious skill to emphasize. |
| **Harold Palmer** | British, 1877–1949 | | *The Principles of Language-Study* (1921) and many others. | He gave practical, detailed advice for the classroom from an experienced teacher. |
| **Basic English** | Mostly in the UK, late 1920s to 1940s | Charles Ogden (British, 1889–1957) | | This was a simplified version of English to serve as an international instrument for science and business. |
| **World War II** | 1939–1945 | | | War occasioned the application of structuralism and anthropology to the urgent need for speakers of many languages. |
| After the War | 1945–1970s | Audio-lingual Method (ALM), US; Situational Approach, UK; SGAV (St-Cloud Method), France | | Common principles included presentation, practice, and production; dialogues and controlled vocabulary; drills to practice structures; comprehension precedes production. It marked the first |

| | | | |
|---|---|---|---|
| | | | widespread use of technology in the classroom. |
| **1970s and Beyond** | | | Cognitive psychology allowed experimentation in foreign-language teaching. The focus was on a relaxed classroom atmosphere and communicative competence. |
| | James Asher (American, born 1929) | Total Physical Response (TPR). | Language learning is aided by movement; students follow increasingly complex commands. |
| | Charles Curran (American, born 1934) | Community Language Learning. | Based on group discussions, the teacher acts as counselor and facilitator who gives any needed language help for students to contribute. These conversations can be recorded and analyzed. |
| | Caleb Gattegno (Egyptian of Spanish descent, 1911–1988) | The Silent Way. | There is a focus on the "spirit" of the language. It involves practice with Cuisenaire rods and the use of limited vocabulary and grammar at the beginning, to allow the teacher to transfer speaking to the students. It uses specified materials such as wall charts, worksheets, readings, recordings, etc. |

*Continued*

*Continued*

| | | |
|---|---|---|
| Georgi Lozanov (Bulgarian, 1926–2012) | Suggestopedia. | It is based on the belief that the brain is capable of more efficient learning than we know. Complete relaxation leads to a hyper-receptive state. |
| Stephen Krashen (American, born 1941) | Associated terms: comprehensible input, learning/ acquisition distinction, monitor theory, affective filter. | His simple, clear theory of language acquisition was (and still is) popular with many teachers. |

# Notes

## NOTES TO THE INTRODUCTION

1. McCullough, "Why History?" 89.
2. The Peace Corps is an organization of the American government that sends teachers and other volunteers to developing countries around the world.
3. Stearns, "Why Study History?"
4. The main points are from Phillips, "American History."
5. Stearns, "Why Study History?"
6. Phillips, "American History."
7. Koerner, *Linguistic Historiography*, 7.
8. Surprisingly, there wasn't even an attempt at sharing ideas in the form of journals or conferences until the early twentieth century.

## NOTES TO CHAPTER 1

1. Among the better-known theories are that language originated with primitive exclamations of pain, surprise, etc.; that it began with onomatopoeia (imitation of sounds); or that its origins lay in the grunting and groaning noises made by groups working together. These have been irreverently dubbed the "pooh-pooh," "bow-wow," and "yo-he-ho" theories, respectively.
2. Germain, *Évolution de l'enseignement des langues*; Titone, *Cinque millenni*. Note that Titone wrote an earlier and more easily found book on this topic in English: *Teaching Foreign Languages: An Historical Sketch*.

## NOTES TO CHAPTER 2

1. Kramer, *Sumerians*, 231.
2. Frayne, "Scribal Education in Ancient Babylonia."
3. Germain, *Évolution de l'enseignement des langues*, 22.
4. Ibid.
5. This is similar to situations we'll encounter in Rome and medieval Europe regarding Greek and Latin.
6. Titone, *Cinque millenni*, 26.

## NOTES TO CHAPTER 3

1. Brunner, "L'éducation en ancienne Égypte," 1:77.

2. Mounin, *Histoire de la linguistique*, 1:34.
3. Brunner, "L'éducation en ancienne Egypte," 1:77.
4. Genesis 1:1–2. Quoted in Pyles and Algeo, *Origins and Development*, 132.
5. Genesis 1:1–2 (New International Version).
6. Both dates from Casson, *Ancient Egypt*, 156–157.
7. Mancini, *Maat Revealed*, chap. 1.
8. Lichtheim, *Ancient Egyptian Literature—A Book of Readings*.
9. Brunner, "L'éducation en ancienne Egypte," 1:73.

## NOTES TO CHAPTER 4

1. Keep in mind that this is a simplified and sanitized description of schools for children from relatively well-to-do families over several centuries. An important source of information is Marrou, *Education in Antiquity*. Marrou's book, written in French in 1948, is a classic and a standard. In recent years, there has been some criticism of his work, mainly for his approach to history, but not the accuracy of the facts. For a modern critique, see Too's "Ancient Education," 1–21.
2. Power, *Legacy of Learning*, 9–11.
3. Kelly, *25 Centuries*, 152.
4. Marrou, *Education in Antiquity*, 155–156; Power, *Legacy of Learning*, 11–12.
5. Kelly, *25 Centuries*, 258. "Booksellers had them copied by slaves, one reader dictating to a roomful of scribes; but the expense of books produced in this way meant that very few could afford them."
6. This quote and variations of it are attributed to several authors. The most likely source is Isocrates, circa 400 BC.
7. Aristotle, *Politics*, 8.4.4.
8. Power, *Legacy of Learning*, 10–11.
9. Marrou, *Education in Antiquity*, 161–170.
10. "pro-jim-NAS-ma-ta."
11. Webb, "The *Progymnasmata* as Practice," 290. "The *progymnasmata* were therefore crucial in laying the foundations for elite discourse, and must have helped to inculcate certain modes of thinking about language, about the classical texts which served as models, and about the relation of the individual to those texts and to language in general."
12. Marrou, *Education in Antiquity*, 174. Marrou attributes this exercise to the *Rhetores Graeci* of Aphtonius [Aphthonius] (fourth century AD).
13. "my-SEE-nee."
14. Power, *Legacy of Learning*, 4–6; Marrou, *Education in Antiquity*, 169.
15. Note, in fact, that "The Lord's Prayer" has resisted modernization and is still often recited in the older form: "Our father, who art in heaven, hallowed be thy name."
16. Marrou, *Education in Antiquity*, 165–170.
17. R. H. Robins, *A Short History of Linguistics*, 31. It's important to note that the first detailed grammar that we know of was written by the great Indian grammarian Pāṇini, in about 350 BC. However, his work was not known to the West for centuries and thus did not have the effect that it merited. Dionysius's work, in contrast, reportedly remained a standard work for thirteen centuries.
18. Ibid.

## NOTES TO CHAPTER 5

1. *Epistles*, 2.1. My translation.
2. Marrou, *Education in Antiquity*, 246.

3. Titone, *Cinque millenni*, 17.
4. Ibid.
5. It's useful to say that it was a smooth transition from Greek to Roman education, but see Power, *Educational Philosophy*, 20–26, for a more critical look at the process.
6. Marrou, *Education in Antiquity*, 265–273.
7. Power, *Educational Philosophy*, 20.
8. Augustine, *Confessions*, 29–30. Translation by R. S. Pine-Coffin.
9. Marrou, *Education in Antiquity*, 274.
10. Quintilian, *Institutionis oratoriae*, 1:43–44. Translation from Kelly, *25 Centuries*, 132.
11. Marrou, *Education in Antiquity*, 255.
12. "SIS-uh-ro" in modern pronunciation.
13. Germain, *Évolution de l'enseignment*, 44.
14. Goetz, *Hermeneumata Pseudodositheana*, 31. My translation.
15. Ibid., 649. My translation.
16. Titone, *Cinque millenni*, 28.
17. Goetz, *Hermeneumata Pseudodositheana*, 645. My translation.
18. "dy-o-MEE-deez."
19. In languages such as Latin or Greek, the grammatical role of each noun in a sentence is indicated by its ending. Taking "woman" as an example, the ending lets us know whether the word is a subject (*femina*) or an object (*feminam*) or if it indicates possession (*feminae*). These grammatical roles are called the noun's "cases." These will be mentioned often in the coming chapters.
20. Keil, *Flavii Sosipatri*, 310. My translation. This is the expression from Isocrates mentioned earlier, but here it is attributed to the politician Cato and changed slightly to refer to the roots of literature rather than of education.
21. Kelly, *25 Centuries*, 140.

## NOTES TO CHAPTER 6

1. Chase, Introduction to *Ars Minor of Donatus*, 12–13.
2. Ibid.
3. "doh-NOT-us."
4. *Donati de partibus orationis ars minor.* He wrote two successful grammar works; this was the shorter or "lesser" one.
5. For example, the narrator in William Langland's *Piers the Plowman* (fourteenth century) uses it to refer to learning the basics of dishonest business practices (passus 5, line 209). Langland, *Piers the Plowman*, 146.
6. Chase, Introduction to *Ars Minor of Donatus*, 10. Chase cites a 1901 Italian list of recent publications, which includes the *Ars minor*. The subtitle indicates that it contains principles of Latin grammar for grammar school students. It was the fiftieth edition.
7. Donatus, *Ars Minor of Donatus*, 29.
8. Ibid., 31.
9. Clerval, *Les Écoles de Chartres*, 221–222. My translation.
10. Kelly, *25 Centuries*, 258. Kelly gives credit to St. Augustine (fourth and fifth centuries AD) for creating this method of learning.
11. "PRISH-en."
12. Norton, *History of Education*, 134–139. As an example of their enduring influence, surviving lists of requirements for a university degree show that they were necessary reading at the universities in Paris in 1254, Oxford in 1267, and Leipzig in 1519.

13. "mo-DIS-ty," from their discussions of "the modes of signifying," or the ways that words related to reality.
14. Thomas of Erfurt, *Grammatica speculativa*. Intrepid readers are directed to G. L. Bursill-Hall's introduction to Thomas of Erfurt for a summary of their theory.
15. It's interesting to note in passing that even the Modistae started their grammatical philosophizing with a framework taken from Priscian.
16. Also known as Alexander de Villa Dei and Alexander Villadei.
17. But R. H. Robins, a noted recent historian of linguistics, wasn't impressed, calling it "2645 lines of rather barbarous verse," though it seems to show, at least, that the preoccupation for correctness was lessening. Robins, *Short History of Linguistics*, 72.
18. Kelly, *25 Centuries*, 141.
19. John of Salisbury, *Metalogicus*, 852–853. Translation from Kelly, *25 Centuries*, 347.
20. This would actually be the early Renaissance, but it is still a reflection of medieval education.
21. "bo-EE-thee-us."Also known as Boetius ("bo-EE-shus"), as in the drawing.
22. "TOL-uh-me" and "puh-THAG-or-us."
23. "PLIN-ee."

## NOTES TO CHAPTER 7

1. *Deductive* learning, in our case, means learning the rules first and then applying them in practice. The opposite, *inductive* learning, means figuring out the rules from practicing the language—the way young children do.
2. Howatt, *History*, 35.
3. Kelly, *25 Centuries*, 34.
4. The book ran through approximately one hundred editions. Flynn, Introduction to Lily, *Short introduction of grammar*, x.
5. Ibid., iv.
6. Howatt, for example, devotes only two paragraphs to him even though "every educated person knew [the book] by heart" in the early sixteen hundreds (*History of English Language Teaching*, 32, 95). Kelly offers just a quote by Lily; the only other reference to him is in a quote by a later scholar, who dismissed the book as "ill contrived" (*25 Centuries*, 172, 221).
7. This introduction was published in the first and in succeeding editions.
8. Lily, *Short introduction of grammar*, "To the Reader," A5v (nonpaginated introduction; second page of the section).
9. Ibid., "An Introduction of the Eight Parts of Latin Speech," B1r (first page of the section).
10. Ibid., "To the Reader," A5v–A6r (second and third pages).
11. The poem was written by the Roman statesman and author Marcus Porcius Cato (234–149 BC), better known as Cato the Elder.
12. Ibid., "Carmen de Moribus," E7r (thirteenth page of the section). My translations.
13. Flynn, Introduction to Lily, x.

## NOTES TO CHAPTER 8

1. The Reformation was a sixteenth-century attempt to "reform" the Catholic Church. It instead resulted in the founding of the Protestant churches.

2. The full title is *De ratione studii ac legendi interpretandique auctores* [On the Method of Study and the Reading and Interpretation of Authors]. It's a short work, approximately twenty pages.
3. Erasmus, *De ratione studii*, 672.
4. Ibid., 667–669.
5. Ibid., 671.
6. Erasmus, *De pueris statim*, 324.
7. Compare his comments on the reality of the day, though:
   > No useless, disreputable scoundrel nowadays is disqualified by general opinion from running a school. . . . There are teachers whose manners are so uncouth that even their wives cannot have any affection for them. . . . They are unable to say anything in a pleasant manner. . . . One might truly say that the Graces frowned upon the hour of their birth. I should scarcely think such men fit to look after my horses. (*De pueris statim*, 324)
8. From the Latin word for "native" or "domestic." In this case it refers to national languages such as English, French, German, etc., as opposed to Latin or ancient Greek.

## NOTES TO CHAPTER 9

1. "ASK-em."
2. Eton College is a famous boarding school, founded in 1440.
3. Ascham, *Scholemaster*, 17–18. I have put many of the quotes in this section into somewhat more modern English.
4. Ibid., 18.
5. Ibid., 19.
6. Ibid., 21.
7. Ibid., 26. All the information on double translation is from the first few pages of "The First Booke for the Youth," the first chapter of *The Schoolmaster*.
8. Ibid.
9. Ibid., 27.
10. Ibid., 29.
11. Ibid., 28.
12. Ibid., 29.
13. Ibid., 96.

## NOTES TO CHAPTER 10

1. Howatt, *History*, 19.
2. *The Schoolmaster* was written for study at home, as its wonderfully long title tells us: *The Frenche Schoolemaister, wherein is most plainlie shewn the true and most perfect way of pronouncinge of the frenche tongue, without any helpe or teacher, set forthe for the furtherance of all those which doo studie privately in their owne study or house: Unto which is annexed a vocabularie for all such wordes as bee used in common talkes*. On the other hand, *The French Littelton. A Most Easie, Perfect, and Absolute way to learne the frenche tongue* was written specifically for the classroom. Its title, borrowed from a well-known introductory law book of the day, indicates that its target audience is beginners.
3. Muriel St Clare Byrne, in her Introduction to *The Littelton*, considers the *Schoolmaster* as "a preliminary experiment" for the writing of *The Littelton* (xiv). Nevertheless, the books competed with each other for more than fifty years (xxii).

4. Byrne, Introduction to Holyband, *Littelton*, xiii.
5. *The Littelton* has a reading on dancing (an indication that it was written for the upper classes), while *The Schoolmaster* has a section on prayers; otherwise, they are very similar in organization.
6. Holyband, *Littelton*, 8, 10. In the books, the dialogues are actually written without any indication of who is speaking or when a change takes place, a custom as old as the *Hermeneumata*.
7. Holyband, *Littelton*, 22.

## NOTES TO CHAPTER 11

1. Herodotus, *Histories*, 2:2.
2. "mee-SHELL de mon-TEN-ya."
3. Montaigne, *Essais*, Vol. 1, 277. All the translations in this section are mine.
4. Ibid., 279.
5. Ibid., 278.
6. Ibid., 281.
7. Ibid., 280.
8. Ibid., 277.

## NOTES TO CHAPTER 12

1. Bush, *English Literature*, 1.
2. Subbiondo, "Universal Language," 178.
3. Adapted from Brinsley, *Ludus Literarius*, 1–8. The language has been updated for easier reading.
4. Ibid., 70.
5. Ibid., xviii.
6. Ibid., 76.
7. The traditional activity of parsing meant studying a sentence by identifying the parts of speech and then determining the relationships of the words.
8. Brinsley, *Ludus Literarius*, 115.
9. Ibid., 92–93. Find the main verb and the subject (nominative case). Translate the subject. Find any adjectives or participles that modify the subject and translate them. Translate the main verb and any following infinitive. Find and translate adverbs. Translate any nouns governed by the verb (accusative case). Translate the remaining nouns in order: genitive (possessive), dative (indirect object), etc.
10. Ibid., 173.
11. Ibid., 215.
12. Ibid., 219.
13. Ibid., 215.
14. Ibid., 212.
15. Ibid.
16. Ibid., chap. 29.
17. Ibid., 32.
18. Ibid., 305.

## NOTES TO CHAPTER 13

1. "ILE-hart lu-BEE-nus."

2. Samuel Hartlib, *The true and readie way*. The preface is dated 1614, seven years before Lubinus's death.
3. Ibid., 17.
4. Ibid., 8.
5. Ibid., 12.
6. Ibid., 19. Note that several of the quotes are from before the standardization of the possessive apostrophe; here he means "the memory's treasury."
7. Ibid., 25. What Lubinus is describing is an *empirical* approach to learning (knowledge is derived through the senses) as opposed to a *rationalist* one (knowledge comes through reason alone, independent of experience). It's an obscure argument today, but was of tremendous significance at the time and will be a recurring theme here. In the current discussion, learning grammar through Lily's rules is rationalist; learning through usage is empirical.
8. Ibid., 34.
9. Ibid., 30.

## NOTES TO CHAPTER 14

1. His birth name was Jan Komensky. Many scholars of his day Latinized all or part of their names. The result was the family name became Comenius. Pronunciations vary, but let's use "Yon Co-MAY-nee-us."
2. Howatt, *History*, 40.
3. Kozik, *Life of John Amos Comenius*.
4. Piaget, "John Amos Comenius," 2.
5. The book was written in Czech in about 1632, translated into Latin in 1657 as the *Didactica Magna*, and retranslated later into English as *The Great Didactic*. "Didactic" means "intended to instruct." The quote "teaching all things to all men" comes from the title page.
6. Comenius, *Great Didactic*, 4. Note that the facsimile reprint of the 1910 edition includes a great deal of introductory material with its own page numbering. The notes here refer to the numbering of the reprinted *Great Didactic* pages.
7. Ibid., 79.
8. Ibid., 93.
9. Ibid., 137.
10. Ibid., 137–138.
11. Ibid., 177.
12. "FLAH-toos VO-chees."
13. Comenius, *Great Didactic*, 179.
14. Ibid., 146.
15. Ibid., 257.
16. Ibid., 124.
17. Ibid., 122.
18. Ibid., 137.
19. Ibid., 272.
20. Ibid., 205.
21. Ibid., 165.
22. Ibid., 139.
23. Ibid., 251.
24. Ibid., 168.
25. Ibid., 249.
26. Ibid., 252.
27. Ibid., 253.

28. Ibid., 68.
29. Ibid., 67.
30. Ibid., 67.
31. Ibid., 254.
32. Ibid., 267.
33. Ibid., 296.
34. "YON-oo-ah."
35. Kelly, *25 Centuries*, 267.
36. "Nihil est in intellectu, quod non prius fuit in sensu."
37. Comenius, Preface to *Orbis*.
38. Piaget, "John Amos Comenius," 1.
39. Kelly, *25 Centuries*, 311.
40. Hoole, Preface to *Orbis*.

## NOTES TO CHAPTER 15

1. Wheeler, "Port-Royal Tradition," 170. Contrast this with the benevolent view of scholars such as Comenius, who saw language mastery as an opportunity to develop a joyful relationship with God.
2. "CLOAD law^n-se-LO." The raised *n* indicates a nasal sound. That is, the first syllable rhymes with "lawn" with the *n* unpronounced.
3. Lancelot, "Avis au lecteur" [Notice to the Reader] in *Nouvelle Méthode*, 2–3. My translation.
4. He noted without details that it had been done before, but it was still not at all the norm. In fact, Port-Royal gets credit as "being the first school of any importance to aim its teaching at the native language." Kelly, *25 Centuries*, 138.
5. Lancelot, *Nouvelle Méthode latine*, 5.
6. Ibid., 9.
7. Ibid., 99. "Rule 14: Of those verbs that take XI in the preterit without the supine: 'To be cold' and 'to shine' will receive [the suffix] XI, but will never have the supine." My translation.
8. Wheeler, "Port-Royal," 171. Lancelot's main influences were Vossius, Scioppius, and especially Sanctius. See the next chapter for more on the Modistae.
9. "Rational," "general," and "universal" grammar are terms often used interchangeably. "Universal" is more descriptive, but "rational," reflecting the influence of Descartes, and "general" are what the Port-Royalists and most others of the era used.
10. "ah^n-TWON ar-NO."
11. Its real title is *La grammaire générale et raisonée* [The General and Rational Grammar].
12. Wheeler, "Port-Royal," 172.
13. Ibid., 173–174.
14. "In many respects, it seems to me quite accurate, then, to regard the theory of transformational generative grammar . . . as essentially a modern and more explicit version of the Port-Royal theory." Chomsky, *Cartesian Linguistics*, 38–39.

## NOTES TO CHAPTER 16

1. Howatt, *History*, 102.

2. The result of his efforts "is acknowledged by historians of linguistics as the standard of the genre." Subbiondo, "Universal Language," 174.
3. Genesis 11:1–8. The story is that the residents of the city of Babel, in a display of both vanity and ability, intended to build a tower so high that it would reach the heavens. Until then, there had been only one language in the world, but a displeased God caused them to begin speaking different languages, making the necessary cooperation impossible.
4. Wilkins, *Essay*, 1. Italics in the original.
5. Ibid., "The Epistle Dedicatory," a2v (nonpaginated introduction, fourth page of section).
6. Ibid., a3r (fifth page).
7. Ibid., a3v (sixth page.)
8. Ibid., a1v (second page).
9. "Essay" in this case means an attempt; "character" here collectively means all his symbols.
10. Robins, *Short History of Linguistics,* 113–114.
11. Wilkins, *Essay*, 421.
12. The page uses "father" only because that is the usual translation.
13. Wilkins, "The Epistle Dedicatory," a2v (fourth page).

## NOTES TO CHAPTER 17

1. John Locke, *Some Thoughts Concerning Education*, 145.
2. Ibid., 145–149.
3. Ibid., 149.
4. Ibid., 138.
5. Ibid., 139.
6. Ibid., 140–141.
7. Ibid., 150–151.
8. Ibid., 172, 173, 150, 151–152.
9. Ibid., 151.
10. Ibid., 150.
11. Ibid., 140–145.
12. Ibid., 156.

## NOTES TO CHAPTER 18

1. A common language used by speakers with different native languages.
2. Kelly, *25 Centuries*, 318.
3. "say-ZAR shay-NO doo-mar-SAY."
4. D'Alembert, "Eloge de du Marsais" [In Praise of du Marsais], lxxii. All translations in this chapter are mine.
5. Ibid., lxix–lxx.
6. Because Latin uses a system of case endings to indicate syntactic relationships, and the verbs are clearly marked for person, the order of Latin words is very flexible and, especially in literature, can be highly unpredictable.
7. Du Marsais, *Éxposition*, 2.
8. Ibid., 5.
9. Ibid., 3.
10. Ibid., 7.
11. Aelfric's *Colloquy* (early eleventh century) is a good example of an earlier use of the technique.

12. Du Marsais, *Éxposition*, 10.
13. A simple example: "You ready?" instead of "Are you ready?"
14. Du Marsais, *Éxposition*, 17.
15. Ibid., 20.
16. This is strongly reminiscent of the exercise advocated by Brinsley, in which an English text is translated into literal Latin and then eloquent Latin.
17. Horace, *Carmen Saeculare* [Secular Hymn], st. 1, line 1.
18. Horace, *Odes of Horace*, 255.
19. Du Marsais, *Éxposition*, 10.
20. Ibid., 35.
21. Ibid., 36.
22. Ibid., v.

## NOTES TO CHAPTER 19

1. Lowth, *Short Introduction to English Grammar*, iii.
2. Ibid., viii.
3. Ibid., v.
4. Ibid.
5. Ibid., vi.
6. Ibid., iv.
7. Ibid., vii.
8. Ibid.
9. Ibid., viii.
10. Ibid., 95–96. Lowth noted this usage and actually approved of it in informal language, calling it "an idiom of the language."
11. Levizac, *Practical Guide*, iv–vi.

## NOTES TO CHAPTER 20

1. Howatt, *History*, 122.
2. Lowth's grammar was for general use, both inside and outside the classroom, while Murray's was written just for schools.
3. Monaghan, "Webster to McGuffey." Lack of copyright laws meant that he received nothing for most of them.
4. Murray, *English Grammar*, iv.
5. Ibid., vii.
6. Ibid., iv.
7. Ibid., vi.
8. Murray, *Exercises*, 12.
9. Ibid., 47. Original punctuation.
10. For example, "Substantives [nouns] are either proper or common. . . . There are exceptions. . . . If my son Toby should act indiscreetly, he would not be a proper fellow. . . . A cat is a common animal, but the winner of the Derby is an uncommon one." *Comic Lindley Murray*, 18.
11. Ibid., 9.
12. Ibid., 10.

## NOTES TO CHAPTER 21

1. Howatt, *History*, 132. I wasn't able to locate this book, but I did examine his *Praktische italienische Grammatik* [Practical Italian Grammar] from

1803. It's nearly five hundred pages and consists of the following sections: general information on grammar, pronunciation, spelling, etc.; short sections of German sentences to translate into Italian (none the other way) with new grammar points introduced every few pages; vocabulary lists by topic; conversations with parallel translations and vocabulary; short readings with vocabulary; one lengthy reading (a description of the Nile, oddly enough); a play by an unattributed author; and numerous examples of business letters in Italian. This format was indeed revolutionary.

2. This wasn't completely new. Comenius is just one example of predecessors who created graded materials, but keep in mind that in the old literature-based classrooms, the readings generally dictated the grammar and vocabulary.

3. It helps that in the early stages, it is possible to use sentences in which French word order closely matches English.

4. Ahn, *French Language*, 30. This shows that sometimes sentences *were* related, though this is about as long as a "passage" gets (in this book, at least). It also demonstrates that moral advice was still freely given.

5. "HINE-rick OH-len-dorf."

6. Foresti, Preface to *Italian Language*, ix.

7. Ibid., x.

8. Ibid.

9. Ibid., ix.

10. G. J. Adler, Preface to *Ollendorff's New Method of Learning to Read, Write, and Speak the German Language*, iv.

11. Ibid., italics in the original.

12. The references to events of the times, however, made for some bizarre sentences: "But must one not be a fool to remain in a place bombarded by Hungarians?" Ollendorff, *German*, 352. Or "I remember well how much I was embarrassed for want of knowing German when I was a prisoner in Prussia during the seven years' war." Ollendorff, *Italian*, 516.

13. Ollendorff, *Italian*, 449–450.

14. Pronunciation for both Ahn and Ollendorff was arrived at through an easy and logical system of transcription, rather like what you'd find in a dictionary for young students today.

15. It should be pointed out that Kelly (*25 Centuries*, 278) held the opinion that Grammar-Translation lowered teaching standards precisely for this same reason. However, he states that incompetence in the classroom was "still unusual" at the time of Comenius (seventeenth century), which is contrary to what we've seen.

## NOTES TO CHAPTER 22

1. Prendergast, Preface to *Hebrew*.

2. Ibid., xii.

3. The Hebrew book kept to sentences of a Biblical nature. In other languages, having to create such long sentences led to highly unlikely utterances. Imagine following Prendergast's instructions with this Text in Latin: "Does he think that the villager will not throw that sword, with which he wounded the servant, into the river?" Prendergast, *Latin*, 12.

4. Prendergast, *Hebrew*, xii.

5. Ibid.

6. That is, 1892, the three-hundredth anniversary of the birth of Comenius.

7. Probably in the sense of natural, or having a relationship to the development of the students.

8. Gouin, *Art of Teaching*, v.

9. Pronounced fraw[n]-SWA GWA[n]; remember that the raised *n* indicates a nasal sound. That is, the first syllable rhymes with "lawn" with the *n* unpronounced, while the last name rhymes with "ran" without the final *n*.

10. Gouin, *Art of Teaching*, 2.

11. Ibid., 5.

12. Ibid., 9.

13. Ibid., 10. He mentions that among his old school materials he had used a book of Greek roots by Lancelot of Port-Royal. This was one of Lancelot's most successful books, as its use two centuries later attests.

14. Ibid., 10–11.

15. Ibid., 11.

16. Ibid., 14.

17. Ibid., 14.

18. Ibid., 16.

19. Ibid., 17.

20. Ibid., 18.

21. Ibid., 21.

22. Ibid.

23. Ibid., 26.

24. Ibid., 29.

25. Ibid., 37.

26. Ibid.

27. Ibid., 38.

28. Ibid., 47.

29. Ibid., 41. What Gouin describes is essentially cognitive psychology of the 1960s: "Existing cognitive structure . . . is the principal factor influencing the learning and retention of meaningful new material." Ausubel, *Verbal Learning*, 217.

30. Gouin, *Art of Teaching*, 42.

31. Ibid., 44–45.

32. Ibid., 45.

33. That is, he chose fifty general areas of human experience, somewhat in the way Wilkins had done more than two centuries earlier. Gouin lists as examples, among others, the following series: river, storm, corn, bee, singing-birds, sheep, young man, trades, etc. Each of the fifty "series" was broken into many "themes," or sequences describing an action. Ibid., 61–62.

34. Ibid., 50

35. Ibid.

36. Ibid., 53. Three types, actually: the third is figurative, but that comes after the development of the objective language, so it is not of immediate interest here.

37. Ibid., 144.

38. Ibid., 294.

39. Descartes: "I think, therefore I am." Hegel: "Absolute nothingness and absolute being are identical."

40. Gouin, *Art of Teaching*, 57.

41. "Nature has furnished us with ears for the study of languages; we have thought it possible to substitute the eye in their place. Here is the primal fall, here the original sin in the present teaching." Ibid., 138.

## NOTES TO CHAPTER 23

1. Ulrich, *Esperanto*, 3.1.

2. Compare participles for "hoping" and related verbs in some Romance languages: Italian *sperando*, French *ésperant*, and Spanish *esperando* ("waiting").

3. Actually, it depends quite a bit on where you live: Esperanto speakers are more easily found in eastern Europe and Israel, for example.

## NOTES TO CHAPTER 24

1. "law$^n$-BAIR so-VUR," with a nasalized vowel in the first syllable.
2. "YO-hon pes-ta-LOAT-see."
3. Sauveur, *Entretiens sur la grammaire*, v.
4. Sauveur, *Causeries avec les enfants*, 7.
5. Sauveur, *Causeries avec mes élèves*, 30. The original text is in French without any translation or notes of any kind. For easier reading, I have put the students' responses in italics. My translation.
6. Sauveur, *Introduction to the Teaching of Living Languages*, 10.
7. Sauveur, *Causeries avec mes élèves*, 108–109. My translation.
8. Ibid., 25–26. My translation.
9. Sauveur, *Entretiens sur la grammaire*.
10. Finotti, "Lambert Sauveur," 16.
11. Ibid., 17–22.
12. The usage of "natural" versus "direct" method is confusing, and we'll consider them to be the same. To be precise, "direct" just means teaching using the target language, while "natural" means a method that imitates the way a child learns. Gouin would probably come closest to a natural method of those we've considered so far. However, Sauveur and Heness called theirs the Natural Method, while the method used in Berlitz schools is usually called the Direct Method.
13. *Berlitz*, accessed July 12, 2010, www.berlitz.com.
14. Berlitz, *Berlitz*, 2.
15. "nee-ko-LA zho-LEE."
16. For a recent discussion of the pedagogical relationship between the two men, see Finotti, "Lambert Sauveur."
17. Berlitz, *Arabic*, xi. The quote is from Berlitz himself.
18. The company today boasts that Berlitz was "the first to select a minimal word list. . . . He established a conversational high-frequency list long before frequency word counts of the literary language became available." Ibid., xi–xii.
19. Ibid., xiii.
20. Aristotle, *Politics*, 8.4.4.
21. Howatt, *History*, 202.

## NOTES TO CHAPTER 25

1. "VIL-helm vee-EH-tor." Titled *Der Sprachunterrict muss umkehren!* [Language Teaching Must Start Afresh], the first edition was published anonymously. An English translation can be found in Howatt, *History*, 340–363.
2. Howatt, *History*, 346.
3. Ibid., 347.
4. Ibid., 359.
5. Ibid., 354–355. "The Reform of Language Teaching," written by Brassai.
6. Ibid., 359.

7. Howatt, *History*, 173–175.
8. It's worth looking at how Grammar-Translation had evolved. As rendered by Ploetz, it is unrecognizable compared to the early days of Ahn and Ollendorff. From his English book for teaching French, we find this example, chosen at random:

> The terminations of the *imparfait du subjonctif* are similar in the second and fourth conjugations; the third has the vowel u and the first the vowel a. In the second, third, and fourth conjugations, the *accent circonflexe* forms the only difference between the third person and the assonant third person of the *passé défini*.

Immediately following are these practice sentences:

> 13. We should not wish that people perceived our faults. 14. The Roman senate ordered the ambassadors of King Tarquin to be driven from Rome. 15. Before the discovery of America it was impossible to work up as much gold and silver as now. (Ploetz, *French Grammar*, 79–80)

The students' book in German (Ploetz, *Elementarbuch*) was very similar.
9. Sweet, *Practical Study of Languages*, vi.
10. Ibid., vii.
11. Ibid.
12. Ibid., 2–3.
13. "The psychological foundation of the practical study of languages is the great law of association." Ibid., 102.
14. And yet Sweet liked long, information-packed sentences, as did Prendergast. We assume Sweet's complaint was the content of the sentences, not the philosophy behind them.
15. Ibid., 177.
16. Ibid., 185.
17. Ibid.
18. Mackin, Introduction to Sweet, *Practical Study of Languages*, iv.
19. Sweet, *Practical Study of Languages*, 102.
20. Mackin points out that Sweet's preoccupation with phonetics should not overshadow his other insights.
21. Sweet, *Practical Study of Languages*, 13.
22. Ibid., 100.
23. Ibid., 163. Sweet noted that one could not do away with isolated sentences altogether, though, because these are needed to illustrate grammar points. They should, however, be self-contained ideas that need no context. He cites as an example, "The sun rises in the east and sets in the west." Ibid., 171.
24. Ibid., 112.
25. Ibid., 113.
26. Ibid., 164–167.

## NOTES TO CHAPTER 26

1. Modern Language Association, *Report*, 14–16.
2. Ibid., 16–19.
3. Ibid., 19.
4. Ibid., 20–22.
5. Ibid., 22–29.
6. Ibid., 29–30.
7. Ibid., 11.
8. Ibid., 29.
9. Ibid., 83.

10. Ibid., 12.
11. Coleman, *Teaching of Modern Languages*, v.
12. Lest there be any doubt as to the thoroughness of their inquiries, a typical table in the report gives us the Approximate Number of Pages of French, German and Spanish Read in the Third and the Fourth Year of Study in Secondary Schools as Reported by Teachers Replying to the Selected Teachers Questionnaire, Divided as 'Read for Class Recitation' and 'Supplementary to Reading for Class Recitation,' with Distribution According to Groups of Teachers Reporting. Ibid., 122.
13. Ibid., 236.
14. Ibid., 124.
15. Ibid., 276.
16. Ibid., 245.
17. Ibid., 237.
18. Ibid., 238.

## NOTES TO CHAPTER 27

1. For example, Henry Sweet's bibliography, in addition to *The Practical Study of Languages* and *A Primer of Spoken English*, consists of such specialized titles as *An Icelandic Primer, A History of English Sounds*, and *A Second Middle English Primer*.
2. Biographical information is from Richard C. Smith's excellent and entertaining biography of Palmer, *The Writings of Harold E. Palmer: An Overview*, Accessed March 18, 2008, homepages.warwick.ac.uk/~elsdr/WritingsofH.E.Palmer.pdf.
3. Palmer noticed that the Berlitz Method, consciously or not, had followed such an approach. He later (1936) stated that this was "one of my reasons for admiring that method—an admiration I still feel." Smith, *Writings*, 36.
4. Ibid., 43.
5. The Institute for Research in Language Teaching, founded in 1923 as the Institute for Research in English Teaching. Smith calls it "the only true 'centre' of EFL expertise worldwide during the pre-war period." Smith, "Origins of *ELT Journal*," 4.
6. Ibid., 4–6. Hornby is known for a number of influential publications; one of them is the *Learner's Dictionary of Current English* (1948), a result of his collaboration with Palmer on vocabulary lists.
7. Palmer, *Principles of Language-Study*, 75–77.
8. Palmer, "Initial Preparation," chap. 7 in *Principles of Language-Study*.
9. Palmer, *Principles of Language-Study*, 36.
10. Ibid., 20.
11. Palmer, "Habit-forming and Habit-adapting," chap. 8 in *Principles of Language-Study*.
12. Palmer, *Principles of Language-Study*, 21.
13. Ibid.
14. Palmer, "Accuracy," chap. 9 in *Principles of Language-Study*.
15. Palmer, "Gradation," chap. 10 in *Principles of Language-Study*.
16. Palmer, "Proportion," chap. 11 in *Principles of Language-Study*.
17. Note that he includes phonetics and pronunciation among these specialized areas, in an apparent reference to the obsession of Henry Sweet and other reformers.
18. Palmer, "Concreteness," chap. 12 in *Principles of Language-Study*.
19. Palmer, "Interest," chap. 13 in *Principles of Language-Study*.
20. Palmer, *Principles of Language-Study*, 136

21. *Intrinsic* motivation comes from within; you are working at something because you want to, for whatever reason. *Extrinsic* comes from outside, usually because you will be rewarded or punished according to the results. If you study a language because you like languages and are going to visit a country where it's spoken, that's intrinsic motivation. If you study it only because your boss will pay you to do it, that's extrinsic.
22. Palmer, *Principles of Language-Study*, 187.
23. Ibid., 141.
24. Palmer, "A Rational Order of Progression," chap. 14 in *Principles of Language-Study*.
25. Palmer, "The Multiple Line of Approach," chap. 15 in *Principles of Language-Study*.
26. Palmer, *Principles of Language-Study*, 161.
27. Ibid.
28. Ibid., 167.
29. Ibid., 164.
30. Palmer, "'Memorized Matter' and 'Constructed Matter,'" chap. 16 in *Principles of Language-Study*.
31. Palmer, *Principles of Language-Study*, 172.
32. Ibid.

## NOTES TO CHAPTER 28

1. Richards, *Basic English*.
2. If the subject interests you, you can find everything you'd like to know about Basic English at http://ogden.basic-english.org.
3. Note that these could form compound nouns, increasing the vocabulary significantly.
4. Cannan, *Wealth*, 163,accessed January 14, 2007, http://ogden.basic-english.org/b4e2.html.
5. Lockhart, *Basic for Economics*, 63. "Cannan on the Grouping of Incomes," accessed January 18, 2007, http://ogden.basic-english.org/b4e2.html.
6. Alcott, *Little Women*, 29.
7. "The Dance," accessed January 17, 2007, http://ogden.basic-english.org/isl440.html#1.
8. It must be noted in his defense that he was referring to a speaker of a European language.
9. West and Swenson, "Critical Examination of Basic English," 34.
10. Howatt, *History*, 254–255.

## NOTES TO CHAPTER 29

1. Conseil scientifique pour l'Afrique, *Colloque sur le multilinguisme*, 72.
2. Barry Velleman's article "The 'Scientific Linguist' Goes to War: The United States A. S. T. Program in Foreign Languages," *Historiographia Linguistica*, was an invaluable source for this section, and interested readers are encouraged to read his article for a deeper understanding of the program.
3. Cowan, "Peace and War," 72.
4. Hockett, "J. Milton Cowan."
5. Palmer, Wiley, and Keast, *Procurement and Training*, 32.

6. Cowan, "Peace and War," 73. Development of the materials was not always an easy task; it sometimes meant assiduous detective work seeking out native speakers all over the country. Cowan tells an amusing story of attempts to locate the only two native Burmese speakers on record in the country at the time. One was found in Manhattan, jobless and reluctant to talk to outsiders. Though his Burmese was rusty, he was hired as a linguistic informant at a very comfortable salary and hustled off to Yale along with his pet dog. However, to the linguists' surprise, he soon wanted to back out—because, it turned out, the money was not equal to his income from the illegal gambling operation he had been running in New York. The linguists had to double his salary to maintain his services. Ibid., 73–76.

7. Agard et al., *Survey of Language Classes,* 5. Cowan, however, says that materials development was done for "roughly five dozen languages." "Peace and War," 76.

8. Murray, "Linguistic Society," 37.

9. Palmer, Wiley, and Keast, *Procurement and Training*, 32. Said one unnamed high-level officer, "With 300,000 men short, we are asked to send men to college!" Ibid., 29.

10. Ibid., 28 and 30.

11. Read, "Personal Journey," 283.

12. Agard et al., *Survey of Language Classes*, 17.

13. Walker, "Language Teaching."

14. Huebener, "Language Teaching," 413.

15. Velleman, "Scientific Linguist," 393.


## NOTES TO CHAPTER 30

1. Although "approach" better describes the Situational viewpoint than "method," we'll call ALM, Situational, and SGAV "methods" for the sake of brevity.

2. "mo-ZHAY."

3. Mauger, *Cours de langue*, vi. My translation.

4. Ibid., v. My translation.

5. There seems to be no standard way to write the name of the method. It appears in every way possible, capitalized or not: Audio-Lingual, audiolingual, audio lingual, etc.

6. Barry Velleman (author of the previously cited "The 'Scientific Linguist' Goes to War") notes, however, that the ASTP encouraged risk-taking and simulation of real-life situations, yet is often unfairly blamed for certain shortcomings of the Audio-lingual method. E-mail message to the author, August 18, 2009.

7. Compare this to the glowing promises expressed in the foreword of one ALM textbook: "flexible and interesting . . . a vicarious adventure in international living . . . promotes positive attitudes . . . seeing is believing." Brenes, *Learning Spanish*, 6.

8. Not all ALM textbooks were this boring visually, but presentation was obviously not one of its strong points.

9. "saⁿ KLOO."

10. This technique eventually spread beyond SGAV, but originated with the method.

11. Quoted in Germain, *Évolution de l'enseignment*, 154. My translation.

12. Ibid.

13. Ibid., 160.

## NOTES TO CHAPTER 31

1. *The American Heritage Dictionary of the English Language,* 4th ed.
2. Despite having their origins in the 1960s, it was not until the next decade that they gained fame and are therefore usually associated with the 1970s and 1980s.
3. Gattegno, Foreword to *Silent Way.*
4. Asher, *Language through Actions,* 3–35.
5. Ibid., 4–42.
6. Asher, "What Is TPR?"
7. Ibid.
8. For more information, see Curran, *Counseling-Learning.*
9. Pronounced "ga-TAYN-yo." His list of achievements is easy to find, but biographical information is not. By far the best source I found is an article that focuses on his career in mathematics: Powell, "Caleb Gattegno."
10. When I was a graduate student in TEFL in Egypt in the 1980s, it never occurred to me that the venerable Gattegno department store in downtown Cairo was somehow linked to the creator of the Silent Way.
11. Gattegno, *Teaching Foreign Languages,* 1.
12. Ibid.,13.
13. For example, Gattegno observes that German speakers, because the verb comes at the end of the sentence, tend to "race through" to the end to convey their meaning. Ibid., 27.
14. Ibid., 38.
15. Ibid., 31.
16. Ibid., 15–16.
17. Ibid., 14.
18. "gay-OR-ghi LO-za-nof."
19. Defined as the "science of the art of liberating and stimulating the personality both under guidance and alone." Lozanov, *Suggestology,* vi.
20. Ibid., 257.
21. The terminology can be confusing. Suggestology is the general theory; Suggestopedy is "an experimental method of Suggestology" (the title of Chapter 5 of Lozanov's *Suggestology*) applied to learning, while Suggestopedia is Suggestopedy for language teaching. Lozanov in more recent times liked to speak of "Desuggestopedia," as it more accurately describes the process of breaking down psychological barriers. Note that Lozanov himself did not normally capitalize any of the terms.
22. Lozanov, *Suggestology,* 284–285.
23. Ibid., 274, 275.
24. Ibid., 279.
25. Ibid., 280.
26. Ibid., 281.
27. Lozanov, "Suggestology and Suggestopedy."
28. Bibeau, *La suggéstopedie,* 276–277.
29. Canale and Swain, "Theoretical Bases," 27–30. Note that in the original, Canale and Swain include discourse competence as a subcategory of sociolinguistic competence, giving three competences instead of the four that are commonly cited.
30. Affective means "relating to, arising from, or influencing feelings or emotions." *Merriam-Webster's Medical Dictionary,* 4th ed.

31. For more on this aspect of Krashen's career, see Wheeler, "Krashen, a Victim of History."

32. Stern, *Fundamental Concepts*, 29.

## NOTES TO THE CONCLUSION

1. The Henry Sweet Society, based in the UK, and the North American Association for the History of the Language Sciences are examples of this type of organization. Though these groups are devoted primarily to linguistics, the history of language teaching is always welcome.

# Bibliography

Adler, G. J. Preface to *Ollendorff's New Method of Learning to Read, Write, and Speak the German Language*, by Heinrich Ollendorff, iii–viii. Rev. ed. New York: D. Appleton and Company, 1850.

Aelfric Grammaticus. *Aelfric's Colloquy*. Edited by G. N. Garmonsway. 2nd ed. London: Methuen, 1947.

Agard, Frederick B., Robert J. Clements, William S. Hendrix, Elton Hocking, Stephen L. Pitcher, Albert Van Eerden, Henry Grattan Doyle. *A Survey of Language Classes in the Army Specialized Training Program*. New York: Commission on Trends in Education, 1944.

Ahn, Franz. *Introductory Practical Course to Acquire the French Language*. 5th ed. New York: D. Appleton and Company, 1862.

Alcott, Louisa May. *Little Women*. Cambridge, MA: John Wilson and Son, 1880.

Aristotle. *Politics*. Translated by H. Rackham. Cambridge, MA: Harvard University Press, 1932. Reprint, London: William Heinemann, 1959.

Ascham, Roger. *The Scholemaster*. 1572. Reprint of a collation of the first and second editions, Boston: D.C. Heath and Co., 1898.

Asher, James. *Learning Another Language through Actions*. 6th ed. Los Gatos, CA: Sky Oaks Productions, 2000.

———. "What Is Total Physical Response?"Accessed March 22, 2009. http://www.tpr-world.com/what.html.

Augustine. *Confessions*. Translated by R. S. Pine-Coffin. Harmondsworth, UK: Penguin, 1961.

Ausubel, David. *The Psychology of Meaningful Verbal Learning*. New York: Grune and Stratton, 1963.

Berlitz International, Inc. *Berlitz: 130 Years of Innovation*. New York: Maya Press, 2008.

Berlitz Languages, Inc. *Arabic*. Princeton, NJ: Berlitz Languages, Inc., 1977.

Bibeau, G. *La suggestopedie*. Vol. 7 of *Rapport de l'étude indépendante sur les programmes de formation linguistique de la fonction publique du Canada*. Ottawa: Bureau de langues, Commission de la fonction publique, 1976.

Brenes, Edin. *Learning Spanish the Modern Way*. New York: McGraw-Hill, 1963.

Brinsley, John. *Ludus Literarius or the Grammar Schoole*. 1612. Edited by E. T. Campagnac. Reprint, Liverpool: The University Press, 1917.

Brunner, Helmut. "L'éducation en ancienne Egypte" [Education in Ancient Egypt]. In *Des origine à 1515*. Vol. 1 of *Histoire mondiale de l'éducation*, edited by Gaston Mialaret and Jean Vial, 65–86. Paris: Presses Universitaires de France, 1981.

Bush, Douglas. *English Literature in the Earlier Seventeenth Century 1600–1660*. 2nd rev. ed. Oxford: Clarendon Press, 1945.

Byrne, Muriel St Clare. Introduction to Holyband, *The French Littelton*, vii–xxxii.

Canale, M. and M. Swain. "Theoretical Bases of Communicative Approaches to Second Language Teaching and Testing." *Applied Linguistics* 1, no. 1 (1980), 27–30.

Cannan, Edwin. *Wealth*. London: P.S. King and Son, 1914.

Casson, Lionel. *Ancient Egypt*. New York: Time Incorporated, 1965.

Chase, Wayland. Introduction to Donatus, *Ars Minor of Donatus*, 3–26.

Chomsky, Noam. *Cartesian Linguistics*. New York: Harper and Row, 1966.

Clerval, A. *Les Écoles de Chartres au moyen-âge*. 1895. Facsimile of the first edition. Frankfurt: Minerva, 1965.

Coleman, Algernon. *The Teaching of Modern Languages in the United States: A Report Prepared for the Modern Foreign Language Study*. New York: Mac-Millan, 1929.

Comenius, John Amos. *Orbis sensualium pictus* [The Visible World in Pictures]. Translated by C. Hoole. 12th ed. London: S. Leacroft, 1777.

———. *The Great Didactic of Comenius*. Translated and edited by M. W. Keatinge. London: Black, 1910. Facsimile of the second edition. Whitefish, MT: Kessinger Publishing, 1992.

*The Comic Lindley Murray; or, the Grammar of Grammars*. Dublin: A. Murray and Co., 1871.

Conseil scientifique pour l'Afrique. *Colloque sur le multilinguisme: Deuxième Réunion du Comité Interafricain de Lingistique, Brazzaville, 16–21. VII. 1962*. Publication Commission de Coopération Technique in Afrique, no. 87 (1964).

Cowan, Milton. "American Linguistics in Peace and War." In Koerner, *First Person Singular II*, 67–82.

Curran, Charles A. *Counseling-Learning in Second Languages*. Apple River, IL: Apple River Press, 1976.

D'Alembert, Jean. "Éloge de du Marsais" [In Praise of du Marsais]. In du Marsais, *Oeuvres de du Marsais*, 1:xxxi–xcii.

Donatus. *The Ars Minor of Donatus: For 1000 Years the Leading Textbook of Grammar*. Vol. 11 of the University of Wisconsin Studies in Social Sciences and History. Edited and translated by Wayland Chase. Madison: University of Wisconsin, 1926.

Du Marsais, César Chesneau. "Éxposition d'une méthode raisonée pour apprendre la langue latine" [Exposition of a Rational Method for Learning the Latin Language]. In du Marsais, *Oeuvres de du Marsais*, 1:1–79.

———. Vol. 1 of *Oeuvres de du Marsais* [Works of du Marsais]. Edited by M. E. G. Duchosal and Charles Millon. Paris: Pougin, 1797.

Erasmus. *Erasmus Reader*. Edited by Erika Rummel. Toronto: University of Toronto Press, 1990.

———. *De pueris statim ac liberaliter instituendis declamatio* [A Declamation on the Subject of Early Liberal Education for Children]. Vol. 26 of *The Collected Works of Erasmus*. Translated by Beert Verstraete. Edited by J. K. Sowards. Toronto: University of Toronto Press, 1985.

———. *De ratione studii ac legendi interpretandique auctores* [On the Method of Study and the Reading and Interpretation of Authors]. Vol. 24 of *The Collected Works of Erasmus*. Translated by Brian McGregor. Edited by C. R. Thompson. Toronto: University of Toronto Press, 1978.

Finotti, Irene. *Lambert Sauveur à l'ombre de Maximilian Berlitz: Les débuts de la methode directe aux États-Unis* [Lambert Sauveur in the Shadow of Maximilian Berlitz: The Beginnings of the Direct Method in the United States]. Bologna: Clueb, 2010.

Flynn, Vincent. Introduction to Lily, *Short Introduction of Grammar*, iii–xii.

Foresti, Felix. Preface to Ollendorff, *Italian Language*, ix–xii.

Frayne, Douglas. "Scribal Education in Ancient Babylonia." Lecture, University of Toronto, Toronto, 1999. Quoted in "Frayne-Scribal Education in Ancient Babylonia." Accessed June 15, 2006. http://www.sumerian.org/Frayne-Scribal Education.htm.

Gattegno, Caleb. *Teaching Foreign Languages in Schools the Silent Way.* 2nd ed. New York: Educational Solutions, 1972.

Germain, Claude. *Évolution de l'enseignement des langues: 5000 ans d'histoire* [Evolution of the Teaching of Languages: Five Thousand Years of History]. Paris: CLE International, 1993.

Goetz, George, ed. *Hermeneumata Pseudodositheana.* Vol. 3 of *Corpus Glossariorum Latinorum* [Collection of Later Latin Works]. Leipzig: Teubner, 1892.

Gouin, François. *The Art of Teaching and Studying Languages.* 2nd ed. Translated by Howard Swan and Victor Bétis. London: George Philip and Son, 1892.

Hartlib, Samuel, trans. and ed. *The true and readie way to learne the latine tongue.* London: R. and W. Laybourn, 1654.

Herodotus. *The Histories.* Translated by Robin Waterfield. Oxford: Oxford University Press, 1998.

Hockett, Charles. "J. Milton Cowan." *Language* 71, no. 2 (1995): 341–348.

Holyband, Claudius. *The French Littelton. A Most Easie, Perfect, and Absolute way to learne the frenche tongue.* 1609. Facsimile of the first edition with an Introduction by Muriel St Clare Byrne. Cambridge: Cambridge University Press, 1953.

———. *The Frenche schoolemaster: Wherin is most plainlie shewed, the true and perfect way of pronouncing the Frenche tongue, to the furtherance of al those which would learn the sayd tongue.* London: William How, 1582?

Hoole, Charles. Preface to Comenius, *Orbis sensualium pictus,* b4v–b6v.

Horace. *The Odes of Horace: Books I–IV and the Saecular Hymn.* Translated by W. S. Marris. Oxford: Oxford University Press, 1912.

Howatt, Anthony P. R. *A History of English Language Teaching.* Oxford: Oxford University Press, 1984.

Huebener, Theodore. "What Shall the Aims of Foreign Language Teaching Be in the Light of Recent Experience?" *Modern Language Journal* 29, no. 5 (1945): 411–413.

John of Salisbury. *Metalogicus.* In Migne, *Patrologia latina,* 199:823–946.

Keatinge, M. W. *Great Didactic of Comenius.* 1910. Facsimile of the second edition. Reprint of *The Great Didactic* by Jan Amos Comenius. Translated, edited, and introduced by M. W. Keatinge. Whitefish, MT: Kessinger Publishing, 1992.

Keil, Heinrich, ed. *Flavii Sosipatri Charisii Artis grammaticae libri V/Diomedis Artis grammaticae libri III* [Flavius Sosipater Charisius, The Art of Grammar, Book V/Diomedes, The Art of Grammar, Book III]. Vol. 1 of *Grammatici latini* [Latin Grammarians]. 1885. Facsimile of the first edition. Hildesheim: Olms, 1961.

Kelly, Louis G. *25 Centuries of Language Teaching.* Rowley, MA: Newbury House, 1969.

Koerner, Konrad, ed. *First Person Singular II: Autobiographies by North American Scholars in the Language Sciences.* Philadelphia: John Benjamins, 1991.

———, ed. *Linguistic Historiography: Projects and Prospects.* Amsterdam: John Benjamins, 1999.

——— and R. E. Asher, eds. *Concise History of the Language Sciences from the Sumerians to the Cognitivists.* Oxford: Pergamon, 1995.

Kozik, Frantizek. *The Sorrowful and Heroic Life of John Amos Comenius.* Translated by Edith Pargeter. Prague: State Educational Publishing House, 1958.

Kramer, Samuel. *The Sumerians: Their History, Culture, and Character.* Chicago: University of Chicago Press, 1963.

Lancelot, Claude. *Nouvelle Méthode pour apprendre facilement et en peu de temps la langue latine* [The New Method for Learning Easily and in a Short Time the Latin Language]. Paris: Pierre le Petit, 1644.

Langland, William. *Piers the Plowman.* Edited by W. W. Skeats. Oxford: Oxford University Press, 1886.

Levizac, Jean-Pont-Victor de. *A Theoretical and Practical Guide to the French Tongue.* London: Baylis, 1799.

Lichtheim, Miriam, ed. and trans. *The Old and Middle Kingdoms.* Vol. 1 of *Ancient Egyptian Literature—A Book of Readings.* Berkeley: University of California Press, 1973.

Lily, William. *A short introduction of grammar generally to be used; compiled and set forth for the bringing up of all those that intend to attain to the Knowledge of the Latin Tongue.* Oxford: At the Theater, 1709.

———. *A shorte introduction of grammar.* 1567. Facsimile of the 1567 edition. Delmar, NY: Scholars' Facsimiles and Reprints, 1945.

Locke, John. *Some Thoughts Concerning Education.* 1693. 2nd ed. Reprint, Cambridge: Cambridge University Press, 1889.

Lockhart, Leonora W. *Basic for Economics.* London: K. Paul Trench Trubner & Co., 1933.

Lowth, Robert. *A Short Introduction to English Grammar.* 1762. Reprint, Philadelphia: R. Aitken, 1799.

Lozanov, Georgi. *Suggestology and Outlines of Suggestopedy.* Translated by Marjorie Hall-Pozharlieva and Krassimira Pashmakova. New York: Gordon and Breach Publishing Group, 1978.

———. "Suggestology and Suggestopedy." Accessed August 9, 2009. http://lozanov.hit.bg (site discontinued).

Lubinus, Eilhard. "Epistolary Discourse." Translated by Samuel Hartlib. In Hartlib, *The true and readie way,* 1–44.

Mackin, R. Introduction to Sweet, *Practical Study of Languages,* x–xiii.

Mancini, Anna. *Maat Revealed: Philosophy of Justice in Ancient Egypt.* New York: Buenos Books America, 2004.

Marrou, H. I. *A History of Education in Antiquity.* Translated by George Lamb. Madison: University of Wisconsin Press, 1956. Originally published as *Histoire de l'éducation dans l'antiquité.* Paris: Éditions du Seuil, 1948.

Mauger, Gaston. Vol. 1 of *Cours de langue et de civilisation françaises* [Course in the French Language and Civilization]. 2nd ed. Paris: Librairie Hachette, 1967.

McCullough, David. "Why History?" *Reader's Digest* (December 2002): 86–89.

Meidinger, Johann. *Praktische italienische Grammatik* [Practical Italian Grammar]. Leipzig, 1803.

Mialaret, G. and J. Vial, eds. *De 1515 à 1815.* Vol. 2 of *Histoire mondiale de l'éducation* [Worldwide History of Education]. Paris: Presses Universitaires de France, 1981.

Migne, Jacque-Paul. *Patrologia latina* [Latin Patrology]. 217 vols. Paris: Garnier, 1844–1855.

Modern Language Association. *Report of the Committee of Twelve of the Modern Language Association of America.* Boston: D.C. Heath and Co., 1911.

Monaghan, Charles. "Webster to McGuffey: A Sketch of American Literacy Textbooks." *History of Reading News* 25, no. 2 (2002): 1–8. Accessed April 1, 2008. http://www.historyliteracy.org/scripts/search_display.php?Article_ID=182.

Montaigne, Michel. Vol. 1 of *Essais.* Paris: Lefèvre, 1818.

Mounin, Georges. *Le linguiste.* Vol. 1 of *Histoire de la linguistique.* Paris: Presses Universitaires de France, 1967.

Murray, Lindley. *English Exercises Adapted to Murray's English Grammar*. 17th ed. Utica, NY: William Williams, 1819.

———. *English Grammar*. 18th ed. New York: Smith and Foreman, 1810.

Murray, Stephen O. "The First Quarter-Century of the Linguistic Society of America." *Historiographia Linguistica* 18, no. 1 (1991): 1–48.

Norton, Arthur O. *Readings in the History of Education: Mediaeval Universities*. Cambridge, MA: Harvard University, 1909. Facsimile of the first edition. Ann Arbor, MI: University Microfilms International, 1982.

Ogden, Charles. *Basic English: International Second Language*. New York: Harcourt, Brace and World, 1968.

Ollendorff, Heinrich. *Ollendorff's New Method of Learning to Read, Write, and Speak the German Language*. New York: American Book Company, 1857.

———. *Ollendorff's New Method of Learning to Read, Write, and Speak the Italian Language*. New York: American Book Company, 1846.

Palmer, Harold. *The Principles of Language-Study*. Yonkers, NY: World Book Company, 1921.

Palmer, Robert R., Bell I. Wiley, and William R. Keast. *The Procurement and Training of Ground Combat Troops*. Vol. 2 of *The United States Army in World War II: The Army Ground Forces*. Washington, DC: Historical Division, Department of the Army, 1948.

Phillips, Brady. "The Importance of American History in Today's Curriculum." Accessed January 6, 2006. members.aol.com/njack18/hist.htm (site discontinued).

Piaget, Jean. "John Amos Comenius." *Prospects* 23, no. 1/2 (1957): 173–196. Accessed November 24, 2006. http://www.ibe.unesco.org/publications/ThinkersPdf/comeniuse.PDF.

Ploetz, Karl. *Easy and Practical French Grammar*. 17th ed. Boston: Carl Schoenhof, 1880.

———. *Elementarbuch der französischen Sprache* [Elementary Book of the French Language]. Berlin: F.A. Herbig, 1898.

Powell, Arthur. "Caleb Gattegno: A Famous Mathematics Educator from Africa." Accessed October 16, 2008. http://andromeda.rutgers.edu/~powellab/docs/other/bio_of_c_gattegno3.pdf.

Power, Edward J. *Educational Philosophy: A History from the Ancient World to Modern America*. Studies in the History of Education. New York: Garland Publishing, 1996.

———. *A Legacy of Learning*. Albany: State University of New York Press, 1991.

Prendergast, Thomas. *Hebrew*. 2nd ed. The Mastery Series. London: Longmans, Green and Co., 1874.

———. *Latin*. The Mastery Series. 2nd ed. London: Longmans, Green and Co., 1875.

Pyles, Thomas and John Algeo. *Origins and Development of English*. San Diego, CA: Harcourt Brace Jovanovich, 1982.

Quintilian, Marcus Fabius. *Institutionis oratoriae libri duodecim* [The Foundations of Public Speaking]. Vol. 1. Edited by Edward Bonnell. Leipzig: Teubner, 1884.

Read, Allen Walker. "A Personal Journey through Linguistics." In Koerner, *First Person Singular II*, 273–288.

Richards, I. A. *Basic English and Its Uses*. London: Kegan Paul, 1943.

Robins, R. H. *A Short History of Linguistics*. 2nd ed. London: Longman, 1979.

Sauveur, Lambert. *Causeries avec les enfants* [Chats with Children]. Boston: Schoenhof and Moeller, 1875.

———. *Causeries avec mes élèves* [Chats with My Students]. New York: William R. Jenkins Co., 1891.

————. *Entretiens sur la grammaire* [Grammar Discussions]. 4th ed. New York: Henry Holt and Company, 1879.

————. *Introduction to the Teaching of Living Languages without Grammar or Dictionary*. Boston: Schoenhof and Moeller, 1875.

Smith, Richard C. "The Origins of *ELT Journal*." Oxford University Press. 2007. Accessed April 6, 2008. http://www.oxfordjournals.org/eltj/about.html.

————. *The Writings of Harold E. Palmer: An Overview*. Tokyo: Hon-no-Tomo-sha, 1999. Accessed March 18, 2008. http://homepages.warwick.ac.uk/~elsdr/WritingsofH.E.Palmer.pdf

Stearns, Peter. "Why Study History?" Last modified July 11, 2008. http://www.historians.org/pubs/Free/WhyStudyHistory.htm.

Stern, H. H. *Fundamental Concepts of Language Teaching*. Oxford: Oxford University Press, 1983.

Subbiondo, Joseph. "Universal Language Schemes and Seventeenth-Century Britain." In Koerner and Asher, *Concise History*, 174–178.

Sweet, Henry. *The Practical Study of Languages: A Guide for Teachers and Learners*. 1899. Reprint, Oxford: Oxford University Press, 1964.

Thomas of Erfurt. *Grammatica speculativa*. Translated and edited by G. L. Bursill-Hall. London: Longman, 1972.

Titone, Renzo. *Cinque millenni di insegnamento delle lingue* [Five Millennia of Language Teaching]. Brescia: Editrice La Scuola, 1986.

————. *Teaching Foreign Languages: An Historical Sketch*. Washington, DC: Georgetown University Press, 1968.

Too, Yun Lee, ed. *Education in Greek and Roman Antiquity*. Leiden: Brill, 2001.

————. "Introduction: Writing the History of Ancient Education." In Too, *Education*, 1–21.

Ulrich, Matthias. *Esperanto: The New Latin for the Church and for Ecumenism*. Translated by Mike Leon and Maire Mullarney. Antwerp: Flandra Esperanto-Ligo, 2002. Accessed January 26, 2009. http://www.u-matthias.de/latino/latin_en.htm#1.

Velleman, Barry. "The 'Scientific Linguist' Goes to War: The United States A. S. T. Program in Foreign Languages." *Historiographia Linguistica* 35, no. 3 (2008): 385–416.

Walker, Charles R. "Language Teaching in a Hurry." *Reader's Digest* (May 1943): 40–42.

Webb, Ruth. "The *Progymnasmata* as Practice." In Too, *Education*, 289–316.

West, Michael and Elaine Swenson. "*A Critical Examination of Basic English*." Bulletin of the Department of Educational Research, Ontario College of Education, no. 2 (1934).

Wheeler, Garon. "Krashen, a Victim of History." *TESL Canada Journal* 20, no. 2 (2003): 92–99.

————. "Port-Royal Tradition of General Grammar." In Koerner and Asher, *Concise History*, 169–174.

Wilkins, John. *An Essay towards a Real Character and a Philosophical Language*. 1668. Facsimile of the first edition. Menston, UK: Scholar Press, 1968.

# Index

## A

abridged works, 26
Aelfric, 31, 97
age of study, 17, 22, 76, 98, 110
Ahn, Johann Franz, 114–115, 119, 147, 152, 215n14, 218n8 (chap 25)
Akkadians, 10–11
Alexander of Villedieu, 32
Alliance française, 178, 182
Aristotle, 17, 20, 31, 34, 78, 143
Army Specialized Training Program, 173–176; criticisms of, 176
Arnauld, Antoine, 86, 87; the Port-Royal Grammar, 86–87
artificial languages. *See* constructed languages
Ascham, Roger, 48–51, 52
Asher, James, 186
Audio-lingual Method, 121, 177, 180–181, 221n1 (chap 30), 221n5–6 (chap 30)
Audio-visual aids, 175, 176, 178, 180, 183, 188
Audiovisual Method. *See* SGAV Method
Augustine, Saint, 22, 207n10 (chap 6)

## B

Basic English, 167–172; criticisms of, 170–171
Berlitz, Maximilian, 138, 141–143, 217n12, 217n18, 219n3
Blair, Hugh, 110
Bloomfield, Leonard, 173
Boas, Franz, 173
books, scarcity of, 16, 28, 30
Brinsley, John, 60–66, 214n16
British Council, 171–172

## C

children: age of first studies, 15, 22, 28; attitude toward as learners, 17, 29, 42, 49–50, 67, 96, 119; unsuited for education, 76
Chomsky, Noam, 59, 87, 181, 187, 191, 212n14
Christian Church: influence of on education, 27–28, 73, 84, 87, 88
Churchill, Winston, 171
Cicero, 23–24, 34, 50, 64, 65, 149
classroom: discipline, 17, 75; in ancient Greece, 16; hours of study, 53, 74–75; need for relaxed atmosphere, 45, 65, 67, 75, 96, 185–186, 187, 189, 190; unpleasantness of learning, 22, 32, 73, 102, 119
Coleman Report, 158, 174, 178, 219n12 (chap 26)
*Colloquy* (Aelfric), 31
Comenius, Jan, 71–83, 124, 134, 211n1, 211n5, 212n1 (chap15), 215n2 (chap 21), 215n6 (chap 22); biography of, 80–82; the Great Didactic, 72–77; *Janua linguarum reserata* (The Gate to Languages Unlocked), 77; *Orbis sensualium pictus* (The Visible World in Pictures), 77–80, 82, 83
Cominius, Georgius, 39
"Committee of Twelve," report of the, 155–157, 158, 174
communication, as the primary goal, 97, 125, 134, 142, 186, 191, 192
communicative competence, 191–192